"Once again, Edward H. Bonekemper has made a significant contribution to the crowded field of Civil War studies. This time he trains his analytical sights on ten blunders committed by leaders wearing both blue and gray. In the process, he shows his remarkable grasp of the many dimensions—some not widely known—in which the Civil War played out. Did the Confederacy suffer from a self-inflicted economic wound when it embargoed cotton in hopes of forcing Great Britain to recognize it? Was there any chance that the South would be driven to use slaves as soldiers, on a promise of emancipation? Read this book and you will see Lee, Grant, and battle after battle in a new light."

—Dr. Eugene Fidell, Senior Research Scholar, Yale Law School

"As he has in previous books, Edward Bonekemper has used original sources and cogent analysis of his own and other historians to take a new look at history. *The 10 Biggest Civil War Blunders* takes to task the Union's and Confederacy's top—and beloved—leaders and puts the blame on them for mistakes that cost tens of thousands of lives. Defenders of those leaders will find it hard to argue with Bonekemper's well-researched reasoning."

—Clint Johnson, author of ten Civil War books

"Armchair strategists and weekend warriors should have hours of enjoyment critiquing and criticizing the politicians and generals whose 'blunders' are collected here. As my friend Arnold Shaukman once said, 'History is supposed to be fun.'"

—Dr. Richard M. McMurry, renowned Civil War scholar and author of *Atlanta 1864* and several other Civil War books

"Ed Bonekemper is a prolific author of Civil War titles, and his latest work, *The 10 Biggest Civil War Blunders*, may be the cream of the crop. Each of the ten chapters of the book focuses on a specific blunder by the political or military leadership of either the North or South—a blunder that, in the author's view, affected either the duration or the outcome of the war. At the beginning of each chapter, Bonekemper summarizes who blundered and how, and he speculates as to its consequences. No sacred cow of the era is spared in the process. Good generals like Grant and Lee come in for their share of the blame, not just maligned generals like McClellan and Bragg. Not even Lincoln escapes the charge of blundering. Readers may not always agree with Bonekemper's choice of blunders or his main culprits. But the author's analysis of the consequences of the ten blunders will both challenge and delight readers who enjoy playing the "what if" game of counterfactual history. I enjoyed the book immensely, and I recommend it whole-heartedly."

    —C. Michael Harrington, Director, Houston Civil War Round Table, B.A. (Yale) and J.D. (Harvard)

THE 10 BIGGEST CIVIL WAR BLUNDERS

THE 10 BIGGEST CIVIL WAR BLUNDERS

EDWARD H. BONEKEMPER III

REGNERY
HISTORY

Regnery® is a registered trademark of Salem Communications Holding Corporation

Regnery History™ is a trademark of Salem Communications Holding Corporation

Cataloging-in-Publication data on file with the Library of Congress

ISBN 978-1-62157-664-8

Published in the United States by
Regnery History
An imprint of Regnery Publishing
A Division of Salem Media Group
300 New Jersey Ave NW
Washington, DC 20001
www.RegneryHistory.com

Manufactured in the United States of America

10 9 8 7 6 5 4 3 2 1

Books are available in quantity for promotional or premium use. For information on discounts and terms, please visit our website: www.Regnery.com.

*This book is dedicated to these exceptional
Muhlenberg College history professors: Edwin R. Baldrige Jr.,
Peyton R. (Randy) Helm (who also served as a great president of the
college), Victor L. Johnson, John Malsberger, Joanne S. Mortimer,
John J. Reed, and Daniel J. Wilson. For more than seven decades,
they informed and inspired thousands of eager and not-so-eager
students of history.*

Ed Bonekemper died suddenly as this book was going to press.
We at Regnery have lost a cherished friend and collaborator,
and every student of the history of the American Civil War
has lost a tireless and perspicacious guide.

———————

*I would not have the anniversaries of our victories celebrated,
nor those of our defeats made fast days and spent in humiliation
and prayer; but I would like to see truthful history written.*
—Ulysses S. Grant

CONTENTS

PROLOGUE

One of the fascinating features of the American Civil War is its wealth of "what ifs"—what could have been done differently that would have affected the outcome of a battle, a campaign, or even the war itself. Some of the "what ifs" involve major failures of Union and Confederate political and military leaders.

After researching and writing six books about the Civil War, I decided to examine some of the more important and interesting blunders of that war—major missteps that had a bearing on the duration or outcome of the war. Each of the six Union blunders discussed extended the war for months or years, causing countless additional casualties on both sides. The four Confederate blunders all resulted in missed opportunities for a possible Southern victory.

I have selected examples that call into question the performance of reputedly great Civil War generals like Robert E. Lee, Ulysses S. Grant, and William T. Sherman, as well as less effective generals such as George B. McClellan, Braxton Bragg, and Henry W. Halleck. Political leaders, including presidents Abraham Lincoln and Jefferson Davis, also committed blunders and, as a result, missed some glorious opportunities.

This book is about glaring blunders that substantially lengthened the Civil War or affected its outcome. That war, with its ten thousand battles and skirmishes, saw so many blunders that it is difficult to select a small number for in-depth examination while putting others to the side.[1] I intend to discuss some of the others in a later book.

I have tried to give leaders the benefit of the doubt. For example, I have not included the Confederates' failure to attack Washington immediately after First Manassas because they had slight chance of success. The post-Gettysburg situation was similar. Many, including Abraham Lincoln,[2] thought that George Meade had missed an opportunity by not successfully pursuing Robert E. Lee's Army of Northern Virginia after that three-day battle. All seven of Meade's corps had been battered, or worse, in the engagement, Meade's cavalry and infantry did pursue in a fairly timely manner, and an attack on the strong Confederate entrenchments at Falling Water, Maryland, at the end of that pursuit likely would have resulted in a Union disaster. Meade did not have a clear chance of success, and his actions are not included here. They are quite different from William T. Sherman's allowing Confederate armies to escape at Atlanta and Savannah without any real effort to hinder their escape, the subject of chapter ten.

This book is undertaken in the spirit expressed by the esteemed Civil War historian Albert Castel: "Of course, this is speculation, yet it is legitimate speculation. History cannot be confined and therefore is not confined to endeavoring to relate accurately what happened; it must and hence often does deal with what might have happened if certain things had occurred or not occurred. Besides, doing this is enjoyable for the writer of history and, evidently, for the reader of it also."[3]

In order to provide a logical flow and explore the connections among these blunders, I will examine them generally in chronological order. Those interested in more details about each example will find sources for further exploration in my notes and bibliography.

COTTON

CONFEDERATES MISPLAY THE COTTON CARD

WHO BLUNDERED?
Jefferson Davis and the Confederate leadership

HOW?
The Confederacy failed to sell large stockpiles of cotton to Britain and France before the Union blockade became effective.

CONSEQUENCES?
The Confederacy lost billions in potential cotton sales that would have resulted in huge credits in Europe for purchases of arms, medicines, vessels, and other critical supplies. Instead most Southern cotton was destroyed or sold to Northern speculators.

O verconfidence in their economic leverage caused Confederate leaders to misplay what might have been a trump card: their dominance in 1860–1861 of the world's cotton market. They believed that King Cotton was certain to win them the support of Great Britain. They could cite David Christy's influential 1855 book *Cotton Is King* to support that belief.[1] A pro-Southern Cincinnatian, Christy summarized all the arguments and data required to show the economic dependence of England and the world on Southern cotton, inspiring the rallying cry of the South, "Cotton is king!" By 1860 the book had been republished and also incorporated into another book.[2]

Senator James Henry Hammond of South Carolina reinforced that belief in an 1858 speech:

> But if there were no other reason why we should never have war, would any sane nation make war on cotton? Without firing a gun, without drawing a sword, should they make war on us we could bring the whole world to our feet. The South is perfectly competent to go on, one, two, or three years without planting a seed of cotton. I believe that if she was to plant but half her cotton, for three years to come, it would be an immense advantage to her. I am not so sure but that after three years' entire abstinence she would come out stronger than ever she was before, and better prepared to enter afresh upon her great career of enterprise. What would happen if no cotton was furnished for three years? I will not stop to depict what every one can imagine, but this is certain: England would topple headlong and carry the whole civilized world with her, save the South. No, you dare not make war on cotton. No power on earth dares to make war upon it. Cotton is king.[3]

Senator Hammond's assertion encapsulated the Confederate confidence that cotton was to be their salvation. Frank L. Owsley, the master of Southern cotton historians, summarized the Confederacy's broad cotton diplomacy plans:

The diplomatic efforts of the Confederacy were directed primarily toward obtaining European intervention in the war. The form of intervention sought differed with the exigencies of the situation. At times the Confederate agents sought European repudiation of the blockade; at other times they sought friendly mediation. Always they sought the recognition of the independence of the Confederacy. Any form of intervention— whether the repudiation of the blockade, mediation, or recognition—would, they believed, end in independence.... It was primarily England and France with whom Confederate diplomacy and propaganda were concerned, for those two maritime powers held the fate of the Confederacy in their hands—and the Confederacy for over a year, because of its monopoly of the cotton supply upon which those two nations depended, believed that it held the fate of those two countries in their hands.[4]

By 1860 the South was exporting two-thirds of the world's supply of "white gold."[5] Europe, especially England, was dependent on the region for the great majority of the cotton that kept its textile mills operating and at least a million workers employed. For example, in 1858, Britain imported cotton worth a total of £931,847,056, of which £732,403,840[6] worth (79 percent) was imported from the American South.[7] The dependence was reciprocal: 80 percent of the South's cotton was imported by the British textile industry.[8] "More than three-fourths of the cotton used in English and French textile industries came from the American South. Between a fifth and a fourth of the English population depended in some way on the textile industry, and half of the export trade of England was in cotton textiles. About a tenth of the nation's wealth was also invested in the cotton business. The English Board of Trade said in 1859 that India was completely inadequate as a source of raw cotton...."[9] Of the twenty-one million people in England, Scotland, Ireland, and Wales, an astounding four to five million (workers and family members) were dependent upon the cotton industry in 1860. In addition, seven hundred thousand French workers depended upon cotton for their livelihood.[10]

It was not just the Americans who realized the power of cotton and the vulnerability of Europe. For example, at the beginning of the war, the London *Times* reported that "so nearly are our interests intertwined with America that civil war in the States means destitution in Lancashire.... [T]he destiny of the world hangs on a thread—never did so much depend on a mere flock of down!"[11]

Confederates saw this European dependence as an opportunity to blackmail the Europeans into supporting the Confederacy. Withholding cotton from the world market would drive cotton prices to unprecedented highs, compelling the foreigners to come to the Confederacy on bended knee. A recent analysis has concluded that "the wealth the American South gained from providing cotton to hungry English textile mills in Lancashire provided much of the self-confidence and wealth that made secession possible."[12] The Confederates believed, writes Craig Symonds, "that [if they starved] the world of the South's white gold the navies of Europe would steam to the Confederacy's doorstep to smash Lincoln's declared blockade and demand access to Southern markets."[13] Therefore, "[s]ome overconfident Confederates even believed that 'King Cotton' would force Britain to intervene on their behalf, lest the British economy starve in the absence of Southern cotton."[14] Owsley wrote that the Confederates put these beliefs into practice: "Until well into the third year of the war the Confederate government and its people relied primarily upon this power of cotton to coerce rather than persuade England and France to interfere in some way with the struggle in America."[15]

Touring the South, the astute London *Times* reporter William Howard Russell noted the nearly universal opinion that the power of cotton would force England to intervene. He heard a Charlestonian tell the British consul, "Why, sir, we have only to shut off your supply of cotton for a few weeks, and we can create a revolution in Great Britain.... [W]e know that England must recognize us."[16] British consuls throughout the South reported the universality of this belief.[17] As Allan Nevins observed, "It was a dangerous theory, for it encouraged a policy which played into the hands of the Northern blockade."[18]

Nevins added, "Altogether, the cotton kingdom flexed its muscles with a sense of exuberant strength.... And never for a moment did the Deep South forget what Senator James H. Hammond and others said of its power to rally European support. A threat to the cotton kingdom would be a stroke at the jugular vein of the greatest naval powers of the globe.... Cotton would maintain peace, for cotton ruled the world."[19]

Two prominent Floridians gave voice to this cotton-based confidence in 1861. Major W. H. Chase declared, "The first demonstration of blockade of the Southern ports would be swept away by English fleets of observation hovering on the Southern coasts, to protect English commerce and especially the free flow of cotton to English and French factories. The flow of cotton must not cease for a day, because the enormous sum of £150,000,000 is annually devoted to the elaboration of raw cotton; and because five millions of people annually derive their daily and immediate support therefrom in England alone, and every interest in the kingdom is connected therewith."[20] Governor R. K. Call expressed similar confidence: "A failure of our cotton crop for three years would be a far greater calamity to England than three years' war with the greatest power on earth."[21]

Owsley summarized the view that was common throughout the South: "The dependence of the English and French cotton industries upon southern cotton, and the seeming dependence upon the cotton industries of England and France for their existence, caused the southern people...to conclude that the need for southern cotton would force England and France to interfere on behalf of the South in case of secession and war. This belief was epitomized in the expression 'Cotton is king,' shortened to 'King Cotton.' By 1860 the belief in the power of cotton to force European intervention was almost universal."[22]

The widespread belief in European, especially English, vulnerability to Southern cotton diplomacy or coercion led the seceding states and the infant Confederacy into a reckless and ultimately counter-productive course of conduct. Instead of reaching out to potential allies, promptly exporting and selling its large surplus of cotton before the establishment of an effective Union naval blockade, reaping large financial benefits, and establishing credit for later purchases of weapons, medicines, and other critical items,[23] Confederate leaders decided to pursue coercion and blackmail. This was a grievous blunder.

What was the cause of the Confederacy's miscalculation on this question? Allan Nevins thought it was based on ignorance and provincialism: "The cotton kingdom cherished its dream because it knew so little of European realities. Few Southerners were students of the economy of other nations; fewer still travelled attentively abroad or talked with foreign businessmen."[24] Southerners and certain British allies calculated that the mill owners, shipbuilders, and bankers of Lancashire, Liverpool, Manchester, and other British textile areas had such a strong economic interest in the cotton trade that they would have to support the Confederacy.[25] In the spring of 1861, the popular British magazine *Punch* reinforced that belief with the following ditty:

> Though with the North we sympathize
> It must not be forgotten
> That with the South we've stronger ties
> Which are composed of cotton.[26]

Rhetoric about King Cotton diplomacy soon turned into action at the national and local levels. President Jefferson Davis was discreet but, according to his wife, "looked to the stringency of the English cotton market, and the suspension of the manufactories to send up a ground swell from the English operatives, that would compel recognition."[27] In March 1861, Confederate Secretary of State Robert Toombs explicitly told his commissioners to Europe that British manufacturing based on Southern cotton totaled $600 million per year, adding, "The British Ministry will comprehend fully the condition to which the British realm would be reduced if the supply of our staple should suddenly fail or even be considerably diminished."[28]

Overestimating the strength of its position, the South immediately began trying to coerce its European customers, encouraged in this policy by cotton merchants, warehouse owners, insurance brokers, cotton brokers, planters, local politicians, and newspapermen. Davis and his advisors unofficially approved this "voluntary" embargo of cotton shipments,[29] and Southerners actually burned much of the 1861 cotton crop to enhance their perceived economic leverage.[30] Finally, the South reduced its production each year of the war, ultimately reaching a low of 20 percent of its prewar levels. Details of these actions follow.

In the summer of 1861, the *Charleston Mercury* threatened every textile factory in England and France with ruin if those countries did not recognize the Confederacy's independence. Its rival *Charleston Courier* advocated the immediate halt of all cotton sales to anyone and added, "[W]e will not allow a bale of our cotton to leave our plantations upon any pretext whatsoever." Almost all Southern papers joined the cry for an immediate embargo on cotton to keep it out of European and Northern hands.[31]

Although the Confederate government did not enact an embargo and blamed the Union's blockade for the dearth of cotton exports, Britain's consuls reported to the Foreign Office that the government and planters were engaged in economic coercion—"no cotton except in return for recognition and the breaking of the Northern blockade!"[32] Robert Bunch, the consul in Charleston, wrote to British Foreign Secretary Lord John Russell in August 1861, "I am sure that the planters of the South will retain upon their plantations every bale of cotton they may grow until the end of the blockade."[33] Indeed, the planters, the political force behind secession, were eager to, and did, withhold their cotton from the market.

Just as important as the planters' support for economic coercion, and perhaps more so, was the support of the cotton exporters or factors (agents), led by those in New Orleans, the South's largest and most important port—especially for cotton. In early August 1861, the city's cotton factors, insurance brokers, and warehousemen issued a circular urging planters not to ship a single bale of cotton to New Orleans, warning that any such shipments would be refused. Their expressed reason was to put pro-Confederate pressure on England and France. The ports of Mobile, Savannah, and Charleston quickly followed suit. "By August 21 Consul [James] Magee [at Mobile] was able to write Lord Russell that all the cotton men in every southern seaport—exporters, merchants, insurance and storage men—had advised the planters against bringing any cotton to the seaports until the southern Confederacy had been acknowledged and the blockade raised."[34]

Although bills were introduced in the Confederate Congress to implement an embargo, they simply disappeared in the legislative process because Jefferson Davis saw no need for government action when the producers and participants in the cotton trade were effectively barring its exportation. Davis valued the public legislative discussions about punishing Europe with an embargo until those countries adopted pro-Confederate positions, but he saw no profit in officially imposing an embargo. He could maintain a more diplomatic posture by keeping formal embargo proposals bottled up in Congress while others actually implemented an embargo. Without Confederate congressional action, a "voluntary" boycott of cotton exports was enforced in Confederate ports by state governments and especially local committees of public safety.[35]

Owsley contended that these local committees were so effective that any congressional or state action was or would have been superfluous. The committees prevented any cotton from being exported for many months—as long as they deemed the embargo policy to be effective. "It was these committees, so effectively preventing the British ships which ran the blockade from carrying out cotton, that caused the British consuls to warn the British government that the South was speaking one language through its diplomatic and administrative organs, but quite another through its more popular and informal mouthpieces."[36]

Even without the congressional imposition of an embargo, therefore, the local committees carried out an embargo policy, preventing virtually all shipments of cotton from the Confederacy for most of the war's first year. The embargo was so effective that the widespread opinion in England was that the Confederate government itself had imposed the ban on cotton shipments. To ratchet up the pressure on Europe, Confederate agents abroad encouraged the view that it was useless to attempt exporting cotton from the South. Ironically, Union agents at the same time were also encouraging this view, intending to blame the hardships on the Confederacy, to discourage blockade running, and to give the impression that the blockade was actually effective, not just a paper blockade, thereby enhancing its legality.[37]

Southerners not only gave the impression of an effective blockade but also carried out the strictest possible embargo and prevented almost all cotton exports from the beginning of the war (April 1861) all the way into the winter of 1861–1862. It was not relaxed until spring 1862. Statistics clearly demonstrate the effectiveness of the embargo in discouraging exports. From September 1860 to January 1861, the major ports of New Orleans, Charleston, Savannah, Mobile, and Memphis received about 1.5 million bales of cotton. During those same months the following year, when the embargo was in full effect, those same ports received fewer than ten thousand bales. Incredibly, even bales left over from the 1860–1861 crop were returned from ports to plantations.[38]

Of the 4.5 million bales of cotton harvested in the Confederacy during the war's first year, virtually none was exported. The embargo itself achieved the economic pressure it was intended to produce, but it failed to accomplish its diplomatic and political goals. As Owsley observed, "The power of cotton in diplomacy had been put to the test, and, as we know, failed to move England and France to intervene."[39]

In carrying out its embargo policy, the Confederate leadership overlooked at least twelve impediments to their plans.

First, the Union was just beginning to build a sizeable navy to implement its announced blockade of the Confederacy. Exporting cotton by running the blockade would only become more difficult as time passed.[40] The fall of New Orleans to a Union naval invasion in April 1862 was a big blow to future cotton exports. "The initial move of embargoing the export of cotton to Europe in 1861, when the Union blockade leaked like a sieve, was only the first in a number of false [Confederate] moves."[41] The tightening Union blockade ultimately precluded Confederate cotton exports sufficient to ameliorate the developing economic crisis in England and France. The South had missed its window of opportunity.[42]

Second, cotton production and export had been so successful before the Civil War that British and French warehouses were filled with large stockpiles. Unusually high American production in 1859 and 1860 had led Europeans to purchase more than eight million bales of cotton in 1860 and 1861, and by mid-1861 England had a stock of more than a million bales, almost double the usual amount.[43]

Third, European countries deprived of cotton could not be expected to sit idly by as their mills closed and unemployment soared. They naturally sought other sources of cotton, finding them in India, Egypt, Brazil, and other countries.[44]

Fourth, some European textile mills switched from cotton to wool or linen. By 1862, some Lancashire mills had switched to production of woolen uniforms for Union soldiers.[45]

Fifth, although much, perhaps most, of the British autocracy was sympathetic to the Southern aristocracy and engaged in cotton speculation and other pro-Confederate money-making schemes, the sympathies of the British working class were with the other side. Strongly anti-slavery, British workers blamed the South for their economic hardships and supported the democratic and increasingly anti-slavery North even though the ranks of the destitute in England ranged from four hundred thousand to two million between late 1862 and mid-1865.[46]

Sixth, because Confederate vessels were not shipping cotton to Europe, there were few Confederate vessels to carry critically needed supplies, purchased at exorbitant prices, from Europe back to the Confederacy. Likewise, British vessels that had run the blockade were discouraged from doing so again when they were denied cotton exports and even precluded at times from exiting Southern ports. Thus, the embargo on cotton exports became an unanticipated embargo on imports of necessities.[47]

Seventh, because the embargo imposed sometimes intolerable hardships on Southern cotton planters and brokers, in 1861 the government purchased more than four hundred thousand bales to aid them.[48] This diversion of scarce financial resources from critically-needed foreign munitions and supplies made cotton a liability instead of an asset.

Eighth, withholding cotton from the world market gave the impression that the Union blockade was effective—an impression that undermined the Confederacy's argument that the blockade violated the 1856 Treaty of Paris, which required nations to honor only those blockades that actually worked.[49]

Ninth, the British government was reluctant to risk war with the Union by blockading Northern ports or taking other hostile actions because it feared losing Canada. Britain's available resources would be no match for American military power, aided by a highly developed rail system, should the United States try to seize Canada in retaliation for British interference in the Civil War.[50]

Tenth, the embargo would have severe economic consequences for the Confederates themselves, depriving them of desperately needed war materiel and other supplies from abroad. By the spring of 1862, Owsley concluded, cotton was "the only medium of exchange left in the South which was acceptable abroad."[51]

Eleventh, the British were unlikely to intervene because, according to Owsley, they believed "that the South could not be conquered and that its independence was inevitable." British confidence in Southern indomitability, making intervention seem unnecessary, was a product of the American Revolution, which convinced the British "that a determined, compact group of people occupying an extensive area could not be conquered." Throughout the war, the British press remained adamant that Southern victory was certain.[52] The London *Economist*, for example, asserted that any politician who believed that "millions of resolute and virulent Anglo Saxons [could] be forcibly retained as citizens of a republic from which they are determined to separate...must have some standard for estimating values and probabilities which is unintelligible to us."[53]

Twelfth, overt British action against the Union blockade was unlikely because British leaders were conscious "of the importance of respecting the right of blockade," as Nevins noted, "for Britain had direly needed that right in Napoleonic times, and might direly need it again."[54] Britain, the world's leading naval power, was predictably uneager to diminish a powerful weapon in its own arsenal.

An early indication that Confederate cotton coercion would not work was the disappointment of a Confederate delegation to London in the spring of 1861. They had hoped to secure British denunciation of the Union blockade, an Anglo-Confederate commercial agreement, or even diplomatic recognition,[55] but the British were uninterested in undercutting the blockade, unconvinced of the necessity of an economic agreement, and disinclined to recognize the Confederacy until it had proved its viability. The Confederate diplomats obtained only British and French recognition of the Confederacy's belligerent status.

With amazing foresight and a keen sense of English feelings on the question of cotton blackmail, the London *Economist* warned in 1851, a decade before the Confederacy's formation: "There is something truly astonishing in the infatuations which seem to possess the Southern States of America.... [In the event of civil war], no bribes, no matter how enormous, would induce the English people—or any class among them...—to lend its aid to a revolt which they believe to be utterly unprovoked, the result of the worst political passions, and likely to end in the degradation of the Southern States."[56]

Renata Long recently observed, "Contrary to the South's belief that a cotton shortage would coerce the population into demanding that the [British] government recognize the Confederacy as a nation, the [English] working-class people of the textile valleys were prepared to stand by their distaste for slavery and suffer whatever hardship the war imposed on them if it ultimately led to emancipation."[57] Even as the huge stockpiles of cotton ran out, British mills closed, and textile workers faced poverty in 1862, the working class became even more supportive of the North. "As the warehouse stocks dwindled, so too did the last vestige of sympathy the workers might have felt for the South. The war was becoming a wedge creating an ever-widening divide within the British system."[58] Relief committees, homelessness, starvation, debt, and soup kitchens pervaded the cotton-manufacturing areas. Although universal male suffrage had not yet arrived in England, politicians could ignore the widespread anti-Confederate feelings only at their peril.[59]

Those feelings were aggravated in the manufacturing districts of Lancashire, which "were reduced to a level of poverty unimagined in the days before the war," when Union wartime efforts to provide relief were stymied by the Confederates. John Bright, the North's strongest supporter in Parliament, wrote to Republican Senator Charles Sumner, who convinced President Abraham Lincoln to send grain to the hard-hit Lancashire area. In the autumn of 1862, Lincoln sent three ships loaded with grain. Two made it through, but the English-built raider CSS *Alabama* captured one of the ships and burned it and its humanitarian cargo.[60] The episode surely reinforced the working class's antipathy toward the Confederacy and the British autocracy.[61]

Even before it became clear, by spring 1862, that the cotton embargo was failing to coerce England or France into supporting the Confederacy in some way, Southerners doubled down on their coercive approach. Not satisfied to withhold existing cotton from the international marketplace, they "undertook to put fear into the hearts of the English and French nations…" writes Owsley, "by destroying the supply on hand with the torch and refusing to produce another crop." In December 1861 and January 1862, newspapers throughout the South urged severe curtailment of cotton production. They reflected a consensus among Confederate leaders that led to a March 1862 joint resolution of the Confederate Congress that "absolutely no cotton ought to be planted in 1862." Georgia limited production to three bales per laborer, and South Carolina set a limit of one bale per laborer. The Confederacy's cotton production dropped from 4.5 million bales in 1861 to 1.5 million bales in 1862, then to 449,000 bales in 1863, and finally 300,000 bales in 1864.[62]

The South not only brought cotton production down to extremely low levels but also proceeded to destroy much of the crop already on hand. Ulysses S. Grant's successful Fort Henry–Fort Donelson campaign of February 1862 allowed the Federals to seize Confederate lands, cotton, and other crops. In response, the Confederate Congress passed a law in March directing the military to destroy cotton, tobacco, and other property that might aid the enemy in prosecuting the war if it fell into their hands.[63] There followed a massive burning of cotton that would have been a valuable resource if not for its vulnerability to seizure by the enemy. Owsley estimated that the Confederate government ultimately destroyed two and a half million bales of cotton.[64]

Burning cotton prevented its falling into enemy hands, but it was also a propaganda tool. Through their own funded London newspaper, the *Index*, and communications with British and French diplomats, the Confederate government ensured that Europeans were aware that the conflagrations aggravated the cotton shortage. In June and July 1862, the *Index* gloatingly published reports of ten million dollars' worth of cotton burned at New Orleans, ten thousand bales in Tennessee, fifty thousand bales in Alabama, one hundred thousand bales near Memphis, and between five hundred thousand and a million bales along the Mississippi. Cotton destruction became another aspect of attempted cotton coercion.[65]

In the middle of the war, the Confederate government finally took some steps to exploit cotton's economic power more productively. In late 1862 it started using cotton to guarantee foreign loans, and in 1863 the desperate Confederacy at long last began exporting the four hundred thousand bales of cotton it had purchased in 1861. Another effort was the New Plan of late 1863, under which the government became directly involved in foreign sales of cotton. Late in the war, the Confederacy assumed total control over cotton exports and blockade running and engaged in cotton sales or barter exchanges with Northerners. "But because of the Confederacy's early confidence in the diplomatic leverage of King Cotton, it did not institute measures such as the New Plan soon enough to make a considerable impact on the war effort."[66]

This Confederate action was too little too late. Owsley provided an illuminating overview of its failed policies:

> Like so many other policies of the Confederacy, the laws and regulations putting cotton and tobacco export under government control in 1864 bore too much the appearance of

locking the stable after the mare had fled. With many ports captured, the blockade was becoming a powerful menace and the accessible cotton had either been swept off by private speculators or burned by the advancing and retreating armies. The belief in foreign intervention to obtain cotton had caused the Confederacy to sacrifice its cotton by an embargo the first year of the war, and the belief that the blockade would be broken if enough private parties could be induced to violate it caused the Confederacy to refrain from taking control of cotton export the second and part of the third year; and it was only after all hopes of intervention or repudiation of the blockade had vanished that the Confederacy made up its mind to make full use of the purchasing power of its cotton.[67]

The Confederacy missed a chance to sell massive quantities of cotton to European buyers for high prices at the beginning of the war, sales that would have provided vast reserves of foreign credit. That credit could then have been used to fund or guarantee purchases of sorely needed weapons, ammunition, uniforms, medicines, and other supplies. As Keith Poulter stated, the Rebel embargo "was not only ineffectual, it also threw away a trump card in the Confederate arsenal—the ability to create credit with potential suppliers of munitions and other vital supplies."[68]

Instead, the bulk of the Confederacy's accumulated cotton remained unsold, was destroyed to avoid seizure by Union troops, or was sold or bartered to Northern speculators, who realized the large profits the South had forfeited. Operating from a false premise that they could coerce Europe into supporting them, Confederate leaders blundered from embargo to burning to crop suppression without converting their key cotton asset into European support. "King Cotton" diplomacy, likely the result of Southern hubris,[69] proved to be a major blunder and a missed economic and military opportunity for the Confederacy.

CORINTH

HENRY HALLECK FAILS TO ELIMINATE A CONFEDERATE ARMY AND HALTS UNION OFFENSIVE ACTIONS

WHO BLUNDERED?

Union Major General Henry Halleck

HOW?

He allowed fifty thousand Confederate troops to escape from Tupelo, Mississippi, in May 1862 and halted Union offensives in the West.

CONSEQUENCES?

The escaped troops provided the backbone of the Rebel invasion of Kentucky in fall 1862 and the bulk of Western Confederate manpower for the next two years. Their escape also cost the Union missed opportunities to proceed promptly against then lightly defended Vicksburg to obtain control of the Mississippi River.

Major General Henry Wager Halleck, commander of the Western Theater, led one of the most painfully slow and disappointing campaigns of the Civil War. The so-called Corinth Campaign in the spring of 1862 was so farcical and such a waste of Union manpower that it scarcely deserves to be called a campaign.

Months before, Halleck had initially rejected Brigadier General Ulysses S. Grant's advice to launch a riverine campaign southward up the Tennessee and Cumberland Rivers. Grant received assistance, however, from President Abraham Lincoln, who in January 1862 ordered all Union armies to go on the offensive, and Halleck authorized Grant to attack Fort Henry on the Tennessee. Grant successfully did so in a joint operation with the navy. On his own volition, Grant next moved against nearby Fort Donelson on the Cumberland, capturing it and a fourteen-thousand-man Rebel army. With this first major Union victory of the war, Grant became a national hero.

Shortly thereafter Halleck inexplicably placed Grant under virtual arrest at Fort Henry while Grant's army moved south up the Tennessee River to Pittsburg Landing, Tennessee, near the Tennessee-Mississippi border. At the same time, Halleck fed false information about Grant to General in Chief George B. McClellan—including rumors that Grant had resumed his old drinking habits. When Washington officials—Lincoln, Secretary of War Edwin Stanton, and McClellan—requested evidence for these accusations, Halleck released Grant, falsely told him he had saved Grant from Washington-based attacks, and sent him to rejoin his army. Halleck's disdainful treatment of a victorious general has been explained as some combination of jealousy and disrespect for Grant's casual approach to military dress and procedures.

Grant proceeded to Pittsburg Landing, where he again took command of his army. Inexcusably unprepared for an enemy attack, Grant was surprised by a huge Confederate assault and then rallied to save his army at the Battle of Shiloh on April 6 and 7, 1862. Halleck then came to Pittsburg Landing to take charge. Angling to become the Union general in chief, he saw an opportunity to put the finishing touches on Western Theater successes—none of which was directly attributable to him. After his arrival on April 11, Halleck took command of Grant's and Don Carlos Buell's armies. With the addition of John Pope's army, Halleck eventually commanded up to 137,000 troops, perhaps the largest single command of the war.[1]

Meanwhile, a disconsolate Grant was pilloried by the press for "Bloody Shiloh" and mourned the recent death of his friend and mentor Major General Charles Smith. Halleck added to his woes with a letter stating that Grant's "army is not now in condition to resist an attack" and directing him to achieve that condition.[2] That same day Halleck also sent Grant a petty directive: "The Major General Commanding desires that, you will again call the attention of your officers to the necessity of forwarding official communications through the proper military channel, to receive the remarks of intermediate commanders. Letters should relate to one matter only, and be properly folded and indorsed."[3]

Grant's morale hit a new low on April 30, when Halleck relieved him of his command, made him his deputy, and replaced him with the newly promoted Major General George H. Thomas as commander of the Army of the Tennessee. In Russell Weigley's words, "Halleck appears to have been jealous of [Grant] for his early successes…, and he did all that he could to deny Grant full credit for his achievements at [Fort] Henry, [Fort] Donelson, and Shiloh and kept him under a shadow as second in command in the West, practically a supernumerary, through the Corinth campaign."[4]

Having thrived as a commander of troops, Grant was extremely frustrated by what he appropriately regarded as a demotion to a meaningless and powerless position. His frustration was aggravated by Halleck's overly cautious, excruciatingly slow "march" on Corinth, Mississippi, to which General P. G. T. Beauregard's Confederates had retreated after Shiloh. Corinth, where the east-west Memphis & Charleston Railroad intersected the north-south Mobile & Ohio, was so critical that it has been called "The Crossroads of the Western Confederacy."[5]

Moving his 130,000 men ever so slowly in the direction of Corinth, Halleck proved himself a match for the notoriously tortoise-like McClellan. Setting out on April 30, he took four weeks to cover the twenty-two miles to Corinth. The army spent four hours entrenching at the end of each day, and none of the three constituent armies—the Tennessee, the Ohio, and the Mississippi—was permitted to edge ahead of the others. Reconnaissance parties were instructed to avoid bringing on battle and to retreat rather than fight.[6] One frustrated soldier wrote in his diary, "Genl Halleck intended taking Corinth without firing a musket." On May 11, Grant wrote to Halleck requesting either a field command or relief from duty. Halleck denied the request. Grant told a fellow officer that he felt like "a fifth wheel to a coach."[7]

During May the Federal armies, with deliberate and frustrating slowness, arrived near Corinth, partially surrounded the town, cut off the railroads to the north and east, and engaged in some minor fighting with Beauregard's troops. Meanwhile, Beauregard was facing greater challenges: bad water, typhoid fever, dysentery, and desertions. Sam R. Watkins, a private in the Confederate Army of Tennessee, reported, "We became starved skeletons; naked and ragged rebels. The chronic diarrhoea became the scourge of the army. Corinth became one vast hospital. Almost the whole army attended the sick call every morning. All the water courses went dry, and we used water out of filthy pools." Apparently in shock from the slaughter at Shiloh, neither Halleck nor Beauregard seemed eager to engage in combat. Beauregard finally ended the standoff with a cleverly executed retreat from Corinth.[8]

The strategic ineffectiveness of Halleck's slow-motion movement against, and partial encirclement of, Corinth became obvious when the fifty thousand Confederates escaped on May 29 and 30. By cheering the arrival of empty evacuation trains as though they were full of fresh troops, the Confederates fooled Halleck into thinking they were reinforcing, not evacuating, Corinth. On the morning of May 30, Halleck had his entire army prepared for defensive battle and issued orders indicating that the Union left was likely to be attacked. After several explosions rocked the town early that morning, Halleck's troops approached cautiously, only to find the town completely abandoned. Entering Corinth, they were greeted by a straw-filled Union uniform with a sign that read, "Halleck outwitted—what will old Abe say?" As Ronald White concludes, "Beauregard had pulled off the largest hoax of the war."[9]

The Confederates' movement fifty miles south to Tupelo, Mississippi, left Corinth in Union hands and forced the Confederate abandonment of the now uncovered city of Memphis. But their retreat also allowed Beauregard's soldiers to fight future battles. With his huge armies in Corinth, Halleck failed to pursue the fifty thousand Confederates to Tupelo or to move on important objectives such as Vicksburg, Chattanooga, Mobile, or Atlanta. Instead, he had his troops dig even more extensive fortifications than the Rebels had abandoned.[10]

Halleck's month-long "movement" to cover a distance Grant believed should have taken two days frustrated and disgusted Grant. These feelings were reinforced by the Rebels' evacuation of all their healthy and wounded troops, artillery, and supplies—with only a few log "Quaker guns" left behind for Halleck's army. As a *Chicago Tribune* correspondent commented, "General Halleck has thus far achieved one of the most barren triumphs of the war. In fact, it was tantamount to a defeat." During the cautious siege, Halleck had sent orders directly to Grant's wing of the army without going through Grant. Believing that he was nothing more than an observer and embarrassed by his position, Grant made several applications to be relieved. Halleck abruptly rejected a suggestion from Grant about how to attack the enemy.[11]

But Grant's concerns went deeper. He believed that the Army of the Tennessee's now-experienced soldiers felt the capture of Corinth was hollow. "They could not see how the mere occupation of places was to close the war while large and effective rebel armies existed. They believed that a well-directed attack would at least have partially destroyed the army defending Corinth." As he wrote in his memoirs, Grant also was disappointed in Halleck's tepid pursuit of the enemy after Corinth and his failure to pursue other opportunities with his large army:

> After the capture of Corinth a movable force of 80,000 men, besides enough to hold all the territory acquired, could have been set in motion for the accomplishment of any great campaign for the suppression of the rebellion.... If [Buell] had been sent directly to Chattanooga as rapidly as he could march, he

could have arrived with but little fighting, and would have saved much of the loss of life which was afterwards incurred in gaining Chattanooga. Bragg would then not have had time to raise an army to contest the possession of middle and east Tennessee and Kentucky; the battles of Stones River and Chickamauga would not necessarily have been fought; Burnside would not have been besieged in Knoxville without the power of helping himself or escaping; the battle of Chattanooga would not have been fought. These are the negative advantages, if the term negative is applicable, which would probably have resulted from prompt movements after Corinth fell into the possession of the National forces. The positive results might have been: a bloodless advance to Atlanta, to Vicksburg, or to any other desired point south of Corinth in the interior of Mississippi.[12]

Williamson Murray and Wayne Hsieh agree that numerous prospects were presented to Halleck: "What to do after the fall of Corinth was the crucial strategic question confronting Halleck.... The most obvious choice would have been for Halleck to move his great army [actually three armies] against Vicksburg, clean up the Mississippi River valley, destroy Beauregard's army, soon to be led by Bragg, and then focus on destroying... Confederate cavalry bands...."[13]

Allan Nevins describes Halleck's weaknesses and his missed opportunities after Corinth:

Excellent in grasp of theory, [Halleck] was inert, muddy-headed, and erratic in action. He had an unmilitary cast of mind, and recoiled from direct control of armies. It was unfortunate that the signal demonstration he had just given of his limitations as a field commander were not yet properly understood. At the beginning of June,... he had possessed at or near Corinth an army of 128,315, of whom 108,538 were fit for duty. Their generals included Grant, Sherman,

Thomas, Sheridan. After the capture of Memphis on June 6, this array, eager for action, was capable, as Grant later said, of rolling up half the Confederate map in the West. It might have taken the remaining river strongholds of Port Hudson and Vicksburg; it might then have marched to the mountain stronghold of Chattanooga, the gateway through which armies from the central Confederacy would have to advance if they ever tried to recover important parts of Tennessee and Kentucky. At the very least, one of these great Union objectives could have been secured before September browned cornfield and meadow.[14]

In any event, a disgusted Grant took leave to visit his family and perhaps seek transfer to another theater. His friend Major General William T. Sherman told him to be patient and hope for reinstatement. That is exactly what happened when Halleck restored him to command of the Army of the Tennessee on June 10. Halleck's intervention after Shiloh, however, had stopped the momentum of Grant's offensive into the Western Confederacy, weakening the prospects of quickly gaining control of the Mississippi River. After Shiloh, writes Russell Weigley, "Halleck dispersed the western armies on garrison and railroad-building work.... [I]t was Halleck who sneered at Lincoln for wanting to violate the principle of concentration by maintaining pressure against the Confederacy everywhere."[15]

T. Harry Williams comments on Halleck's legacy to the Western Theater:

> Before he left he split the Western Department into two commands under Buell and Grant. Characteristically, he assigned to Buell, who had done practically no fighting, a fighting mission—the seizure of well-guarded Chattanooga. To Grant, who had done much hard and victorious fighting, he gave the relatively inactive mission of protecting communications along the Mississippi River.[16]

Not only had Halleck stopped Grant's momentum, but his wait-and-see approach left the North vulnerable to Confederate counteroffensives. In the fall of 1862, Confederates took advantage and went on the offensive. After the Confederate movement to Tupelo, Jefferson Davis relieved Beauregard, a personal adversary, of command for taking unauthorized sick leave and replaced him with Davis's friend Braxton Bragg. Although Bragg would ultimately prove to be an incompetent commander and general, he outfoxed the hapless Halleck, the limits of whose talents were becoming clear.

Beauregard's and Bragg's troops remained vulnerable to attack at Tupelo for seven weeks after Halleck's occupation of vacated Corinth. But Bragg realized the need to return to action the fifty thousand troops Halleck had essentially ignored. After leaving fifteen thousand to defend Vicksburg, he moved eastward with thirty-five thousand. Despite the South's disjointed transportation system, Bragg found a way to transport them 776 miles to Chattanooga. Beginning on July 23, he transported them by rail to Mobile and then by boat to Montgomery, where they made rail connections to Atlanta. From there Bragg's soldiers moved by rail to Chattanooga and then on foot through eastern Tennessee and into eastern Kentucky.[17] Thus, while Robert E. Lee campaigned in Maryland, Bragg and Edmund Kirby Smith, coming from southwest Virginia, invaded eastern Tennessee and Kentucky. The western segment of these dual invasions had been enabled by Halleck's inept Corinth Campaign and his allowing an entire Rebel army to escape.

The invasion of Tennessee and Kentucky compelled Buell to terminate his slow movement toward Chattanooga across southern Tennessee and move north to stymie the threat to Kentucky and the Midwest. As Buell moved north to intercept Bragg and Smith in Kentucky, Grant was directed to send three of Major General William Rosecrans's divisions as reinforcements to Buell. Grant then faced the challenge of defending his assigned territory with reduced forces.[18] With many of his troops having been sent away to battle the Rebel forces Halleck had allowed to escape, Grant found himself handicapped in fighting the Confederates who remained in Mississippi.

In summary, Halleck had missed a grand opportunity to put fifty thousand Confederate troops out of action for the war's duration. He had carried out a tepid campaign with a 130,000-man, three-army force against Corinth that allowed fifty thousand Confederates to escape and form the bulk of the Rebel force that invaded Kentucky and fought at the Battle of Perryville in the fall of 1862. Moreover, those soldiers formed the core of Rebel forces composing Braxton Bragg's Army of Tennessee at the 1862–1863 battle of Stones River (Murfreesboro) in eastern Tennessee, the mid-1863 Tullahoma Campaign in eastern Tennessee, and the fierce late-1863 Battles of Chickamauga (Georgia) and Chattanooga (southeastern Tennessee). They also fought in the mid-1864 Atlanta Campaign and then the bloody Battles of Franklin and Nashville, Tennessee, in late 1864. In addition, some of the Corinth-Tupelo survivors even joined General Joseph Johnston in resisting Sherman's Carolinas campaign in early 1865. In addition to his failure at Corinth, Halleck missed the opportunity to seize Vicksburg and gain control of the Mississippi River by mid-1862—more than a year before Grant would actually achieve this decisive objective.

ANTIETAM CAMPAIGN

GEORGE McCLELLAN FAILS TO DESTROY ROBERT E. LEE'S ARMY

WHO BLUNDERED?

Union Major General George McClellan

HOW?

He botched several opportunities to destroy Lee's army during the Maryland (Antietam) Campaign.

CONSEQUENCES?

McClellan's blunders in this campaign enabled the Confederacy to maintain an Eastern army and continue the war for more than two years. Ironically, McClellan's failures also resulted in the Emancipation Proclamation and in the legal termination of slavery, two actions he strongly opposed.

The September 1862 Maryland Campaign (also known as the Antie-tam Campaign) is the sad tale of Major General George McClellan's failure to use his massively superior Army of the Potomac to destroy General Robert E. Lee's Army of Northern Virginia, which had invaded Maryland in an attempt to reach Pennsylvania. McClellan was presented with repeated opportunities to do so and consistently squandered them.[1]

SUMMARY OF BLUNDERS

First, with the fortuitous discovery of Lee's famous campaign order (the "Lost Order"), McClellan learned of the divided and vulnerable state of Lee's army, but he "pursued" that opportunity and Lee's army with his usual slowness, sacrificed the 11,500 Union troops taken prisoner at Harpers Ferry, and allowed all of Lee's separated troops to reunite.

Second, McClellan arrived at Sharpsburg, Maryland, (site of the Battle of Antietam) before any of the Rebel troops from Harpers Ferry had returned to Lee, but he failed to attack when he had a four-to-one and then a three-to-one advantage.

Third, he squandered his manpower superiority on the day of the fierce Battle of Antietam, September 17, by attacking ineffectively and sequentially with a portion of his army on the north of the field, then a portion in the center, and finally yet another portion in the south—a process that enabled Lee to switch his defenders from one front to another during the day.

Fourth, McClellan kept more than one-quarter of his army in reserve and unused during that entire battle—even on occasions when he could have used it to destroy Lee's army.

Fifth, he misused his cavalry by failing to harass Lee's wings, discover fords across the Antietam, or scout for threats such as Major General Ambrose Powell Hill's late-day arrival. Instead, he kept his cavalry in reserve in the rear, apparently to protect his artillery and his headquarters.

Sixth, he passed up a glorious opportunity to destroy Lee's army on September 18 when Lee recklessly remained at Sharpsburg even though McClellan had more fresh troops than Lee's entire surviving army. By his timidity, slowness, and lack of moral courage, McClellan missed a great chance to end the war in the East.

BEGINNING OF THE CAMPAIGN

After the McClellan-assisted Union defeat at Second Manassas on August 28–30, 1862, Union survivors from John Pope's and McClellan's armies fled to Washington. Lincoln, hoping to bring order out of chaos and quickly mold the soldiers into an organized fighting force, appointed McClellan to command the combined armies in the Washington area. He did so over the opposition of most of his cabinet and much of Washington, who urged removal of the "traitorous" McClellan. Although aware of McClellan's shameful behavior in withholding troops and undercutting Pope at Second Manassas,[2] Lincoln recognized his organizational ability and the soldiers' loyalty to him. Under the circumstances, the president had few, if any, other options.

On September 5, after Lee had crossed the Potomac into Maryland, Lincoln expanded McClellan's command to the army in the field that would oppose Lee. That decision must have pleased Lee, whose low opinion of McClellan's "speed" and "aggressiveness" had been confirmed in the Peninsula Campaign that spring and summer. Lincoln agreed with Lee's assessment, confiding to Secretary of the Navy Gideon Welles on September 12, "[McClellan] can't go ahead—he can't strike a blow."[3] Nevertheless, McClellan let his command go to his head. In a letter on September 5 he beamed, "Again I have been called upon to save the country—the case is desperate, but with God's help I will try unselfishly to do my best & if he wills it accomplish the salvation of the nation."[4]

On the eve of his departure from Washington, McClellan was still bragging to his wife: "I shall have nearly 100,000 men, old & new, & hope with God's blessing to gain a decisive victory. I think we shall win for the men are now in good spirits—confident in their general & all united in sentiment.... I have now the entire confidence of the Govt & the love of the army—my enemies [in Washington and the army] are crushed, silent & disarmed—if I defeat the rebels I shall be master of the situation...."[5] In McClellan's mind, there were "enemies" and "rebels"—an interesting and telling distinction. Although McClellan had almost one hundred thousand troops, outnumbering Lee by about two to one, he would be gripped by his usual delusion that the numbers were reversed. He was also deluded about having "the entire confidence" of the government.

Meanwhile Lee moved quickly and dangerously. He "knew McClellan well and believed his opponent would move with glacial slowness and the Army of Northern Virginia could take substantial risks."[6] On September 7, Lee's army completed its arrival at Frederick, Maryland, where he posed a threat to Washington, Baltimore, Harrisburg, and Philadelphia. He told one of his brigadiers that before McClellan was aroused, "I hope to be on the Susquehanna."[7]

By the next evening, McClellan was at Rockville, Maryland, about twenty miles northwest of Washington and thirty miles southeast of Frederick. Without knowing Lee's location, he assured General in Chief Halleck, "As soon as I find out where to strike, I will be after them without an hour's delay."[8] That same day Lee issued a proclamation to the people of Maryland, informing them that he came to free, not harm, them, asking them to rally to the Confederate cause, and disclaiming any use of compulsion to recruit. His expectation of receiving numerous volunteers was unrealized for two reasons. First, he had entered the non-slaveholding western section of the state, where there was minimal sympathy for the Confederate cause. Second, those Marylanders who wished to join his army—generally from the Eastern Shore or areas southeast of Washington—had already done so.

LEE'S CAMPAIGN PLAN

Against the advice of Major Generals James Longstreet and Stonewall Jackson, Lee issued the crucial Special Orders No. 191 on September 9. To secure his communication and supply line through the Shenandoah, the order divided his army into four (which became five) segments to

Boteler's Ford, Potomac River, near Shepherdstown. Point at which the Confederate Army crossed after the Battle of Antietam. *Courtesy of the Library of Congress*

capture Harpers Ferry before moving on toward Pennsylvania. The next day his army began executing the order and left Frederick. Brigadier General John Walker backtracked to Loudon Heights, Virginia, overlooking Harpers Ferry from the south. Major Generals Lafayette McLaws and Richard H. Anderson went southwest from Frederick through Crampton's Gap in South Mountain to attack Union troops guarding Maryland Heights, overlooking Harpers Ferry from the east.

The major Rebel movement involved Jackson. He led three divisions west-northwest on the National Road through Turner's Gap at South Mountain, crossed the Potomac at Williamsport, and then moved through Martinsburg, Virginia, to close the trap on Harpers Ferry from the west. Lee, with Longstreet's corps, followed Jackson through Turner's Gap, left Daniel Harvey Hill's division at Boonsboro, and continued northwest to Hagerstown, near Pennsylvania. On September 10, Lee's entire two corps left Frederick to carry out their assigned missions.

McCLELLAN'S OVERESTIMATION OF ENEMY STRENGTH

On September 9, McClellan forwarded to Halleck a "not fully reliable" cavalry report that one hundred thousand Rebels had crossed the Potomac and a subsequent report that the enemy numbered 110,000 near Frederick.[9] That afternoon he told his wife about the 110,000-troop report and commented, "I have not so many, so I must watch them closely & try to catch them in some mistake, which I hope to do."[10] By the next afternoon, the general sent a further inflated estimate to Lincoln: "I have scouts and spies pushed forward in every direction and shall soon be in possession of reliable and definite information. The statements I get regarding the enemy's forces that have crossed to this side range from 80,000 to 150,000...."[11] That same day, the tenth, he advised Halleck, "All the evidence that has accumulated from various sources since we left Washington goes to prove most conclusively that almost the entire Rebel army in Virginia, amounting to not less than 120,000 men, is in the vicinity of Frederick City."[12]

In a meeting on September 12, an unimpressed Lincoln again complained to Gideon Welles about McClellan's slowness: "He got to Rockville, for instance, last Sunday night, and in four days he advanced to Middlebrook, ten miles, in pursuit of an invading enemy. This was rapid movement for him."[13] McClellan was proving Lincoln correct. Between September 7 and 13, his troops marched a total of thirty miles.[14] On the morning of the eleventh, McClellan suggested that Colonel Dixon Miles and his nine thousand troops at Harpers Ferry be ordered to join him. Halleck's immediate response was, "There is no way for Colonel Miles to join you at present. His only chance is to defend his works till you can open communication with him."[15] In other words, McClellan and his large force would have to break through to Harpers Ferry rather than expecting that small garrison, one-tenth the size of McClellan's force, to force its way to him through all those Confederate troops he kept writing about.

Throughout the Maryland Campaign McClellan, as usual, repeatedly asserted that he was grossly outnumbered by the enemy. The historian Edward Fishel has demonstrated that McClellan made up his figures from whole cloth, while his intelligence chief, Allan Pinkerton, was kept busy trying to find evidence to support the general's already-issued pronouncements about enemy strength. Fishel points out that Lee's army miraculously doubled in size when McClellan replaced John Pope. McClellan's estimate of 120,000 men was based on rumors and guesses from uninformed sources, and "The record does not show that Pinkerton contributed to this estimate."[16]

Even Gregory A. Thiele, in a sympathetic assessment of McClellan at Antietam, concludes that McClellan himself was responsible for overestimating Rebel strength. Thiele notes in McClellan's defense that in this he was "no worse than many other *unsuccessful* Civil War generals."[17] In reality, McClellan exceeded every other Civil War general in his consistent and gross overestimates of enemy strength, overestimates that he used as an excuse for inaction or tepid action. Lincoln noticed this tendency, remarking on July 25 that if McClellan were miraculously given a hundred thousand reinforcements to advance on Richmond (which McClellan claimed was defended by two hundred thousand troops), "he would telegraph that he had certain information that the enemy had 400,000 men and that he could not advance without reinforcements."[18]

Many of McClellan's blunders in the Maryland Campaign resulted from his self-deception about enemy strength. On the basis of the supposed Rebel numerical superiority of "at least 25 per cent" and the apparent secure condition of Washington, McClellan requested that "every available man be at once added to this army." He provided his usual pessimistic assessment: "[T]he result of a general battle, with such odds as the enemy now appears to have against us, might, to say the least, be doubtful; and if we should be defeated, the consequences to the country would be disastrous in the extreme."[19]

McClellan made daily pleas for more troops. On September 11, he requested Halleck to "[p]lease send forward all the troops you can spare from Washington, particularly [Fitz John] Porter's, [Samuel] Heintzelman's, [Franz] Sigel's, and all other old troops." At six o'clock that evening, Lincoln responded that Porter, with twenty-one thousand troops, "is ordered to-night to join you as quick as possible. I am for sending you all that can be spared, & hope others can follow Porter very soon."[20] McClellan's failure to use Porter's large corps at the Battle of Antietam six days later would nullify this addition to his army.

SETTING THE STAGE FOR BATTLE

While McClellan pleaded for reinforcements, Jackson began tightening the noose on Harpers Ferry. On September 11, he crossed the Potomac back into Virginia at Williamsport, attacked the Union garrison at Martinsburg, and drove it back toward Harpers Ferry. Lincoln reported the news of Jackson's crossing to McClellan, speculating that the "whole rebel army…is recrossing the Potomac," and pleaded, "Please do not let him get off without being hurt."[21] McClellan responded that he was afraid the Rebels would escape by way of Williamsport but assured the president, "If Harpers Ferry is still in our possession I think I can save the garrison if they fight at all."[22]

On September 12, McClellan's troops began reaching Frederick, where they were welcomed by the majority of the residents. McClellan advised Lincoln, Halleck, and his wife of his troops' entry into Frederick, his intent to pursue the enemy into Pennsylvania or cut off their retreat to Virginia, and his concern about the need to save the garrison at Harpers Ferry. To Halleck, he wrote, "I have heard no firing in that direction [Harpers Ferry], and if he [Miles] resists at all, I think I cannot only relieve him, but place the rebels who attack him in great danger of being cut off. Everything moves at daylight tomorrow."[23] In fact, no Union soldiers advanced the next day.

THE "LOST ORDER"

McClellan, however, was presented with a golden opportunity to do just what he had suggested to Halleck—cut off isolated portions of Lee's army that were planning to attack Harpers Ferry. On the morning of September 13, two Indiana soldiers found a copy of Lee's Special Orders

No. 191 wrapped in paper with three cigars in a field near Frederick. The famous "Lost Order" was sent up the chain of command to the commanding general. Here was a virtually unprecedented opportunity. McClellan possessed Lee's orders showing that the Army of Northern Virginia likely was spread all over western Maryland and northwestern Virginia, its components separated by rivers, and vulnerable to a swift Union attack on its divided forces.

McClellan was meeting with a delegation of citizens of Frederick when, some time between noon and three o'clock, he was presented with the intercepted orders. Recognizing their significance, he allowed his excitement to overcome his discretion. Throwing his hands up, he exclaimed in the presence of his visitors, "Now I know what to do!" Lee later reported that one of the visiting townsmen informed J. E. B. Stuart of what had happened. Lee knew that something important was up.

McClellan sent a dispatch to the president bragging of the coup and appearing to promise quick action: "I have the whole rebel force in front of me, but am confident, and no time shall be lost. I have a difficult task to perform but with God's blessing will accomplish it. I think Lee has made a gross mistake, and that he will be severely punished for it. The Army is in motion as rapidly as possible. I hope for a great success if the plans of the rebels remain unchanged.... I have all the plans of the rebels, and will catch them in their own trap if my men are equal to the emergency."[24] His men were equal to the emergency, but he was not.

McClellan waited until after six o'clock to issue orders, so it was fifteen to eighteen hours before his troops were underway toward Harpers Ferry. Stephen Sears points out that McClellan had everything to gain and nothing to lose by at least prepositioning his army for dawn attacks on the Confederate-controlled mountain gaps.[25] "Nothing displays McClellan's weaknesses more than his failure to act with dispatch before Antietam when Lee's plans fell into his hands and the opportunity existed to bag the Army of Northern Virginia."[26]

McClellan's hesitance in the face of opportunity has earned him universal criticism. The historian A. Wilson Greene explains why:

Every writer agrees that Little Mac erred egregiously when he failed to order an immediate march toward the west on the afternoon of September 13. Two important possibilities beckoned seductively to an energized Federal army. By breaking through Crampton's Gap on his left, McClellan might have overwhelmed Lafayette McLaws's force in Pleasant Valley and seized Maryland Heights, thus relieving Harpers Ferry. An offensive thrust through Turner's Gap and Boonsboro on the Union right would have isolated D. H. Hill and James Longstreet from Jackson's forces south of the Potomac, creating the opportunity to crush a wing of Lee's army.[27]

LACKADAISICAL PURSUIT

McClellan decided to divide his army into three wings. The right wing would march northwest from Frederick on the National Road, the left wing would march southwest after McLaws on Maryland Heights above Harpers Ferry, and the center would act as a reserve. It was 6:20 p.m., between three and seven hours after he saw Lee's order, before McClellan—who knew that a large contingent of Union troops was trapped at Harpers Ferry—issued orders to William Franklin, commanding the critical left wing that needed to break through to Harpers Ferry. Those orders called for him to head toward Harpers Ferry through Crampton's Gap by moving "at daybreak in the morning" of the fourteenth.[28]

That evening McClellan told Brigadier General John Gibbon of the Iron Brigade, "Here is a paper with which if I cannot whip Bobby Lee, I will be willing to go home. I will not show you the document now, but here is the signature, and it gives the movement of every division of Lee's army. Tomorrow we will pitch into his center and if you people will do two good, hard days' marching I will put Lee in a position he will find it hard to get out of."[29] At the same time, McClellan already was fatally delaying his army's attack.

Late on the thirteenth, McClellan informed Halleck of the Lost Order and cited evidence that Lee's army consisted of at least 120,000: "This

General George B. McClellan. *Courtesy of the Library of Congress*

Army marches forward [to Harpers Ferry] early to-morrow morning and will make forced marches, to endeavor to relieve Col. Miles, but I fear unless he makes a stout resistance, we may be too late. A report came in just this moment that Miles was attacked to-day and repulsed the enemy, but I do not know what credit to attach to the statement. I shall do everything in my power to save Miles if he still holds out."[30] In reality, McClellan moved with sluggishness instead of determination and alacrity.

The next morning, the fourteenth, McClellan's forces moved deliberately westward toward Turner's and Fox's gaps in South Mountain. For the balance of the day, D. H. Hill's and Longstreet's infantry and some of Stuart's cavalry barely held the gaps. Hill's twenty-three hundred troops most likely would have been quickly swept aside had McClellan started his army forward promptly on the thirteenth. McClellan remained miles from the fighting, which he left to Generals Jesse Reno (who was killed), Ambrose Burnside, Joe Hooker, George Meade, Jacob Cox, John Gibbon, and others.[31] He apparently admired the fighting on South Mountain from a lookout back on the Catoctin Range; if so, it was the first time he had actually observed an army under his command in combat. Rebel forces grimly hung on there until night, when they withdrew southwest toward the small town of Sharpsburg on Antietam Creek.

FALL OF HARPERS FERRY

South of those gaps was Crampton's Gap, where the most critical fighting of the day, and perhaps the campaign, occurred. Franklin's thirteen-thousand-man Sixth Corps was supposed to break through to Maryland Heights, foil Jackson's plans to capture Harpers Ferry, and save the twelve thousand Union troops trapped there. Franklin proved that he was McClellan's disciple by delaying his march in a fruitless wait for Darius Couch's division (a wait ordered by McClellan, according to Franklin) and then finally attacking in mid-afternoon. He probably felt no urgency after receiving McClellan's routine 11:45 a.m. dispatch concluding with the words, "Continue to bear in mind the necessity of relieving Colonel [Nelson] Miles *if possible*."[32]

Franklin and his commanders did not realize they were being opposed by a mere thousand soldiers in four Rebel regiments. Finally, at four o'clock and on their own initiative, Major General Henry Slocum's division attacked and defeated the well-positioned defenders. Howell Cobb's thirteen-hundred-man Georgia brigade then reinforced the defense as it was collapsing and held out until dark. The greatly outnumbered Confederates had held Crampton's Gap throughout the fourteenth at a cost of eight hundred casualties (to the Union's five hundred). After the gap fell, Franklin did nothing all night to fight his way onward toward Harpers Ferry and rescue the troops trapped there. Instead he waited for the arrival of an unneeded additional six thousand troops.[33]

It was imperative for Franklin, having reached the gap by nightfall, to keep the pressure on McLaws and, at least by the noise of fighting, alert the Union garrison at Harpers Ferry that relief was on the way. By ten o'clock, Franklin received seven thousand additional troops and had twenty thousand troops to attack the minuscule Confederate force between Harpers Ferry and his troops. But Franklin continued McClellan-like in his reluctance to engage and even failed to attack into Pleasant Valley west of South Mountain at first light on the fifteenth. Instead, he assumed that he was outnumbered and requested more reinforcements. Franklin's failure to attack overnight or early that morning led directly to the surrender of Harpers Ferry at 7:15 on the morning of the fifteenth.[34]

The Federal commander of the Martinsburg and Harpers Ferry detachments huddled in Harpers Ferry was the incompetent Colonel Dixon S. Miles. As Jackson and his three separate commands were closing the trap on him, Miles made no effort to move to Maryland Heights or escape along the Potomac. After a brief cannonading from Maryland Heights on the east and Loudon Heights, Virginia, on the south, Miles surrendered the garrison and its 11,500 troops, seventy-three guns, thirteen thousand small arms, two hundred wagons, and thousands of blue uniforms.[35] The Harpers Ferry disaster was the direct result of McClellan's and Franklin's shameful slowness and lack of aggressiveness, as well as Miles's timidity.

This largest surrender of Union troops during the war was directly attributable to McClellan's usual slowness, excessive caution, and gross overestimation of enemy strength. His failure to save this large contingent of soldiers and their valuable equipment deprived him of those troops for the duration of the campaign and allowed Jackson to send his victorious troops to aid Lee's army at Sharpsburg. That assistance strengthened Lee during the entire Battle of Antietam and likely saved his army when A. P. Hill's troops arrived from Harpers Ferry on the Union flank in the final stage of the battle.

Although the Harpers Ferry fiasco was an important Rebel victory, Allan Nevins concludes, "the South would have paid too high a price if Lee had been smashed before Jackson could get back to him."[36] McClellan's typical dallying at Sharpsburg would keep that from happening.

FIRST DAYS AT SHARPSBURG

Aware of McClellan's slowness and reluctance to fight, Lee had gambled even more than usual at Antietam when he placed the remnants of Longstreet's corps and D. H. Hill's division with their backs to the Potomac and its single shaky ford. In the words of Murray and Hsieh, "Here indeed was the man named 'audacity.' Lee was taking an enormous gamble in deploying portions of his army east of the Potomac in the belief McClellan would fail to attack until Jackson had rounded up the Harper's Ferry booty. He also counted on Jackson being able to drive his troops to Sharpsburg in time to meet a potential Union attack. The gamble came within hours of destroying the Army of Northern Virginia."[37]

McClellan's failure to destroy Lee's bottled-up and outnumbered army at Sharpsburg was a major missed opportunity to shorten or end the war. As Steven Woodworth points out, "George B. McClellan's failure to attack Lee at Antietam on September 16 or 18, 1862, or to launch a coordinated, all-out attack on the 17th [was a major blunder]. With Lee's army backed up against the Potomac and outnumbered more than two-to-one, McClellan had the opportunity to win the war in Virginia in an afternoon."[38]

Indeed, McClellan failed to attack a disorganized, outnumbered, and battered Rebel army on September 15, 16, and 18. Further, his attack on September 17 was piecemeal, failed to utilize twenty-five thousand Union reserves, and made no effective use of his cavalry. As Confederate Colonel Porter Alexander, Longstreet's chief of artillery, tartly observed, "not only did McClellan bring upon the field his 87,176, well equipped men, against Lee's 35,255 ragged and poorly equipped; but he brought *himself* also."[39] What follows here is a description of the many blunders

McClellan committed at Sharpsburg—causing him to miss several more grand opportunities to destroy Lee's army.

On the morning of the fifteenth, McClellan sent a typically inaccurate message to Halleck claiming a "glorious" and "complete" victory at the gaps. He then asserted, falsely, that the routed and demoralized enemy was "in a perfect panic," that Lee had admitted losses of fifteen thousand and that his army was "shockingly whipped," and that Lee had been wounded.[40] In fact, the uninjured Lee's army had suffered losses of about 3,400 and retreated in good order to Sharpsburg.[41] Lincoln acknowledged the wires and responded, "God bless you, and all with you. Destroy the rebel army, if possible."[42] McClellan would fail to do that. Jackson assigned the mopping up at Harpers Ferry to A. P. Hill's division and force-marched the rest of his troops north to join Lee at Sharpsburg.

Fifteen miles to the north of Harpers Ferry, McClellan arrived on the afternoon and early evening of the fifteenth at Sharpsburg with sixty to seventy thousand troops on the east side of Antietam Creek, while Lee aligned his paltry fifteen to eighteen thousand troops in the woods and on a slight ridge on the western side of the creek. Lee's soldiers were trapped in a horseshoe bend of the Potomac River with only a single ford as an escape route. Ordering his army to gather and engage the enemy at Sharpsburg instead of victoriously departing Maryland after Harpers Ferry was, in Porter Alexander's words, "the greatest military blunder that Gen. Lee ever made." He pointed out that Lee's army was tired, sick, and badly outnumbered and that McClellan's was continually being reinforced.[43]

Although Joe Hooker and George Custer reported Rebel strength at a mere fifteen thousand,[44] McClellan did nothing on the fifteenth even though he enjoyed a more than four-to-one advantage. Despite assuring Halleck that "our troops are now advancing in pursuit of them,"[45] he pursued slowly, and "orders to move were inexcusably delayed."[46] But fearing he was outnumbered, he "launched no probing attacks and sent no cavalry reconnaissance across the two undefended bridges or the several fords to determine Confederate strength."[47] The first day at Antietam was wasted.

Things got no better for the Union side on the sixteenth. At seven o'clock in the morning, McClellan wired Halleck that his troops had arrived too late on the fifteenth to attack, that heavy fog was preventing an attack that morning, and that he would attack "as soon as the situation of the enemy is developed." Early in the day, he had seventy thousand troops to oppose Lee's eighteen thousand, who later that day were reinforced by Jackson but still numbered no more than about twenty-five thousand. According to McClellan's post-campaign report, he spent the sixteenth reconnoitering the enemy and planning for battle. There is no indication that he used his cavalry to find fords across the Antietam, determine the true nature of enemy strength, screen his own activities, or secure the battlefield perimeter against Rebel reinforcements (foreseeably likely to be coming from Harpers Ferry). "McClellan's failure to conduct a thorough reconnaissance using all means available was a gross error."[48]

The historian Robert C. Cheeks has summarized the situation on the sixteenth well:

> On the morning of Tuesday, September 16, McClellan had nearly 60,000 soldiers facing Lee's 15,000. His heavy 20-pound Parrott rifles were sending case shot across the creek, feeling out the enemy. As Longstreet ordered a vigorous response—more for bluff than effect—Lee realized his one chance for salvation lay with McClellan reverting to his old, timid behavior. McClellan did not disappoint him. Across the creek, the commander of the Federal Army rode about on his horse, Dan Webster, taking the salutes of his admiring infantry and superbly equipped artillery. His boys would pay dearly for their general's indecisiveness.[49]

Porter Alexander marveled at McClellan's failure to attack on the sixteenth: "And now McClellan's chance had come. He must have known that Lee's whole army was not yet on the field, & pushed it with all possible vigor & all his force."[50]

Harpers Ferry, photographed immediately after its evacuation by the Rebels, 1861. *Courtesy of the Library of Congress*

In summary, on either the fifteenth or sixteenth, McClellan could have reaped the benefits of the discovery of the Lost Order and decimated Lee's minuscule force—as he had said he would do—with his own army of seventy to seventy-five thousand. Instead, McClellan convinced himself that Lee had 120,000 troops and declined to attack until he was ready—and Lee was increasingly reinforced.[51]

BATTLE OF ANTIETAM (SHARPSBURG)

September 17, 1862, was the bloodiest single day of the entire war—and in American military history. In a full day of unbelievably brave and foolish charges and countercharges, the troops of both armies cut each other to pieces in the Battle of Antietam—known in the South as the Battle of Sharpsburg.[52] McClellan squandered his huge numerical superiority by attacking sequentially instead of simultaneously and never even using a quarter of his troops.

Alexander later wrote, "Had McClellan attacked along the whole line at dawn we had not the force to have withstood him long. He let us get through the day only by making partial attacks & giving us the chance to concentrate nearly all we had to meet each one in succession."[53] According to Gregory Thiele, "Given the Confederate ability to rapidly reinforce due to their interior lines, McClellan's best course would have been to conduct a coordinated assault along his entire line. This would have tied down all of the Confederate troops and made it difficult for Lee to plug any holes that developed."[54]

THE NORTH END

From before dawn until mid-morning, disjointed attacks by Hooker's and later Joseph K. F. Mansfield's troops from the North Woods and the East Woods on the north end of the lines were driven back from the West Woods and the immortal Miller's Cornfield by Jackson's defenders, who then counterattacked. The Cornfield was the scene of about fourteen attacks and counterattacks, as each side took turns massacring the other before Union troops finally seized that field. Reinforcements from the southern end of the Rebel line and the arrival at seven o'clock of more of Jackson's troops, who had marched all night to get to the battlefield, kept the Confederate north flank from breaking. Had McClellan attacked on the fifteenth or sixteenth, those troops would not have been there to augment Lee's force.[55]

As the northern portion of the battle deteriorated into a bloody stalemate during the early to mid-morning hours, McClellan finally sent Edwin V. Sumner's fifteen thousand men into the north and middle of the battlefield. He did so only after Sumner had come to his headquarters seeking such orders, having been stalled by McClellan's staff, who assured him that all was going well—although battlefield smoke and full-leafed trees in the East Woods precluded their viewing the early combat from their faraway "command" post. Many of Sumner's disorganized troops marched into a trap and were killed or wounded. John Sedgwick's division of Sumner's corps suffered 42 percent casualties, the highest of any Union division on the field that day.[56]

THE MIDDLE

Next, in late morning, waves of Union troops, fully twelve thousand and including Brigadier General Thomas F. Meagher's famous Irish Brigade, attacked a strong Confederate position at the Sunken Road in the center of the field. They were mowed down by Rebels firing from the Sunken Road, which they had fortified with a breastwork of fence rails. One union division lost 40 percent of its men and another lost 10 percent attacking that position. Only a mistaken withdrawal of Rebel troops from both ends of the Sunken Road made it vulnerable to a deadly enfilade attack by Union troops that turned the depressed road into "Bloody Lane."[57] The Confederates fled from that position, leaving the heart of the battlefield open to Union assault and ripe for victory. Small numbers of Confederate reinforcements rushed to bolster the center and briefly repelled Union progress. General Longstreet himself directed the fire from a single battery. Lee's army was spread thin. Its center, having been broken, was wide open to attack.

But the only Federal movement at that time was a ponderous effort by Brigadier General George Sykes's few battalions, which were halted after they crossed the Middle Bridge. Sykes believed that supporting troops would have enabled him to reach the high ground at Sharpsburg in the center of the collapsed Rebel line.[58] Generals Sumner and Porter convinced McClellan not to send in twenty-five thousand Union reinforcements who were just back of the bridge. McClellan agreed with them that it would not be prudent to attack with those reserves of Porter and Franklin, although the latter general wanted to attack. "Lee's army was ruined, and the end of the Confederacy was in sight," Alexander would recall. Longstreet himself later said that a mere ten thousand Union reserves sent in at that point could have swept the Rebels from the field.[59] Thiele concurs: "Had McClellan ruthlessly pressed this assault, he could have pierced the weak Confederate center, with potentially disastrous results for the Confederates."[60]

Another opportunity to break the Confederate center arose around midday. General Franklin moved up with five fresh brigades to join Sumner in a renewed assault. When Sumner declined to participate in an attack, McClellan characteristically called off the attack that would, alone or in conjunction with Burnside's delayed efforts, have decimated Lee's army. According to Alexander, "some congenital defect made McClellan keep Fitz John Porter's fine, large corps entirely out of action, though it stood there looking on about 20,000 strong within a mile of our centre."[61] Pois and Langer conclude, "When one more assault might have routed the Confederate left flank, [McClellan] chose to believe a demoralized Maj. Gen. Edwin Sumner...that failure could result in defeat."[62]

Late in the morning, in the same middle sector of the battlefield, Union artillerymen moved across the Middle Bridge and fired their guns from Cherry Hill west-southwest into the town of Sharpsburg. McClellan did not support their efforts. Paul Chiles writes, "There was no timely follow-up by McClellan, so the Confederates had time to reinforce the position...and hold on. McClellan's failure to exploit his numerical advantage in this sector was another missed opportunity for the Union to win the battle and possibly end the war."[63]

THE SOUTH END

Meanwhile, on the south end of the battlefield, nothing happened until McClellan, after nine o'clock, belatedly ordered Burnside's Ninth Corps to cross the Antietam, get behind Lee's army, and cut off its only retreat across the Potomac at Boteler's Ford. Burnside—resentful at having been rebuked by McClellan for his allegedly nonaggressive pursuit of the enemy after the South Mountain fighting and effectively stripped of his wing command by McClellan's removal of Hooker's corps from his control—was tepid in his response.[64]

McClellan had delayed ordering Burnside to attack until even more troops arrived—Franklin's Sixth Corps from near Crampton's Gap.

President Lincoln and General George B. McClellan in the general's tent at Antietam. *Courtesy of the Library of Congress*

While Burnside had waited with 12,500 troops on the south end of the Antietam battlefield, Lee had shifted troops away from that quiescent front. Starting six hours after the battle had begun, Burnside tried unsuccessfully to cross Rohrbach's Bridge, which since then has been ingloriously called Burnside's Bridge.[65]

McClellan had failed to have his cavalry reconnoiter the area during the two days his army was on scene before the seventeenth, and Burnside had failed to do the same, so Burnside's troops were unaware of the depth and fords of Antietam Creek near the bridge. The creek was four to five feet deep in the vicinity of the bridge, and its depth in many nearby places was only three feet. Primarily because McClellan kept his cavalry back at his headquarters, Burnside's troops were slow to discover the fords in the area, including Snavely's Ford (two miles to the south). The situation, writes John Waugh, was ridiculous: "Every resident within miles of the Antietam knew that all around the bridge, above and below, there were fords closer than Snavely's that could have been easily crossed out of range of the rebel guns on the heights. But nobody in the single-minded fixation with getting across that damnable bridge had seemed to consider that."[66]

That bridge was vulnerable to descending Confederate fire from a plateau to the immediate west. Riflemen and sharpshooters of the Second and Twentieth Georgia regiments easily and bloodily repelled assaults at the bridge and along a road paralleling the stream. The Eleventh Connecticut, Second Maryland, and Sixth New Hampshire regiments suffered heavy casualties attempting to reach the bridge in the late morning of the seventeenth and finally retreated.

McClellan's inspector general then appeared at Burnside's headquarters to order another attack, this one commanded by Colonel Edward Ferraro, who promised to restore the whisky rations of the Fifty-first Pennsylvania and Fifty-first New York regiments if they took the bridge. Their attack was preceded by a Union artillery barrage of canister on the Georgia defenders across the creek. Instead of exposing themselves on the creekside road, as their predecessors had done, the two regiments charged directly toward the bridge from the east—perpendicular to the Georgians' line. After a brief pause, they successfully charged across. Finally, at about one o'clock in the afternoon, Burnside's men, taking advantage of the Confederates' low ammunition and cumulative losses, crossed to the west bank of the Antietam—along with compatriots who at long last had crossed at Snavely's Ford.[67]

In what became a turning point in the battle, Burnside delayed his advance for two hours while he brought up ammunition and reinforcements—a disastrous mistake. Deferring to Burnside's delayed assault, McClellan failed to use his other resources to attack the open Rebel right flank. As the historian Robert Barr Smith observes, "McClellan still had all his cavalry and a fresh infantry corps [Porter's], but as usual he dithered, his head filled with visions of hordes of imaginary Rebels. The final push to victory, then, would have to come from Burnside's men."[68]

Finally Burnside's troops advanced up the slopes toward Sharpsburg, facing about thirty Rebel guns and infantry that Lee had rushed into place from the now-quiet central and northern portions of the battlefield. To Burnside's right were Union regulars, who joined in the attack until they were recalled by McClellan.[69] As Burnside's attackers were about to overwhelm Lee's south flank, they were suddenly assaulted from their left by Rebel troops of A. P. Hill, the last of Jackson's force to arrive from Harpers Ferry, many of them dressed in the blue uniforms confiscated there. Burnside's men were decimated by this unexpected attack from the south, and those on his left flank fled back to and even across Burnside's Bridge. Although Burnside's right flank was still in a strong position to break Lee's line, McClellan again declined to send in Porter's Fifth Corps when Porter, his protégé, told him, "Remember, General! I command the last reserve of the last Army of the Republic!" Burnside's unsupported attack faltered and ceased. Lee's army was saved.[70]

While not excusing Burnside's abysmal performance, Stephen Sears describes McClellan's failures related to Burnside's wing:

> …McClellan's catalog of failures is lengthy and manifest. The Ninth Corps made its battle under an unwieldy command structure he imposed on it and without clearly stated objectives. Reconnaissance of the Antietam fords was ineptly performed, and by McClellan's staff rather than by cavalry. No use was made of the potential reinforcement of Couch's [just-arrived] division. The decision to open the attack was taken not only inexplicably late but without coordination with the rest of the army. The elementary precaution of guarding the army's left flank with cavalry was ignored, granting Powell Hill the decisive advantages of surprise and position. Finally, the Ninth Corps was denied any support from the more than ample reserve, either to exploit victory or to salvage defeat.[71]

Thiele points out that McClellan never visited Burnside or his operations and "is ultimately to blame for Burnside's failure to attack earlier, not simply because he was the army commander, but because his passivity permitted it."[72]

A WEALTH OF BLUNDERS

McClellan's only substantial communiqué that day was a short telegram to Halleck, in which he reported:

> We are in the midst of the most terrible battle of the war— perhaps of history. Thus far it looks well, but I have great odds against me. Hurry up all the troops possible. Our loss has been terrific, but we have gained much ground. I have thrown the mass of the army on their left flank. Burnside is now attacking their right, and I hold my small reserve consisting of Porter's Fifth Corps, ready to attack the center as soon as the flank movements are developed. I hope that God will give us a glorious victory.[73]

This missive is classic McClellan. He did *not* have great odds against him. He threw in his usual plea for reinforcements. His army had *not* gained much ground. His "small" reserve consisted of between twenty and twenty-five thousand troops—in addition to Couch's thousands of arriving reinforcements. McClellan apparently never believed his flank movements were sufficiently developed (the one on his right had ceased hours before) because he failed to use his massive, fresh reserves to attack the center.[74]

That misleading message epitomizes McClellan's bungling leadership and command on that bloody day. Safe on a hillside, he gave minimal direction to his army, ordering a piecemeal attack on an inferior foe, failing to use his massive superiority in a simultaneous attack all along the lines, leaving a quarter of his troops unused, and squandering an opportunity to decimate or trap Lee's Army of Northern Virginia.

THE FINAL BLUNDER

McClellan's blundering continued on the eighteenth. In light of his army's battered condition, Lee's subordinate generals advised him to retreat the night of the seventeenth,[75] but he foolishly decided to stay at

Sharpsburg for another full day—a decision, writes Gary Gallagher, that "seemed to pass beyond audacity to recklessness."[76] Particularly risky for Lee was the vulnerability of Boteler's Ford, his only possible avenue of retreat across the Potomac in his rear. General Alexander described the ford as rocky, deep, and narrow. It could be blocked by a few wrecked wagons and was vulnerable to fire from many positions on the Maryland side's rolling hills. He concluded, "[I]t requires no argument to see that no army could retreat over such a road as that under fire."[77] Remaining at Sharpsburg gained Lee nothing, and it would have cost him his army had almost any general other than McClellan been commanding the Union forces.

The military force available to McClellan that day was substantial. Across the way, Lee's army was in shambles. As Burnside later told the Joint Committee on the Conduct of the War, he had offered to attack Lee on the Union left with his more than nine thousand troops if McClellan would give him an additional five thousand. The commanding general declined although he had thirty thousand troops available from the First, Second, Ninth, and Twelfth Corps, more than twenty thousand from the virtually unused Fifth and Sixth Corps, six thousand freshly recruited Pennsylvania troops who arrived early that morning, and another six thousand Fourth Corps soldiers who arrived at midday. Similarly, McClellan had rejected Franklin's recommendation to attack on the Union right. McClellan had more fresh troops than Lee had total troops. With Lee still trapped by the Potomac and his army reduced to fewer than thirty thousand men, what did McClellan do with his more than sixty thousand able-bodied soldiers on September 18? Nothing.[78]

Porter Alexander later recalled that the "Confederate army was worn & fought to a frazzle," while McClellan still had Porter's unused corps and Burnside's lightly used one. Alexander found it strange, therefore, that Lee did not retreat overnight into Virginia. He forecast that "surely military historians will say that McClellan again threw away a chance which no other Federal commander ever had, before or since."[79]

Murray and Hsieh, exploring the broader ramifications of McClellan's Antietam Campaign failures, come to a similar conclusion: "Had

McClellan driven forward on 18 September, he had every possibility of winning a great victory, which would have destroyed the Army of Northern Virginia utterly and completely.... As he had done throughout his tenure as commander of the Army of the Potomac, McClellan hesitated, and Lee escaped."[80]

He failed to press or move toward Lee, even though he wrote to his wife that morning, "The contest will probably be renewed today," and "[The battle] was a success, but whether a decided victory depends upon what occurs today." After Lee retreated that night, McClellan told her, "Our victory complete."[81] In two messages to Halleck on September 19, McClellan explained that his army was fully occupied on the eighteenth "replenishing ammunition, taking care of wounded, &c.," and claimed a "complete victory" because the Confederates had been driven across the river.[82] Unlike Lincoln, McClellan thought it was sufficient—a great victory, even—merely to chase Lee out of Maryland without disabling his army. McClellan's public claim of a "complete victory" did at least make it easier for Lincoln to issue his Preliminary Emancipation Proclamation on September 22, since the president had been waiting for an occasion on which his action would not be deemed one of desperation growing out of defeat.

In a report on his army's operations written nearly a year later, McClellan composed two small-print pages explaining why he did not attack at Antietam on the eighteenth. The introduction reflected his perennial fear of failure: "...at this critical juncture I should have had a narrow view of the condition of the country had I been willing to hazard another battle with less than an absolute assurance of success. At that moment—Virginia lost, Washington menaced, Maryland invaded—the national cause could afford no risks of defeat. One battle lost, and almost all would have been lost. Lee's army might then have marched as it pleased on Washington, Baltimore, Philadelphia, or New York."[83] As usual, McClellan's fear of defeat had eliminated any possibility of a decisive victory and the destruction of Lee's army.

Thus, in Alan Nolan's words, he "contented himself with a token pursuit."[84] Some of McClellan's own officers disagreed with his

General Robert E. Lee. *Courtesy of the Library of Congress*

characterization of Antietam as a "complete victory." A captain from Maine wrote, "We should have followed them up the next day." And a Connecticut officer could "imagine no earthly reason why we did not go at them the next day with a vengeance."[85] As the historian Patrick J. Brennan concludes, "What should have been a moment of triumph for the beleaguered president swiftly turned into a season of frustration.... Washington whispers of treasonous insubordination targeted McClellan and his 'Potomac Army Clique.'" When John J. Key of Halleck's staff (the brother of McClellan's judge advocate) boasted that an Antietam victory was "not the game" and that a battle of mutual exhaustion had been agreed upon to save the institution of slavery, Lincoln had him summarily court-martialed and dismissed from the Army.[86]

SUMMARY

On September 18, 1862, the sun set on perhaps the greatest series of blunders and lost opportunities of the Civil War. Instead of destroying Lee's divided army in detail after being handed its operational order; quickly rescuing besieged Union troops at Harpers Ferry; attacking the vastly outnumbered Rebel army on September 15 or 16 at Sharpsburg; using all of his army (including his reserves and cavalry) to attack Lee's forces simultaneously and aggressively on September 17; or attacking the decimated Southerners on September 18, McClellan had settled for a tactical draw, losing an opportunity to close out the war years before it would finally end. As Alexander reflected from a Confederate perspective, "A drawn battle, such as we did actually fight, was the best *possible* outcome one could hope for. Even that we only accomplished by the Good Lord's putting it in McClellan's heart to keep Fitz John Porter's corps entirely out of the battle, & Franklin's nearly all out."[87] Porter later wrote, "I commanded the Reserve. At no time did I receive any order to put troops in action on the 17th—or even a suggestion." John M. Priest concludes, "Both he and his commanding general feared being overrun by the numerically inferior Army of Northern Virginia."[88]

Gregory Thiele, however, argues that military historians' searing criticism of McClellan's Antietam performance may not be deserved, citing the judgment of none other than Robert E. Lee, who after the war was reputed to have emphatically said that "McClellan by all odds" was the greatest Union general.[89] Assuming that Lee said this and was not joking (something he did not do), how do we explain such an assessment? It is likely that Lee disdained the "hard-war" approach of Grant, Sherman, and Sheridan and that he preferred not to recognize Meade, the victor at Gettysburg. Almost by default, then, and probably with gratitude, he might have bestowed the accolade on McClellan. Lee had read McClellan like a book. He played him for a fool again and again and benefitted from his blunders on the Peninsula and in the Maryland Campaign. He understood that McClellan had undermined Pope at Second Manassas, and he appreciated that Mac had wanted to fight a gentlemen's war, a virtually bloodless contest of maneuvers that would not disturb slavery. Perhaps Lee thought that the better McClellan looked, the better Lee himself appeared for outsmarting him.

In his sympathy for McClellan, Thiele offers as credible a defense of his performance at Antietam as one could come up with:

> Based on his actions, the picture that emerges of McClellan is simply of a very conservative general who was averse to taking risks. McClellan did not seek to win as much as he sought not to lose, but he may not deserve all the scorn that has been heaped upon him. As a further handicap, McClellan faced an extremely skillful foe in Robert E. Lee. Given the difficulty of the task that Lee had set before him, McClellan had turned in a creditable performance. An audacious general might have destroyed Lee's army. If Lee had been faced with a solid, energetic adversary, it is unlikely that he would have decided to make a stand behind Antietam Creek with the Potomac River to his rear. Lee knew McClellan very well, however, and knew that McClellan was intelligent, but saw difficulties everywhere. He had the love of his men, but he loved them too much to ask them to make the sacrifices necessary to achieve victory. This ultimately spelled his doom as army commander.[90]

Eighteen months into the war, the Union needed more than mediocre performances. It bore the burden of winning, not stalemating, the war and thus desperately needed audacious generals. Thiele's sympathetic evaluation confirms that McClellan's blunders at Antietam were caused by his hesitancy, rather than action, when opportunities for Union success were handed to him.

Porter Alexander captured the sense of frustration that McClellan's lack of aggression engendered:

> Common sense was just shouting, "Your adversary is backed against a river, with no bridge & only one ford, & that the worst one on the whole river. If you whip him now, you destroy him utterly, root & branch & bag & baggage. Not twice in a life time does such a chance come to any general. Lee for once had made a mistake, & given you a chance to ruin him if you can break his lines, & such game is worth great risk. Every man must fight & keep on fighting for all he is worth." For no military genius, but only the commonest of every day common sense, was necessary to appreciate that.[91]

Gary Gallagher concurs: "Priceless openings had come and gone over three crucial days, and Lee's decision to hold his lines on September 18 was McClellan's ultimate opportunity.... The Army of the Potomac possessed the requisite elements to deliver a fatal blow. Destruction of Lee's army would have uncovered Richmond and crippled Southern morale; it might have ended the war. Because McClellan chose not to force the issue, his military performance in Maryland must be judged harshly."[92]

The consequences of McClellan's blunders during the Maryland Campaign were huge. Instead of eliminating the only major Confederate army in the East in late 1862, he left the door open for Lee to contest the war until early 1865. His missed opportunities extended the war for as much as two and a half years and resulted in hundreds of thousands of additional casualties. The irony in this history is that the extension of the Civil War led to the abolition of slavery—an outcome that McClellan vehemently opposed.

BLACK SOLDIERS

CONFEDERATES FAIL TO USE SLAVES AS SOLDIERS

WHO BLUNDERED?

Confederate President Jefferson Davis and other Confederate leaders

HOW?

They failed to arm and use black slaves as Confederate soldiers.

CONSEQUENCES?

If the Confederates intended to win the war and maintain their independence (as opposed to maintaining slavery), they needed to use this great source of manpower. Since they failed to do so, their manpower shortage became increasingly debilitating as the Civil War progressed.

A major obstacle facing the Confederacy was that the Union had an almost four-to-one advantage in white men of fighting age. The ten million Southern whites desperately needed to fill their armies with every last man they could find. Drafting boys and old men was not sufficient. One obvious source of manpower was the four million slaves, about a million of whom were males of military age, but the Confederacy committed a grievous error by not using slaves as soldiers, one of its biggest missed opportunities of the war.[1]

Part of the Myth of the Lost Cause[2] has been the false contention that many, perhaps thousands, of blacks, fought for the Confederacy. Soon after the war, the Southern journalist J. D. B. DeBow asserted, "So firmly fixed did our people remain in the faith that the negro would be true to his master that it was finally proposed to receive him into the ranks of the army as a soldier.... [S]o popular was the idea, that enlistments began to take place, and had the war continued the negro must have formed a large element of our military strength." He concluded that three or four hundred thousand black troops *could have been* "thrown into field."[3] DeBow did not explain why the Confederacy waited until the war was essentially lost before enlisting any blacks, and he made no mention of the violent opposition to arming blacks or of the paltry number that were enlisted.

Even today, unsubstantiated claims are made that regiments consisting of thousands of blacks fought for the Confederacy and that slaves who fought for the Confederacy received their freedom.[4] There is no credible evidence to support such claims. The Confederacy forbade the use of black soldiers until the last month of Lee's army's existence, and then the move was so conditional and tardy that it produced no black combat troops.

Most of the purported thousands of soldiers were nothing more than slaves who were compelled to accompany their masters or masters' sons to war. Their role was not that of soldiers, but of slaves performing menial tasks. They were whipped or otherwise punished for misbehavior—not exactly a court-martial procedure. Although postwar Southerners' accounts mentioned their slaves' battlefield exploits, "the vast majority of these stories of servants braving the battlefield to fight Yankees or rescue wounded masters...tell us much about how whites chose to remember their former slaves during the postwar period, but very little about what motivated camp servants during these moments of intense danger."[5]

White soldiers' wartime correspondence referred to their slaves merely as negro, boy, uncle, or other unsoldierly terms. When a slave named Luke asked for a parole so he could accompany his master after their military incarceration, his master told him he did not need a parole because "[y]ou have never been a soldier."[6]

In summary, "Following the war the relationships between Confederate officers and their black camp servants were transformed into stories of loyal slaves and used as a pillar of the Lost Cause narrative.... [The stories and other postwar developments] made it easier to distance the Confederates' experiment in independence from their 'peculiar institution.'"[7]

Just after the Confederate victory in the first battle of Bull Run (Manassas) in mid-1861, Brigadier General Richard Ewell suggested to an exuberant President Davis the necessity of emancipating and arming slaves to ensure Southern independence. Davis rejected this private plea as "stark madness that would revolt and disgust the whole South." Ewell rejoined that this step would "paralyze the North." Davis said the scheme was impossible and asked who would command a brigade of Negroes. When Ewell said he would, the president again rejected the proposal as simply impossible. Ewell's recommendation to arm and emancipate Southern slaves would never be implemented by the Confederate government.[8]

From late 1863 through March 1865, other Southerners, seeing the Confederacy in serious jeopardy, proposed that slaves be armed as Confederate soldiers and possibly granted their freedom for doing so. In December 1863, Major General Thomas Hindman, an Arkansan, anonymously made such a suggestion in an open letter to a Tennessee newspaper then being published in Georgia.[9] The stage was set for the most serious and thoughtful proposal on this subject, which came from Hindman's former law partner, Major General Patrick Cleburne, the Rebels' best general in the Western Theater. Cleburne's rear-guard action at Ringgold

Gap after the rout at Chattanooga had saved the Army of Tennessee and, by February 1864, earned him the official thanks of the Confederate Congress.[10] But his prospects for promotion ended on January 2, 1864, when he and thirteen subordinate officers proposed arming and freeing slaves after Confederate forces had been driven out of Tennessee.

A native of Ireland, Cleburne had a broader perspective than most Southerners. His proposal was designed to address Confederate manpower shortages and the lack of foreign recognition. He read his proposal at a meeting with the commander of the Army of Tennessee, General Joseph Johnston, and almost all his corps and division commanders. Cleburne first described the Confederacy's desperate situation, which he said was due to its inferior numbers, inferior supply of potential soldiers, and "the fact that slavery, from being one of our chief sources of strength at the commencement of the war, has now become, in a military point of view, one of our chief sources of weakness." Although recognizing that the slavery issue "may rouse prejudice and passion," he said with understatement, "it would be madness" not to probe all relevant possibilities.[11]

He described President Davis's recent proposals to increase the army's manpower by a series of actions involving white men, including "placing in the ranks such of the able-bodied men now employed as wagoners [sic], nurses, cooks and other employés [sic], as are doing service for which the negroes may be found competent." Cleburne somewhat brazenly concluded that Davis's proposals would not provide adequate manpower, adding,

> [W]e propose…that we immediately commence training a large reserve of the most courageous of our slaves, and further that we guarantee freedom within a reasonable time to every slave in the South who shall remain true to the Confederacy in this war. As between the loss of independence and the loss of slavery, we assume that every patriot will freely give up the latter—give up the negro slave rather than be a slave himself.[12]

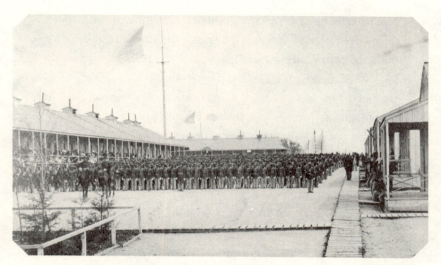

The 26th U.S. Colored Volunteer Infantry on parade, Camp William Penn, PA, 1865. *Courtesy of the National Archives*

Cleburne was advocating nothing less than the abolition of slavery and the recruitment of blacks to fight for the Confederacy. Among the benefits of these actions, he said, were the attraction of foreign support for the Confederacy and the destruction of the purpose for which Northern abolitionists and black Union troops were fighting. He also answered the question "Will slaves fight?" by citing numerous historical examples, including ex-slaves in Jamaica and, reluctantly, Union blacks ("...the experience of this war has been so far that half-trained negroes have fought as bravely as half-trained Yankees...").[13]

In explaining his long and thoughtful proposal, Cleburne made some justifying observations that obviously upset supporters of slavery. For example, he said that his proposal

> would instantly remove all the vulnerability, embarrassment, and inherent weakness which result from slavery. The approach of the enemy would no longer find every household surrounded by spies; the fear that sealed the master's lips and the avarice that

has, in so many cases, tempted him practically to desert us would alike be removed. There would be no recruits awaiting the enemy with open arms, no complete history of every neighborhood with ready guides, no fear of insurrection in the rear, or anxieties for the fate of loved ones when our armies moved forward.... *It would remove forever all selfish taint from our cause and place independence above every question of property.*[14]

Cleburne not only had to justify arming slaves, but he also had to explain the reasons for freeing them—and their families and all "loyal" slaves. His arguments included the following:

If we arm and train [the Negro] and make him fight for the country in her hour of dire distress, every consideration of principle and policy demand [sic] that we should set him and his whole race who side with us free. It is a first principle with mankind that he who offers his life in defense of the State should receive from her in return his freedom and his happiness, and we believe in acknowledgment of this principle, . . . The slaves are dangerous now, but armed, trained and collected in an army they would be a thousand fold more dangerous; therefore when we make soldiers of them we must make free men of them beyond all question, and thus enlist their sympathies also. We can do this more effectually than the North can now do, for we can give the negro not only his own freedom, but that of his wife and child, and can secure it to him in his old home. To do this, we must immediately make his marriage and parental relations sacred in the eyes of the law and forbid their sale.[15]

The proposal concluded, "It is said that slavery is all we are fighting for, and if we give it up we give up all. Even if this were true, which we deny, slavery is not all our enemies are fighting for.... We have now briefly proposed a plan which we believe will save our country.... No objection ought to outweigh it which is not weightier than independence."[16]

Cleburne had carefully and thoroughly thought through his startling proposal. This was not a flippant verbal recommendation. His was a serious "white-paper." He saw that the Confederates desperately needed more manpower, that the South's slave population comprised a large pool of fighting-age men, that blacks had historically and were concurrently showing for the North[17] an ability to fight, that freedom for black soldiers and their families was a necessity, and that the Southern practice of not recognizing slave marriages and family units would have to end.

But the Irishman had not reckoned with the deep-seated belief in the social and economic necessity of slavery. The well-to-do, whose wealth consisted primarily of slaves, were reluctant to give up their valuable "property." According to the 1860 census, slaves constituted one-half of Southern wealth (property value) and one-fifth of the nation's wealth.[18] Just as significantly, Southern whites would perceive armed slaves and liberated slaves as a threat to white society.

After two centuries of justifying slavery partially on the grounds that Negroes were incapable of performing skilled functions, the shock of their being allowed to act as armed soldiers was too astounding to absorb. As Benjamin Quarles noted, Southerners "were enslaved by a system of values which stamped the blacks as inferiors, and to make the Negro a soldier would be to call into question the very foundation of their mythology, or compel them to invent new myths."[19] These foes of Cleburne's proposal ignored the success of black soldiers in the Revolution and the War of 1812, as well as those fighting for the Union in the Civil War.[20]

Even if there had been support for awarding freedom to black soldiers, extending it to their wives and children would have undermined slavery's remaining economic viability. Cleburne's call to arm the slaves amounted to a call for the end of slavery itself as the price of Southern victory, and despite his assurances to the contrary, it was a challenge to white supremacy. As one historian observed in the late nineteenth century, for many Southerners, slavery "had been so long and so thoroughly interwoven with the domestic economy, the comfort, and the traditions of Southern society, that the common thought revolted at any suggestion which contemplated its eradication either proximate or remote."[21]

The reaction to Cleburne's proposal reveals much about Southern priorities—slavery trumped independence. All officers at the meeting with Johnston, except Hindman and the silent Johnston, condemned the proposal. An "awestruck horror apparently grew in the minds of several of the assembled generals as they were faced with this moment: they must choose either slavery or independence *but could not have both*," writes Daniel Mallock. "For the majority at the meeting the choice was an impossible one; they chose instead to make no decision at all and condemned both the conundrum itself and its proponent."[22] No decision meant no slave soldiers.

The hostile reaction was just beginning. Major General W. H. T. Walker called the proposal "incendiary," and Major General A. P. Stewart wrote that arming and emancipating slaves was "at war with my social, moral and political principles." They were joined by Major General James Patton Anderson, who called the idea "monstrous" and wrote that he would not "attempt to describe my feelings on being confronted with a project so startling in its character,—may I say *so revolting to southern sentiment, southern pride, and southern honor*?"[23]

Although Cleburne had hoped his written proposal would be forwarded to Richmond for high-level consideration, Johnston temporarily stymied that hope by sitting on it. For better or worse, Walker took matters into his own hands and, completely outside the chain of command, sent the paper to Jefferson Davis. Johnston had denied Walker's request to forward the document to the War Department. But Walker sent it directly to President Davis anyway because, in his dramatic and self-serving words, "The gravity of the subject, the magnitude of the issues involved, my strong convictions that the further agitation of such sentiments and propositions would ruin the efficacy of our Army and involve our cause in ruin and disgrace constitute my reasons for bringing the document before the Executive."[24]

When the proposal reached Davis, he responded to Walker that it was "injurious to the public service [and] that the best policy under the circumstances will be to avoid all publicity...it should be kept private. If it be kept out of the public journals its ill effect will be much lessened."[25] Davis had Secretary of War James Seddon tell Johnston that "the dissemination or even promulgation of such opinions under the present circumstances of the Confederacy, whether in the Army or among the people can be productive only of discouragement, distraction, and dissension."

He instructed Johnston to tell those who had attended the meeting of the president's disapproval and "urge on them the suppression, not only of the memorial itself, but likewise of all discussion and controversy respecting or growing out of it."[26] Johnston did so in a communication to his division commanders in which he simply reproduced the letter from Seddon. He added a note on Cleburne's copy requesting him to pass this information to his divisional officers.[27]

Suppression of the proposal, embarrassing to many ex-Confederates, lasted thirty years until its discovery and publication in the *Official Records*.[28] The important point is that, as of January 1864, Cleburne's idea was viewed by Jefferson Davis himself and other involved Confederate leaders as inconsistent with the Confederacy's *raison d'être*.

General Braxton Bragg, now a military advisor to Jefferson Davis,[29] called Cleburne and his allies "abolitionist men" who "should be watched." He described the proposal as "treasonous" and stated, "I should like to know as a matter of safety the names of the traitors."[30] Bragg had no love for Cleburne, who had been one of many subordinate officers who had urged his removal from command the prior year.

Bragg warned, "We must mark the men." And indeed the more-than-deserving Cleburne was never to receive a promotion to lieutenant general and corps command, even though there were three openings in the first eleven months of 1864, before his death in the suicidal attack that November at Franklin, Tennessee. As one officer much later described the situation,

> [T]he entire army recognized the gallantry, devotion, and military prowess of Cleburne, and for a year prior, and up to the day of his death, officers and men were anxiously expecting his promotion to the grade of lieutenant general, and few, very

few knew why he was not so commissioned.... [His proposal]
cost him promotion, yea, ever after kept him from attaining
his just and well merited deserts—a lieutenant generalship.[31]

Bruce Levine summarizes the Confederate position on arming black
soldiers that prevailed for most of the war: "[D]uring the war's first three
and a half years, Richmond refused to consider this policy because it
seemed to threaten both slavery and white supremacy, the twin pillars
of southern economy, social relations, culture, and ideology. *Having
seceded from the Union and gone to war to protect those institutions*,
few southern political and community leaders were ready to seek military
victory through a policy that apparently abandoned the original purpose
of the struggle."[32]

But cumulative calamities caused some reconsideration of this position. Confederate losses mounted, and their prospects declined in 1864.
Lee lost thirty-three thousand irreplaceable soldiers opposing Grant's
Overland Campaign movement to Richmond, Rebels suffered heavy
casualties opposing Sherman in Georgia, crucial Atlanta fell at the beginning of September, and the Army of Tennessee was decimated at Franklin and Nashville in November and December. Lincoln's reelection
dashed Southern hopes for a political victory and finally convinced
Davis, Secretary of State Judah Benjamin, and eventually Robert E. Lee
to urge the military use of slaves. None of them favored general emancipation—just military use of slaves in return for their freedom. Lee's
support was conditioned on approval of the slaves' owners.[33]

To make such recommendations, Davis had to backtrack from the
previous statement, made on his behalf by Secretary of War Seddon, that
the Cleburne proposals "in their scope pass beyond the bounds of Confederate action, and could under our constitutional system neither be
recommended by the Executive to Congress nor be entertained by that
body."[34] Lee, in January 1865, had to explain that military necessity
drove this proposal, although he still agreed that the "relation of master
and slave, controlled by humane laws and influenced by Christianity and

enlightened public sentiment [was] the best that can exist between the white and black races while intermingled as at present in this country."[35]

So just over a year after Cleburne's spurned proposal, even Robert E. Lee recommended that slaves be armed. On January 11, 1865, he wrote, "I think, therefore, we must decide whether slavery shall be extinguished by our enemies and the slaves be used against us, or use them ourselves at the risk of the effects which may be produced upon our social institutions. My own opinion is that we should employ them without delay."[36] In a letter published late the next month, Lee wrote that arming slaves was "not only expedient but necessary" and "those who are employed should be freed."[37]

Even in those desperate final months of the war, the idea of some form of emancipation, supported by the Confederacy's top political and military leaders, Davis and Lee, was widely opposed in the Southern press—often on grounds of inconsistency with the reasons for the Confederacy's existence. Georgia's *Macon Telegraph and Confederate* declared, "This terrible war and extreme peril of our country" were "occasioned…more by the institution of negro slavery" than "by any other subject of quarrel." "For it and its perpetuation, we commenced and have kept at war," said the *Memphis Appeal*. The *Richmond Examiner* succinctly concluded that the proposal was "opposite to all the sentiments and principles which have heretofore governed the Southern people."[38]

Robert Barnwell Rhett Jr.'s *Charleston Mercury* protested, "[T]he mere agitation in the Northern States to effect the emancipation of our slaves largely contributed to our separation from them.… [But incredibly] before a Confederacy which we established to put at rest forever all such agitation is four years old, we find the proposition gravely submitted that the Confederate Government should emancipate slaves in the States."[39]

The *Richmond Whig* launched a broad attack on the enlist-and-emancipate proposals, affirming its longstanding position that "servitude is a divinely appointed condition for the highest good of the slave [and] is that condition in which the negro race especially may attain the highest moral and intellectual advancement of which they are capable."

Emancipation would therefore "be an act of cruelty to deprive the slave of the care and guardianship of a master."[40]

Most Southern politicians opposed abolition. Former Confederate Secretary of State Robert M. T. Hunter urged the rejection of European pressure for emancipation: "What did we go to war for, if not to protect our property?" Tennessee Congressman Henry S. Foote asked, "If this government is to destroy slavery, why fight for it?"[41]

The proposed arming of slaves—a Southern nightmare for about two hundred years—aroused more heated opposition. On January 8, 1865, Major General Howell Cobb of Georgia, the first speaker of the Provisional Confederate Congress, wrote to Secretary of War Seddon, "I think that the proposition to make soldiers of our slaves is the most pernicious idea that has been suggested since the war began. It is to me a source of deep mortification and regret to see the name of that good and great man and soldier, General R. E. Lee, given as authority for such a policy.... You cannot make soldiers of slaves, nor slaves of soldiers.... The day you make soldiers of [Negroes] is the beginning of the end of the revolution. If slaves will make good soldiers our whole theory of slavery is wrong—but they won't make soldiers." Ignoring the successful Union experience with black soldiers,[42] Cobb added, "As a class they are wanting in every qualification of a soldier." He said it was better to abolish slavery to win British and French support than to pursue "the suicidal policy of arming our slaves."[43] Numerous sources reported widespread opposition from Confederate soldiers, who had little desire to fight alongside blacks.[44]

Georgia Governor Joseph E. Brown, the *Richmond Whig*, and R. M. T. Hunter contended that the proposed limited abolishment of slavery would violate the Confederate Constitution. Hunter said, "[T]he Government had no power under the Constitution to arm and emancipate the slaves, and the Constitution granted no such great powers by implication."[45]

The debate in late 1864 and early 1865 about arming slaves or other blacks sharply contradicts those who argue that blacks were fighting for the Confederacy all along. Confederate soldiers in the field did not report

City Point, VA, Negro soldier guarding 12-pdr. Napoleon. *Courtesy of the Library of Congress*

that ex-slaves were fighting alongside them. The problem with arming blacks was that it undercut the South's rationale for secession—opposition to abolition. For example, the *Richmond Examiner* opined in November 1864, "If a negro is fit to be a soldier he is not fit to be a slave. The employment of negroes as soldiers in our armies, either with or without prospective emancipation, would be the first step, but a step which would involve all the rest, to universal abolition." As the historian Kevin Levin concludes, "The evidence is overwhelming that Confederate plans to arm slaves were considered a radical and dangerous step, not a continuation of the slave impressment policies that accepted slaves in camps as servants."[46]

In *Confederate Emancipation*, Bruce Levine details the widespread opposition throughout the South to arming and freeing slaves, concluding that "opponents of the Davis administration's last-minute plan...agreed on one central and fundamental point, one that they considered nearly self-evident—that the South had withdrawn from and made war upon the old Union primarily to safeguard its 'peculiar institution.'"[47]

Because similar views on emancipation and arming blacks prevailed among the Southern people, politicians, and press, the Confederate Congress never approved the military use of slaves in return for their freedom. On March 8, 1865, a watered-down program for the use of slaves with their owners' and states' permission and without manumission passed the Senate by one vote. Even the support of Robert E. Lee, the Confederacy's national hero, was insufficient to convince the Confederate Congress to arm and free slaves—let alone approve a general manumission.

A disappointed Davis signed the weak legislation into law on March 13. After deliberation, he decided to go beyond the new law and implement some form of emancipation incentive, issuing on March 23 a general order declining to accept any slaves as soldiers without their own consent and their owners' consent to their freedom (a still unlikely prospect).[48] Davis's action came two and a half weeks before Lee's surrender—too late for meaningful implementation.

The Confederacy's last-minute acceptance of black soldiers was something of a farce. Two companies of mixed free blacks and slaves were paraded before thousands of onlookers in Richmond a week before the city fell.[49] At least one such review was canceled because black soldiers had not been issued uniforms, equipment, or arms.[50] The use of black soldiers in the Confederacy began late and ended with a whimper.

In contrast, the Union made use of 180,000 black soldiers and twenty thousand black sailors. Black Union soldiers fought in forty major engagements and about 450 other firefights. Among their major fights were Port Hudson, Milliken's Bend, Fort Pillow, Yorktown, Petersburg, New Market Heights, Fort Fisher, Fort Wagner, and Nashville. They demonstrated extreme bravery and suffered a higher rate of casualties than their white comrades. Sixteen blacks received the Medal of Honor.[51]

No black units fought for the Confederacy. The proposal to arm and liberate slaves failed, writes Levine, "because of opposition by both blinkered masters and clear-eyed slaves—slaves who had their eyes on a much bigger prize than the one that Jefferson Davis was belatedly and grudgingly offering."[52] Protection of slavery had trumped the military needs of the Confederacy and demonstrated the extent to which slavery and white supremacy were the primary foundations of that would-be nation. The Confederacy's failure to use its extensive black slave man-power as soldiers was one of the biggest blunders of the Civil War.

GETTYSBURG

ROBERT E. LEE CONDUCTS A BLUNDERING CAMPAIGN

WHO BLUNDERED?

Confederate General Robert E. Lee

HOW?

Lee blundered by initiating a strategic offensive, missing a grand opportunity on Day One at Gettysburg, and launching uncoordinated piecemeal assaults against strong Union positions on Days Two and Three.

CONSEQUENCES?

He deprived the Confederacy of resources needed in other theaters, incurred intolerable losses, and caused a triple, morale-deflating disaster for the Confederacy.

Robert E. Lee's blunder-filled Gettysburg Campaign (June 3–July 24, 1863) proved to be a disaster for the Confederacy. It was an unnecessary strategic offensive that the resource-challenged Confederates could not afford. It deprived other theaters of desperately needed Rebel reinforcements. And it featured numerous tactical blunders by Lee: failure to push aggressively for control of the high ground at the end of Day One of the Battle of Gettysburg (July 1), failure to coordinate his three attacks on the final two days of battle (July 2 and 3), failure to adequately reinforce James Longstreet's and William Barksdale's combined assault on Cemetery Ridge on Day Two, and failure to compel the Federals to attack his army instead of playing into George Meade's hands by haphazardly attacking Union forces who had seized and held the high ground. All of these blunders not only resulted in a major tactical and strategic defeat at Gettysburg, but also contributed to Union successes at Vicksburg and in eastern Tennessee (the Tullahoma Campaign and ultimately the fall of Chattanooga).

LEE'S STRATEGIC PLAN

Capitalizing on his acclaim after a major strategic victory at Chancellorsville in early May 1863, Lee in mid-May pushed Jefferson Davis into making a crucial mistake that cost the Confederacy major defeats in the three primary theaters of the war (Eastern, Middle, and Western). Lee strongly opposed the transfer of Lieutenant General James Longstreet and any portion of his First Corps outside the Virginia Theater. He convinced Davis and most of his cabinet to leave Longstreet with Lee for an offensive into the North, which became the disastrous Gettysburg Campaign.[1]

With both Vicksburg and Chattanooga threatened, Lee, on May 10, opposed sending one of Longstreet's divisions to the West and argued to Secretary of War James Seddon that unless he was reinforced he would have "to withdraw into the defences around Richmond.... The strength of this army has been reduced by the casualties in the late battles."[2] The next day Lee even pleaded with Davis for reinforcements—without specifying where they might come from.[3]

Perhaps as damaging as Lee's actual losses at Chancellorsville was the over-confidence that the victory inspired in Confederate minds—particularly in the mind of Robert E. Lee.[4] His badly outnumbered army had embarrassed Major General Joe Hooker by thwarting his offensive and driving him back across the Rappahannock River. On May 21, Lee wrote to Hood about the men in the Army of Northern Virginia: "I agree with you in believing that our army would be invincible if it could be properly organized and officered. There never were such men in an army before. They will go anywhere and do anything if properly led."[5] Lee's enormous confidence in his soldiers, tempered by a concern about his officers, thus led him to believe that the Army of Northern Virginia was invincible[6]—a belief, according to Confederate General Porter Alexander, shared by his army:

> But, like the rest of the army generally, nothing gave me much concern so long as I knew that Gen. Lee was in command. I am sure there can never have been an army with more supreme confidence in its commander than that army had in Gen. Lee. We looked forward to victory under him as confidently as to successive sunrises.[7]

Lee's overconfident army, however, had seen its last major strategic "victory."

Lee finalized his plans to invade Pennsylvania only after rejecting pleas that he send part of his army to rescue the thirty thousand troops that Ulysses S. Grant had bottled up near Vicksburg, Mississippi. Seddon and Longstreet had recommended such a rescue to President Davis—that or a reinforcement of the outnumbered Braxton Bragg in Middle Tennessee.[8]

Between May 14 and 17, while Grant took Jackson, Mississippi, and moved toward Vicksburg, the Confederacy's leadership met in Richmond to debate whether to send some of Lee's troops to trap Grant between Jackson and John Pemberton's thirty-thousand-man army in Vicksburg. Using all his Chancellorsville political capital, Lee convinced Davis that Richmond would be threatened if Lee's army was reduced in strength and that the best defense of Richmond would be an offensive campaign into the North. Lee revealed his biased and flawed national strategic vision in his argument that this was a "question between Virginia and the Mississippi." He also desperately argued that the oppressive Mississippi climate would cause Grant to withdraw from the Vicksburg area.[9] Allan Nevins contends that Lee saw only the East clearly and thought only of Virginia: "On the evidence available, it is difficult to believe that Lee either knew or cared much about the Mississippi front."[10]

On May 26, Davis authorized a Northern offensive in the East. Moving north, Lee wrote to Davis, quite unrealistically, that his Eastern offensive might even induce the Union to recall some of its troops from the West, but he hedged his bet with a request that troops be transferred to Virginia from the Carolinas to protect Richmond, threaten Washington, and aid his advance.[11] Although Longstreet acquiesced in Lee's strategic offensive, he spent a great deal of time trying to convince Lee to go on the tactical defensive once in the North so as to repeat the prior December's defensive victory at Fredericksburg. Confederate General Wade Hampton later wrote with regret that while he had thought the Pennsylvania campaign would enable the Confederates to choose a battlefield, instead "we let Meade choose his position & we then attacked."[12]

Lee's correspondence indicates that he went north with mixed intentions. These are reflected in two letters to Davis of June 25. In the first, he wrote, "I think I can throw Genl Hooker's army across the Potomac and draw troops from the south, embarrassing their plan of campaign in a measure, if I can do nothing more and have to return."[13] In the second letter, he seemed to reflect Longstreet's view: "It seems to me that we cannot afford to keep our troops awaiting possible movements of the enemy, but that our true policy is, as far as we can, so to employ our own forces as to give occupation to his at points of our own selection."[14]

Porter Alexander later remarked that the troops would have been better used by sending them to the West, a strategy that would have taken advantage of the South's interior lines and was successful that autumn at Chickamauga under less favorable circumstances.[15] The Confederates' failure to send troops to either Vicksburg or middle

Depiction of the Battle of Gettysburg, possibly Pickett's Charge, by P. F. Rothermel. *Courtesy of the Library of Congress*

Tennessee in order to maintain Lee's own army at full strength contributed to the fall of Vicksburg, the loss of the Mississippi Valley to Union control, and a retreat by Bragg through southeastern Tennessee and Chattanooga after he had sent troops to aid Vicksburg. As Archer Jones explains, "This opening of the Mississippi had a profound effect by spreading hope in the North for an early victory and in the South widespread pessimism."[16]

The Confederate commissary in Atlanta shipped massive foodstuffs to Lee that spring and summer and virtually nothing to Bragg, considerably weakening the Army of Tennessee.[17] Not only did Lee refuse to send troops to the West, but he unrealistically implored Bragg to invade Ohio to complement Lee's planned incursion into Pennsylvania[18]—this at a time when Bragg had only fifty thousand troops in Tennessee, either to hold that state or to send assistance to Vicksburg. Union strength in the Western and Middle Theaters was 214,000.[19]

Gettysburg—the finale to Confederate military prospects in the East—exposed Lee at his worst. The numbers dictated, as they had when he went north in 1862, that at the very least an embarrassing retreat and perceived strategic defeat would be the result.[20] General Alexander later expressed his concern that Lee's nearest ammunition supply railhead was at Staunton, Virginia, one hundred fifty wagon-miles from Gettysburg.[21] As in 1862, Lee was moving north with a badly weakened army, blinded by its prior tactical success.[22]

In going north again, Lee pursued his flawed strategy that the best defense was a good offense.[23] Hoping to draw Hooker's army out of Virginia and have the two armies live off the Pennsylvania countryside during the summer and early fall, he succeeded in taking everyone north, but his stay there was shorter than he had hoped, and his eventual retreat to the Rappahannock line, following a huge tactical defeat, itself constituted a strategic defeat. His losses ensured that Gettysburg was Lee's final major strategic offensive campaign.[24]

THE MOVEMENT NORTH

Lee's offensive strategy and tactics had weakened the entire command structure of his army.[25] Following Jackson's death at Chancellorsville, he felt compelled to reorganize his army into three corps. Longstreet commanded the First Corps, Ewell the Second, and A. P. Hill the Third. Neither Ewell nor Hill had worked directly under Lee's command, and neither of them had Stonewall Jackson's experience and aggressiveness. Lee's failure after Chancellorsville to adjust his style, expectations, and orders to the poorer and less experienced generals in his army would prove disastrous.

The swashbuckling style of Jeb Stuart, in command of the cavalry division, led to serious problems soon after Lee's army started north on June 3. Lee's lax oversight of Stuart and the cavalry arm of his army led to one near-disaster and to one actual disaster. Stuart's cavalry was supposed to be protecting Lee's right flank and hiding his northward movement from Yankee eyes. On June 5, Stuart's approximately 9,500 officers and men held a grand parade at Brandy Station, Virginia—to the joy of the local ladies and to the disgust of the Confederate infantry.[26] At Lee's request, the cavalry's spectacle was repeated on June 8,[27] one day before they were to move across the Rappahannock to cover Ewell's and Longstreet's continuing northward march. A pleased Lee wrote to his wife, "I reviewed the cavalry in this section yesterday. It was a splendid sight. The men & horses looked well.... Stuart was in all his glory."[28] Lee gloried in his fellow Virginian's showmanship. As Allen Guelzo notes, "People do not often see what deleterious effects resulted from Lee's tendency to play favorites; on the other hand, that was how he had advanced in his own career, by serving as a protégé, first of [Charles] Gratiot, then [Joseph] Totten, and finally [Winfield] Scott."[29]

Early the next morning, June 9, the Confederates were caught off guard at Brandy Station by a dawn attack launched by Brigadier General Alfred Pleasonton's Union cavalry. Stuart almost lost his artillery, and an all-day battle swirled around Fleetwood Hill. The Northern horsemen achieved their goal of determining the probable location of the bulk of the Army of Northern Virginia while demonstrating, for the first time, their ability to initiate and sustain a credible offensive. Embarrassed by his lack of preparedness and near-defeat, Stuart sought to redeem himself later in June by setting off on a third swing around a Union army. Lee, instead of reining in the flamboyant Stuart, provided him with such ambiguous orders that Lee's invasion of Pennsylvania and most of the battle at Gettysburg were carried out without precise knowledge of where his adversaries were. Lee allowed Stuart to depart with half his cavalry and his best subordinate commanders, Major General Wade Hampton and Brigadier General Fitzhugh Lee, while leaving the weak Brigadier General Beverly Robertson to screen and scout for the army commander.

With a variety of orders to choose from, Stuart decided on the most exciting and glorious opportunity offered to him. Exercising the confusing discretion Lee had given him, Stuart engaged in a meaningless frolic and detour, not rejoining Lee until late the second day at Gettysburg. Beginning on June 24, he swung east behind, and east of, the northward-moving Union army and thus separated his troopers from the rest of Lee's army. Although he entered Pennsylvania only about twenty miles east of Gettysburg, Stuart had no idea where Lee was and therefore headed farther north to Carlisle instead of west to Gettysburg. A captured wagon train that he regarded as precious booty slowed him down.

At the end of this eight-day ego trip, Stuart arrived at Gettysburg too late to be of any real assistance. On June 28 Lee had learned from a spy of Longstreet's about George Meade's appointment to succeed Hooker and about Meade's ninety-five-thousand-man army's northward movement to the area around Frederick, Maryland. When Lee then decided to concentrate his army in the Cashtown-Gettysburg area, he greatly missed Stuart's cavalry, which would have screened the converging movements of Lee's scattered units—an often overlooked consequence of Stuart's absence.[30]

Lee had no idea which Union corps were going to arrive when at Gettysburg, and on the critical second day of July he had to base his plan of battle on skimpy and incorrect information about Union strength in the area of the Round Tops south of Gettysburg. Lee had only himself to blame for letting his strong-willed cavalry commander get away from his army.[31] Indeed, his vague orders to Stuart were among a number of such orders that plagued the Confederates throughout the Gettysburg campaign.

While Stuart campaigned east of the Blue Ridge, Lee was having success to the west. Ewell's Second Corps led the northward sweep and routed nine thousand Yankee defenders at Winchester, Virginia, on June 14 and 15. When word of the rout reached Richmond the next day, the Confederate chief of ordnance, Josiah Gorgas, ominously noted in his journal: "What the movement means it is difficult to divine. I trust we are not to have the Maryland [Antietam] campaign over again."[32] After Winchester, Ewell, A. P. Hill, and Longstreet moved their corps into Pennsylvania's Cumberland Valley. Ewell moved his leading corps through Chambersburg and then eastward through the mountains to York and Carlisle. Lee spread his forces all around south-central Pennsylvania without knowing the location of the Army of the Potomac and without cavalry to screen his operations.

In the midst of these movements, Lee finally revealed to Davis the scope of his planned offensive by belatedly requesting back-up diversionary reinforcements. On June 23 and twice on June 25, he wrote to Davis that an army should be raised in the southeast under General Beauregard and moved to Culpeper Court House to threaten Washington.[33] Lee's unrealistic but typical suggestion to reinforce Virginia overlooked the known facts that Grant by then had Pemberton trapped in Vicksburg and that Beauregard already had sent reinforcements to Tennessee.

By June 28 Ewell was in position to move on the Pennsylvania capital of Harrisburg. Lee, unaware of the Union army's precise whereabouts, was with Hill and Longstreet back at Chambersburg. After learning of the enemy's movement to Frederick, Maryland, Lee decided to meet them east of the mountains. Recognizing the need to concentrate his numerically inferior force but not sure where the enemy was and how quickly he could move, Lee sent discretionary orders to Ewell to head back toward either Cashtown or Gettysburg.[34]

BATTLE OF GETTYSBURG: DAY ONE

Day One of Gettysburg—July 1, 1863—brought Lee's army a stiff rebuff, a fortuitous success, and finally a missed opportunity for victory.[35] The prior day the Confederates had discovered a Federal cavalry division under Brigadier General John Buford at Gettysburg. The next morning a stronger Confederate force, the divisions of Major Generals Henry Heth and Dorsey Pender of Hill's Corps, headed east from Cashtown toward Gettysburg under orders not to bring on a general engagement. Because of Stuart's absence and Lee's ignorance about the timing of Meade's corps' approaches to Gettysburg, Heth's and Pender's infantry divisions found more than they had bargained for. Initially they were handicapped because two-thirds of Lee's army was going to have to use a single road, the Chambersburg Pike-Cashtown Road, to get to Gettysburg. Heth pushed ahead with two brigades. Why did A. P. Hill send Heth against a position known to be held by Union forces if he was not to bring on a general engagement? Was he to stand in place when he encountered resistance and back up at least two-thirds of Lee's army on a single road?

On June 30 Buford had astutely recognized the tactical value of the high ground south and east of Gettysburg and decided to save it for the main Union army once it arrived. Instead of putting his cavalry on those hills, therefore, he deployed them during the night west and north of the town so they could delay the Confederates until Union infantry arrived. He sent word to Pleasonton that A. P. Hill's corps was massed back of Cashtown nine miles west and that Hill's infantry and artillery pickets were in sight. He also passed along accurate rumors that Ewell was coming south over the mountains from Carlisle.[36] In a fierce struggle that began around 7:30 a.m. on July 1, Buford's cavalry stubbornly resisted the 7,500-man advance of two of Heth's brigades. With the firing of the first shot, Buford sent word of the fighting to Major General John F. Reynolds, commander of the Union First Corps. Reynolds, then five miles away, ordered his 9,500 men to shed their baggage and speedily march to Gettysburg.

The evening before, Buford had posted videttes (advance mounted sentries) on the Chambersburg Pike at and beyond Herr's and Belmont School House ridges west of his main camp in town. Their determined resistance forced the Confederates to spend more than a precious hour deploying into a battle line. Meanwhile, Reynolds arrived and conferred with Buford about the critical situation. Reynolds then went back to hasten his infantry to the front, sent word to Major General Oliver O. Howard to speed his Eleventh Corps to Gettysburg, and sent a message to Meade that Gettysburg would be the collision point of the East's two armies.

Heth, enjoying momentary superiority, ordered his two brigades forward. Buford's skirmishers grudgingly gave up the forward ridges and a small stream called Willoughby Run, gradually falling back to McPherson's Ridge only a mile west of Gettysburg. Buford sent a message to Pleasanton describing the battle. A. P. Hill's entire corps was moving on Gettysburg, Buford informed him, and Confederate troops had been discovered approaching Gettysburg from the north.[37]

Late Day Two—Part of Ewell's attack, by Edwin Forbes. *Courtesy of the Library of Congress*

The nature of the battle changed when Reynolds's men, led by Cutler's brigade and then the Iron Brigade, began arriving at the scene shortly after ten o'clock in the morning. The latter, composed of proud, stalwart black-hatted troops from the upper Midwest, was the First Brigade of the First Division of the First Corps of the Army of the Potomac. A Rebel bullet killed Reynolds while he was directing his troops in an assault on James Archer's brigade. Nevertheless, this devastating Union counterattack drove the Confederates back toward Herr's Ridge. Buford's brilliant delaying tactics had saved the day and perhaps the entire battle, and Reynolds had arrived in the nick of time to repel the first serious Confederate assault.

Back at Cashtown, Lee heard the sounds of battle and started toward Gettysburg. His distress at Stuart's absence was reflected in a comment he is said to have made as he headed toward the fateful battlefield: "I cannot think what has become of Stuart; I ought to have heard from him long before now.... In the absence of reports from him, I am in ignorance of what we have in front of us here. It may be the whole Federal army, or it may be only a detachment. If it is the whole Federal force, we must fight a battle here...."[38]

As the Union forces gained strength, so did Lee's. Down the Carlisle Road and over Oak Hill from the northwest of town came Rodes's eight-thousand-man division of Ewell's Second Corps, which had been as far north as Carlisle. They arrived about eleven o'clock, the same time as advance elements of Oliver O. Howard's Eleventh Corps arrived to impede their advance. After Reynolds's death, Howard assumed overall command of the Union forces, and Major General Carl Schurz took command of the Eleventh Corps. At about noon Rodes's artillery began shelling the Union lines, and by two o'clock his infantry launched an assault on Schurz's and Doubleday's troops northwest of town. At about the same time, Meade learned of Reynolds's death and dispatched Major General Winfield Hancock to Gettysburg to take command (even though Howard was senior to him).

Rodes's five-brigade attack from the northwest was uncoordinated and ineffective. Soldiers of Brigadier General Alfred Iverson Jr.'s brigade were either slaughtered or pinned down by Union troops.[39] Rodes failed to break through the Eleventh Corps' lines, and the Confederate situation looked bleak. Their fortune changed, however, around three o'clock, when Jubal Early and his 5,500-man division (also of Ewell's Corps) arrived. Moving from the northeast and north, Early had heard the battle and headed south on roads approaching Gettysburg from the north and north-northeast. These approaches brought Early's division in on Schurz's right and, more importantly, east of Schurz's exposed right flank.

Although the arrival of Rodes's and Early's divisions of Ewell's Second Corps prevented a disastrous defeat of Hill's men coming east on the bottlenecked Chambersburg Pike, an earlier arrival would have been even better. Because Lee was ignorant of the Union army's precise whereabouts, he had ordered Ewell to march from Carlisle to either Cashtown or Gettysburg. Ewell's initial choice of Cashtown resulted in a delay of several hours in his corps' arrival at Gettysburg. At Arendtsville, northwest of Gettysburg, Ewell learned about the Gettysburg fighting and sent Rodes's division in that direction. But Johnson's division had gone farther west, toward Cashtown with Ewell's trains. Had Ewell been ordered to march directly to Gettysburg, his men could have driven out Buford's and Reynolds's troops, reduced Hill's and their own casualties, and occupied the high ground just south and east of the town before Union reinforcements arrived. Lee could not have known this, but he had to know that giving Ewell discretion to go to Cashtown risked a logjam on the Chambersburg Pike.

But this was not the end of the problems that resulted from Lee's ignorance of the Union army's whereabouts. Lee, still at Cashtown as the morning fighting erupted in Gettysburg, was advised by a messenger from Ewell that Ewell was heading south toward the sounds of battle. Lee asked about Stuart, ordered Ewell to send scouting parties to look for Stuart, and then told the messenger that he did not want a major engagement brought on that day.[40]

Lee then used the critical Chambersburg Pike to send Ewell's third division, under Major General Edward "Old Allegheny" Johnson, and Ewell's entire wagon train east toward Gettysburg. That division and Ewell's train were on the same road as Hill's and Longstreet's corps because of Lee's Cashtown-or-Gettysburg orders to Ewell. Lee's use of the Chambersburg Pike for a crucial ten-hour period to move Ewell's wagon train, estimated at fourteen miles long,[41] compounded the bottleneck on that road. Meade, on the other hand, had his army marching full-bore for Gettysburg on several roads with their trains behind. Lee's action delayed the initial arrival near Gettysburg of Longstreet's leading divisions, those of Hood and McLaws, until midnight and dawn, respectively, as well as the completion of their divisions' arrivals until dawn and noon, respectively.[42] Not expecting a major engagement until July 2, Lee had bottlenecked seven of his nine divisions on a single road,[43] retarding their arrival for both the first and second days of battle.

Nevertheless, as a result of Early's fortunate afternoon arrival on the field, when Lee arrived on Herr Ridge from Cashtown he observed the pleasing panorama of the Eleventh Corps' line crumbling and its troops starting to retreat. Lee hastily sent the remainder of Heth's badly beaten-up division and Abner Perrin's fresh division into the fray with the First Corps west of town around 3:30. Lee, then, initially did not hesitate to take advantage of his momentary numerical and positional superiority and the opportunity to destroy two Union corps before Meade had his whole army up.

Between three and five o'clock in the afternoon of Day One, it looked like Gettysburg was going to be a great victory for Lee. Ewell's two-division attack from the north forced the outflanked Eleventh Corps to flee south in disarray into Gettysburg and through the town to Cemetery Hill. Uncovered by that retreat and flanked on their left, the exhausted Union First Corps troops, who had been defending the Chambersburg Pike approach west of town for many hours, had no choice but to retreat to Seminary Ridge by four o'clock and ultimately to Cemetery Hill.

Hancock, arriving at Cemetery Hill before four o'clock, in time to see the massive retreat of two Union corps, sent some troops east to the unoccupied Culp's Hill and started the men entrenching. Although Hancock later would take credit, Howard already had laid out the Union defensive line. Between 6:00 and 6:30, Slocum began arriving with his 8,500-man Twelfth Corps, but it deployed primarily along Cemetery Ridge south of the high ground. An immediate attack by all of Lee's forces had a good chance of dislodging the minimal Union forces from their position on Culp's Hill and possibly Cemetery Hill. The likelihood of their success is demonstrated by Ewell's near-success on those same hills twenty-four hours later. Although some argue that Lee was unlikely to capture the high ground late on July 1, that afternoon was his best opportunity to do so during the three-day battle. Instead, he attacked against stronger, reinforced Union lines the next two days with less chance of success. Because he was unaware of the enemy army's proximity, Lee apparently thought he could wait until the next morning to take the high ground. He underestimated the speed of Meade's soldiers in approaching and reaching Gettysburg.

Even though Stonewall Jackson was dead, Lee persisted in issuing ambiguous orders that only Jackson could have turned into victories. With an advantage in manpower of at least thirty-five thousand to twenty-one thousand through the late afternoon and evening, Lee did not aggressively take charge of the field or order any of Hill's troops to move ahead or to their left to join or support an attack by Ewell on the two hills. Ewell and Early were on their own. At this point, Ewell should have had more than ten thousand men still able to attack—particularly the five thousand relatively fresh men in four brigades of Early's division. Early's men were actively pursuing the Union troops through the town and could have tried moving ahead to higher ground; disruption in the town, however, hindered the Confederates' movements. Instead, Early halted the pursuit and sent two brigades off to the east because Union troops were reported coming from that direction.[44] Receiving Early's report and conflicting information concerning Union strength on Culp's Hill, Ewell decided not to attack.

With Union troops in chaotic retreat through the town, Lee committed two egregious errors. First, he failed to deploy all the troops on hand in a maximum-strength attack on the eighty-foot-high Cemetery Hill or the hundred-foot-high Culp's Hill, the dominant heights in the immediate vicinity of the town. He ignored all troops other than Ewell's, particularly Hill's, and thus failed to take advantage of his numerical superiority.

Second, at 4:30 he issued a merely discretionary order, by way of Major Walter Taylor, to the stalled Ewell to take the high ground. Given the critical importance of the objective, Lee's verbal orders to Ewell were appallingly vague: Ewell was to take the heights "if he found it practicable, but to avoid a general engagement until the arrival of the other divisions of the army,"[45] which was going to take many more hours. This order seems inexplicable because there had been a general engagement since about dawn that day,[46] the Confederate forces were caught in a traffic jam on the Chambersburg Pike, and the Union presence would only become stronger. In the absence of a mandatory order immediately to take those critical positions, Ewell not surprisingly failed to move on Culp's Hill and Cemetery Hill before the outnumbered and disorganized Union forces there had dug in and been reinforced.

Even the arrival at dusk of Ewell's third division—"Old Allegheny" Johnson's—did not encourage him to take the high ground—at the very least the dominant heights of Culp's Hill. Virtually all of Ewell's generals urged an assault on the high ground, including Early, who had passed up the earlier opportunity to do so when he alone would have been responsible.[47] Major General Isaac R. Trimble asked for a single regiment to take the two hills and stalked away in disgust when Ewell declined to attack.[48]

At the same time, Lee deliberately and inexplicably held in reserve the nearby unbloodied troops of Major General Richard H. Anderson's division in Hill's corps and two brigades of Dorsey Pender's—apparently because Lee's whole army was not yet concentrated and he lacked information on the enemy's strength.[49] For these reasons, Edwin B. Coddington writes, "Responsibility for the failure of the Confederates to make an all-out assault on Cemetery Hill on July 1 must rest with Lee."[50] This was the only time on July 1 that either side did not immediately use (usually successfully) all the forces it had gotten to Gettysburg.

As to Lee's responsibility for Hill's failure to get involved late that day, Guelzo concludes, "Perhaps, in the end, it was the great mistake of Robert E. Lee at Gettysburg that, having had to reach past his corps commanders to direct operations that afternoon, he did not keep reaching past them. Whatever blame attaches to Ambrose Powell Hill in the twilight of July First also attached to Robert E. Lee for not overriding him."[51]

The hesitation of Lee, Ewell, and Early proved disastrous. Lee's failure to take full advantage of his temporary superiority with a definitive attack on Cemetery Hill or Culp's Hill or both left Union forces on the final two days of the battle in control of the commanding heights that Buford, Reynolds, Howard, and Hancock had determined to protect and hold because they were the key to battlefield control at Gettysburg.

Lee's reluctance to *command* an all-out assault on the first day at Gettysburg seems to have been due to his desire to have his entire army on the field before undertaking a "general engagement," a wishful approach that is difficult to explain in light of his knowledge that a large portion of the Union army had not arrived. On the afternoon of July 1 Lee substantially outnumbered his adversary, and every passing hour allowed the Yankees to move toward numerical and positional parity and then superiority. No one can say with certainty that a Rebel attack on the high ground late on July 1—even if Stonewall Jackson himself were leading it—would have been successful. But that opportunity was far superior to those Lee had the next two days, after the rest of the Union army had arrived to strengthen its hold on the high ground.

Was Ewell or Early responsible for the failure to attack pursuant to Lee's discretionary order? Chris Mackowski and Kristopher White have shown that after Ewell's reconnaissance discovered that Culp's Hill was unoccupied, Ewell suggested that Early occupy it. Early declined, however, and recommended the assignment be given to "Allegheny" Johnson's newly arrived troops, and Ewell followed his advice. By the time Johnson's troops arrived, Culp's Hill was occupied. "The chance to take the ground without a fight slipped away," write Mackowski and White, and Confederates took 2,500 casualties trying to take Culp's Hill over the next two days. "After the war, Early contended that he had vigorously supported an assault on Cemetery Hill, yet on the evening of the battle he claimed his men were too tired and disorganized to occupy unoccupied Culp's Hill. If his men were in no condition to move unopposed to an empty hilltop, how could they have led an attack against a heavily fortified enemy position?"[52]

On the morning of July 2, Lee expressed his disappointment at the prior afternoon's events: "We did not or could not pursue our advantage of yesterday and now the enemy are in a good position."[53] This amounted to a rebuke of Ewell and Early, but Lee must have known that he bore at least as much responsibility as they for the army's failure to seize the commanding heights on that vital first day. With Confederate casualties at 6,500 to the Union's nine thousand, Lee had won an engagement but missed an opportunity to win the battle of Gettysburg.

BATTLE OF GETTYSBURG: DAY TWO

By the morning of July 2, the situation had radically changed. Hancock's thirteen-thousand-man Second Corps and Major General Dan Sickles's twelve-thousand-man Third Corps arrived by early morning. Instead of three corps with twenty-one thousand men on the battlefield, the Union now had five corps and forty-six thousand men. Two more corps (the Fifth and Sixth) with twenty-eight thousand more men were being force-marched about fifteen and thirty-four miles, respectively, to get there that day. Instead of scrambling to find any kind of position as they had done the prior day, the Northerners had established a strong line running from near Little Round Top (two miles south of town) north along Taneytown Road and Cemetery Ridge to Cemetery Hill and then curving east to Culp's Hill and southeast parallel to the Baltimore Pike. The Yankees now had superior numbers, an imposing defensive position, and the advantage of interior lines, which permitted them to move soldiers quickly to threatened points in their lines. Meade's army had twenty-seven thousand men per mile along a three-mile inverted-fishhook line while Lee's army had ten thousand men per mile along a five-mile semi-circle.[54] That disparity augured ill for Lee's army.

On July 2 Lee erred again—in several ways.[55] Without Stuart's cavalry to accurately advise him of enemy positions and movements, Lee ordered a small scouting expedition under Captain Samuel Johnston, his staff engineer, to conduct what turned out to be inadequate reconnaissance of the Union left. Johnston reported that he had ascended Little Round Top, that there were no Union troops south of Cemetery Hill, and that there was a clear route to the area west of the Round Tops from which Lee wanted to attack. Somehow Johnston's small scouting parties failed to detect Federal forces on the south end of Cemetery Ridge and on and in front of the Round Tops. Guelzo speculates that Johnston, in the morning fog, may have climbed the wrong hill.[56] Because of the faulty reconnaissance, Lee erroneously believed that the prominent hills, Little Round Top and Big Round Top, and the areas around them were not occupied by Union troops.[57]

Contrary to Longstreet's advice, Lee ordered his two delayed and exhausted divisions to march several miles and attack the left flank of the Union forces. Late the prior afternoon Longstreet and Lee had watched Yankee forces retreat to the high ground immediately south of Gettysburg and discussed what to do the following day. Longstreet wanted to turn the Union left flank, establish a strong position, and await an attack.[58] At about that same hour, Hancock was sending a message to Meade that the Union's strong position would be difficult to take but could be turned.[59] Longstreet argued that the Union forces would be compelled to attack any Confederate force placed between them and Washington and that inviting a confrontation like that at Fredericksburg was consistent with a strategically offensive and tactically defensive campaign, which is what Longstreet thought had been agreed upon. Perhaps desperate for a convincing victory to justify his rash invasion of the North and concerned about his medium-term supplies, Lee insisted upon an attack. To Lee's assertion, "If the enemy is there tomorrow, we must attack him," Longstreet apparently replied, "If he is there tomorrow, it will be because he wants you to attack—a good reason, in my judgment, for not doing so."[60]

In his Gettysburg Battle Report, Lee later justified his cobbled-together offensives of July 2 and 3 on the grounds that retreat would have been difficult and awaiting attack was impracticable because of foraging difficulties.[61] General Porter Alexander had the following thoughts about Lee's rationale:

Now when it is remembered that we stayed for three days longer on that very ground, two of them days of desperate battle, ending in the discouragement of a bloody repulse, & then successfully withdrew all our trains & most of the wounded through the mountains; and, finding the Potomac too high to ford, protected them all & foraged successfully for over a week in a very restricted territory along the river, until we could build a bridge, it does not seem improbable that we could have faced Meade safely on the Second at Gettysburg without assaulting him in his wonderfully strong position. We had the prestige of victory with us, having chased him off the field & through the town. We had a fine defensive position on Seminary Ridge ready at our hand to occupy. It was not such a really *wonderful* position as the enemy happened to fall into, but it was no bad one, & it could *never have been successfully assaulted.... We could even have fallen back to Cashtown & held the mountain passes with all the prestige of victory, & popular sentiment would have forced Meade to take the aggressive.*[62]

Alexander's suggestion that the Confederates might have defended Seminary Ridge and then perhaps fallen back to the ridges and hills west of Gettysburg is an intriguing option that Longstreet did not recommend and Lee did not exercise—or possibly even consider—but it appears to have great merit. Nevins agrees with Alexander: "The two armies were so fairly matched in strength that, had the South defended the ridges and the North attacked, as Longstreet had hoped, the result might well have been different."[63] Daniel Bauer has studied the food supplies that would have been available to Lee had he gone on the defensive in Pennsylvania. Lee had the necessary resources, Bauer concludes, and erred when he let such concerns drive him to dismiss that alternative.[64] One reason Lee did not go on the defensive was that he was on a roll. His army had wrecked two Union corps the day before, and he sensed a great opportunity, in Guelzo's view, to "not only bag the remnants, but seize Cemetery Hill, the most advantageous ground in the entire region."[65]

There were problems with Lee's offensive strategy on July 2, and his execution of it proved disastrous. Lee again failed to give clear and forceful orders to Ewell's corps, undermining the coordination between the Confederate left and right flanks. Lee's plan called for Ewell to demonstrate against the Union right, attacking if an opportunity developed, and for Longstreet to attack the Union left. Even though Ewell had clearly demonstrated his reluctance to attack the previous day, Lee failed to oversee his efforts on Day Two, which passed with no assault by the Confederate left wing to divert attention from Longstreet's attack on the Confederate right or to prevent Union reinforcements being sent from Ewell's front to oppose that attack.[66]

Likewise, Lee failed to oversee, personally or through staff, the execution of his orders on the right flank. No one, including Lee's early morning scouting party, ascertained the precise secure route that Hood's and McLaws's divisions of Longstreet's corps (actually accompanied by Captain Johnston) needed to take to reach their attack positions. This lack of oversight compounded Longstreet's difficulties in proceeding to the southern Union flank without being observed by the Yankees. Alexander assessed the resulting damage:

> That is just one illustration of how time may be lost in handling troops, and of the need of an abundance of competent staff officers by the generals in command. Scarcely any of our generals had half of what they needed to keep a *constant & close supervision on the execution of important orders*. An army is like a great machine, and in putting it into battle it is not enough for its commander to merely issue the necessary orders. He should have a staff ample to supervise the execution of each step, & to promptly report any difficulty or misunderstanding. There is no telling the value of the hours which were lost by that division that morning.[67]

Some of the postwar promoters of Lee and critics of Longstreet, such as Early[68] and William Nelson Pendleton,[69] falsely contended that Lee had ordered Longstreet to attack at dawn on Day Two. There is no credible evidence to support this contention. Alexander found it unbelievable since Lee would have ordered Longstreet's troops into position during the night if he had desired a dawn attack, and the enemy's position was not determined until morning, and then inaccurately.[70] Having personally delayed Longstreet's divisions on the Chambersburg Pike for ten hours the previous afternoon and thus caused them to arrive near Gettysburg in the wee hours of July 2, Lee was well aware of their inability to initiate an early morning assault in a position miles away from their bivouac. Because of the Chambersburg Pike congestion, Longstreet's two primary divisions to be used in the attack had finished arriving near Gettysburg between midnight and noon on Day Two.

Lee had ordered a scouting expedition around dawn, and he was not in a position to order an attack until he had specific information, based on daylight observations, on whom should be attacked where. At about eleven o'clock in the morning, Lee finally issued his only specific attack order of the day, directing Longstreet to proceed south to get into position to attack.[71] In addition, Lee at that time specifically consented to Longstreet's request that his attack be delayed until Brigadier General Evander Law's brigade of Hood's division could be brought up.[72] Law, another victim of the Chambersburg Pike bottleneck, had set out at about 3:00 a.m. and arrived on scene around noon. Lee could not have expected an attack before mid-afternoon—let alone at dawn. Douglas Southall Freeman, an idolizer of Lee who severely criticized Longstreet for allegedly delaying the attack, contended that Lee virtually surrendered control to Longstreet and concluded, "It is scarcely too much to say that on July 2 the Army of Northern Virginia was without a commander."[73] As commanding general of that army and on-scene commander of the battle, Lee was responsible for where and when Longstreet attacked.

As Longstreet proceeded on his southward march toward the Union left, he received reliable scouting reports that the Union left flank was "hanging in the air" and could be rolled up. Twice he passed this information on to Lee and requested permission to launch a flanking attack. Lee declined, however, and repeated his order to attack—probably under the erroneous impression that he still was ordering a flanking attack of some sort. McLaws's and Hood's divisions had difficulty finding their way on unfamiliar roads to their designated attack positions and even had to retrace their steps when they discovered that a point on the line of march was visible from a Union signal station on Little Round Top. They were being guided by the previously mentioned Captain Johnston of Lee's staff, and Lee himself rode part of the way south with Longstreet.[74] Lee oversaw and approved Longstreet's troop dispositions.[75]

Beginning their attack after 4:00 p.m., Longstreet's forces fought bravely in the Wheatfield, Peach Orchard, and Devil's Den and almost succeeded in capturing both Big Round Top and the critical Little Round Top. The near success indicates what might have been achieved if Lee had turned Longstreet's men loose for a flanking attack instead of squandering them in frontal assaults along the Union lines on Emmitsburg Road and Cemetery Ridge. The magic that Lee had worked with Stonewall Jackson at Second Manassas and Chancellorsville could not be replicated at Gettysburg, but even the frontal attack could have come closer to success if it had been properly planned, executed, and supervised.

Union General Daniel Sickles had advanced his Third Corps, contrary to orders, into a vulnerable position in and near the soon-to-be-famous Peach Orchard along Emmitsburg Road, well in front of the intended Union line along Cemetery Ridge. But Sickles's men received a brief reprieve. Instead of simultaneously attacking the north-to-south Union line along their entire front, the Confederates attacked piecemeal. Hood's division carried out an extended attack on the Union left flank before McLaws's division was ordered to attack Sickles's center and right. This staggered, or *en echelon*, attack enabled the Union defenders to respond to each successively threatened position.

When Hood, McLaws, and their brigadiers moved into position, they were surprised to find large Union troop concentrations in areas they had been informed were devoid of enemy forces. Both Hood and McLaws sought Longstreet's permission to avoid the desperate frontal assault they envisioned, but Longstreet, having failed numerous times to change Lee's mind over the prior twenty-four hours, directed that Lee's attack order be carried out.[76] In addition, Lee personally refused Hood's final request to send a brigade around the Union flank on the Round Tops.[77]

Each of the individual Confederate attacks was successful in driving back the enemy and capturing territory, but their overall effect was greatly reduced by uncoordinated timing. The attacks did not begin until 4:30 p.m. First, Hood's men attacked on the far south of the battlefield, crossed and followed Plum Run, and captured Devil's Den below the Round Tops. They would have captured Little Round Top but for the courage of four Union regiments of Colonel Strong Vincent's brigade—the Third Pennsylvania, Twentieth Maine, Fourth New York, and Sixth Michigan—and others who came to their aid. In fierce fighting, the Confederates drove Sickles's corps from the Peach Orchard, engaged in bitter combat for control of the adjoining Wheatfield, and finally drove the defenders back to the northern base of Little Round Top.

To their north, Dick Anderson's division of A. P. Hill's Third Corps participated very ineffectively in the late stages of the attack. Brigadier General Carnot Posey's brigade advanced haphazardly, and Brigadier General William Mahone's brigade never moved off Seminary Ridge despite division orders to do so. Lee and Hill failed to reinforce the aggressive attacks by Brigadier Generals William Barksdale and Ambrose Wright. Throughout the day, Hill's corps and much of Anderson's division acted as though they were unaware of Lee's plans or any role for them in the struggle. Lee apparently had intended for them to join in the sequential attacks beginning at the southern end of his line, but despite being nearby, he took no actions to get them properly aligned or bring all of them into the fray as the afternoon turned to evening.[78]

On the Union side, Hancock took advantage of the disjointed Confederate attack and sent reinforcements to each successively attacked position. The Fifth Corps went to the Round Tops and to Sickles's left, and the Second Corps reinforced Sickles. The Sixth Corps, which arrived at 2:00 p.m. after marching thirty-four miles in seventeen hours, and the Twelfth Corps backed up the others and stopped the Confederates before they could puncture Cemetery Ridge. By the time Sickles's line finally was broken and the Wheatfield secured, darkness was beginning to fall and additional Union troops had moved into position to back up Sickles and hold the Cemetery Ridge line. At one critical juncture, the Rebels broke the Union's Emmitsburg Road line and were about to advance onto Cemetery Ridge. Hancock sent in the 262-man First Minnesota Regiment to push them back at all costs—which they did with 82 percent casualties. The failed Confederate frontal attack *en echelon* cost them 6,500 casualties (to the Union's six thousand) and was reminiscent of similar tactical failures by Lee's army during the Seven Days' Campaign.

Where was Lee while this major uncoordinated and costly attack was falling apart? He was overlooking the battle from the cupola and elsewhere at the Lutheran Seminary on Seminary Ridge, at times with Generals Hill and Heth. He neither sent nor received more than a message or two and apparently sent only one order during the battle. Having given his orders many hours before, when conditions were radically different, he now stood by and watched the bloody assault falter and fail. Lee's inaction prompted Arthur J. L. Fremantle, a British military observer at Gettysburg, to comment, "It is evidently his system to arrange the plan thoroughly with the three corps commanders, and then leave to them the duty of modifying and carrying it out to the best of their abilities."[79] In a prelude to the more famous events of the next day, Lee allowed one-third of his force to attack while the others remained in place.[80] In sharp contrast, George Meade moved his forces all over the battlefield to meet each new attack, took corrective actions when he discovered Sickles's disastrous abandonment of his assigned position, and used a "hands-on" approach throughout the entire battle to prevent a Rebel breakthrough along his critical Cemetery Ridge line.[81]

Lee's uncoordinated assaults continued that night when Ewell's forces finally attacked Cemetery Hill. They were twenty-four hours too late for likely success and several hours too late to coordinate with Longstreet. Nevertheless, the brave men of two brigades fought their way to the top of Cemetery Hill. Failures of high command to provide support, however, compelled them to retreat. Ewell failed to commit his artillery to support the assault, while Early never committed the reserve brigade of Brigadier General John Brown Gordon to the battle. Once again, the attack on Cemetery Hill was planned *en echelon*—Johnson to attack first, followed by Early, and then Rodes. The reality was an ineffective assault by one brigade after another and the failure of many brigades to engage at all. In fact, Avery's and Hays's brigades had completed their successful attacks and been compelled to withdraw before Rodes launched his forces from the town itself. The strategy was poor and the execution was worse. The result was a failure to secure and hold critical Cemetery Hill, which dominated the north end and most of the battlefield.[82] Early on the morning of July 3, Confederate General Johnson assaulted Culp's Hill with even less success.[83]

As Porter Alexander pointed out, Lee wasted Ewell's Second Corps by leaving it in an isolated and harmless position northeast of the primary struggles on the second and third days of Gettysburg:

Ewell's troops were all placed beyond, or N.E. of Gettysburg, bent around toward the point of the fish hook of the enemy's position. It was an awkward place, far from our line of retreat in case of disaster, & not convenient either for re-inforcing others or being reinforced. And...this part of the enemy's position was in itself the strongest & it was practically almost unassailable. On the night of the First Gen. Lee ordered him withdrawn & brought around to our right of the town. Gen. Ewell had seen some ground he thought he could take & asked permission to stay & to take it. Gen. Lee consented, but it turned out early next morning that the position could not be taken. Yet the orders to come out from the awkward place he was in—where there was no reasonable probability of his accomplishing any good on the enemy's line in his front & where his artillery was of no service—were never renewed & he stayed there till the last. The ground is there still for any military engineer to pronounce whether or not Ewell's corps & all its artillery was not practically paralysed & useless by its position during the last two days of the battle.[84]

In conclusion, the second day of Gettysburg was another lost opportunity for which the commanding general of the Army of Northern Virginia must be held responsible. Over the objection of his corps and division commanders, Lee ordered Longstreet's First Corps to launch a frontal, *en echelon* assault on strong Union positions. Lee stood by while Hill's Third Corps in the center of the Confederate lines and directly in front of Lee did little to assist Longstreet.[85] Finally, Lee neither moved Ewell's Second Corps to an effective supporting attack position nor ensured that it attacked the Union right flank at the same time Longstreet was attacking the Union left. Lee had accomplished something: he put two more Union corps, the Third and Fifth, and a division of the Second out of action. But the opportunity for even greater success had been missed.

BATTLE OF GETTYSBURG: DAY THREE

Lee's performance on the final day at Gettysburg, July 3, was even worse. Frustrated by his two successive days of failure, he compounded his errors on the third.[86] His original plan for that day again involved simultaneous attacks by Ewell on the Confederate left and Longstreet on the right. This plan was thwarted when Meade ordered a night attack on Ewell's forces, which had occupied Union trenches the prior evening. A seven-hour battle at the north end of the battlefield ensued as Johnson's division of Ewell's corps unsuccessfully tried again and again to capture Culp's Hill. The attack tied down the Twelfth and remnants of the Union First Corps. Federal forces still held that critical position as dawn broke on the fateful third of July.[87] With Ewell engaged, Lee changed his mind and decided to attack the center of the Union line. The previous evening Union Major General John Newton, Reynolds's replacement as First Corps commander, had told Meade that he should be concerned about a flanking movement by Lee, who would not be "fool enough" to attack frontally the Union army in the strong position into which the first two days' fighting had consolidated it.[88] Around midnight Meade told Gibbon that his troops in the center of the Union line would be attacked if Lee went on the offensive the next day. Gibbon told Meade that if that occurred, Lee would be defeated.[89]

Lee, however, saw things differently. Again ignoring Longstreet's advice and pleas, Lee canceled Longstreet's early morning orders for a right wing attack and instead ordered the suicidal assault in the battlefield's center that would be known forever as Pickett's Charge.[90] After studying the ground over which the attack would occur, Longstreet said to Lee, "The 15,000 men who could make a successful assault over that field had never been arrayed for battle."[91] Longstreet was not alone in his bleak assessment of the chances for success. Brigadier General Ambrose "Rans" Wright said there would be no difficulty reaching Cemetery Ridge but that staying there was another matter, because the "whole Yankee army is there in a bunch."[92] On the morning of the third, Brigadier General Cadmus Wilcox told his fellow brigadier, Richard

Garnett, that the Union position was twice as strong as Gaines' Mill at the Seven Days' Battles.[93]

Demonstrating the extreme, almost blind, faith Confederate troops had in Lee, Alexander commented that "like all the rest of the army I believed that it would come out right, because Gen. Lee had planned it."[94] But the historian Bevin Alexander severely criticizes Lee's order: "When his direct efforts to knock aside the Union forces failed, Lee compounded his error by destroying the last offensive power of the Army of Northern Virginia in Pickett's charge across nearly a mile of open, bullet-and-shell-torn ground. This frontal assault was doomed before it started."[95]

The famous attack was preceded by a massive artillery exchange— so violent and loud that it was heard 140 miles away. Just after one o'clock, Alexander unleashed his 140 Rebel cannon against the Union forces on Cemetery Ridge. Eighty of the two hundred Federal cannon responded. Across a mile of slightly rolling fields, the opposing cannons blasted away for ninety minutes. The Confederate goal was to soften up the Union line, particularly to weaken its defensive artillery capacity, prior to a massive assault on the center of that line. Some Federal batteries were hit, as were horses and caissons (ammunition-carrying vehicles) on the reverse slope near General Meade's headquarters.

Alexander's cannonade continued until his supply of ammunition was dangerously low. A slowdown in the Union artillery response gave the false impression that the Confederate cannonade had inflicted serious damage. Although Alexander received some artillery assistance from Hill's guns to Alexander's north, Ewell's five artillery battalions northeast of the main Confederate line fired almost no rounds. Artillery fire was one thing that Ewell could have provided, but the commanding general and his chief of artillery also failed to coordinate this facet of the offensive.[96]

The time of decision and death was at hand for many of the remaining forty thousand Confederates and sixty thousand Yankees. The Rebels were about to assault a position that Porter Alexander described as "almost as badly chosen as it was possible to be." His rationale:

Briefly described, the point we attacked is upon the long *shank* of the fishhook of the enemy's position, & our advance was exposed to the fire of the whole length of that shank some two miles. Not only that, that shank is not perfectly straight, but it bends forward at the Round Top end, so that rifled guns there, in secure position, could & did enfilade the assaulting lines. Now add that the advance must be over 1,400 yards of open ground, none of it sheltered from fire, & very little from view, & without a single position for artillery where a battery could get its horses & caissons under cover.

I think any military engineer would, instead, select for attack the *bend* of the fishhook just west of Gettysburg. There, at least, the assaulting lines cannot be enfiladed, and, on the other hand the places selected for assault may be enfiladed, & upon shorter ranges than any other parts of the Federal lines. Again there the assaulting column will only be exposed to the fire of the front less than half, even if over one fourth, of the firing front upon the shank.[97]

Around 2:30, Alexander ordered a ceasefire and hurried a note off to General Longstreet. It read, "If you are coming at all, you must come at once or I cannot give you proper support, but the enemy's fire has not slackened at all. At least 18 guns are still firing from the cemetery itself."[98] Longstreet, convinced of the impending disaster, could not bring himself to give a verbal attack order to Major General George E. Pickett. When Pickett asked him, "General, shall I advance?" he merely nodded.[99]

On the hidden western slopes of Seminary Ridge, nine brigades of thirteen thousand men began forming two mile-and-a-half-long lines for the assault on Cemetery Ridge. Their three division commanders were Pickett, Major General Isaac Trimble (in place of the wounded Dorsey Pender), and Brigadier General J. Johnston Pettigrew (in place of the wounded Henry Heth). Pickett gave the order: "Up men, and to your posts! Don't forget today that you are from old Virginia!"[100] With that, they moved out.

After sending his "come at once" message, Alexander noticed a distinct pause in the firing from the cemetery and then clearly observed the withdrawal of artillery from that planned point of attack. Ten minutes after his earlier message and while Longstreet was silently assenting to the attack, Alexander sent another urgent note: "For God's sake come quick. The 18 guns are gone. Come quick or I can't support you."[101] To Alexander's chagrin, however, Union Chief of Artillery Henry J. Hunt moved five replacement batteries into the crucial center of the line. What Alexander did not yet know was that the Union firing had virtually ceased in order to save ammunition to repel the coming attack and to bring up fresh guns from the artillery reserve. Hunt had seventy-seven short-range guns in the position the Rebels intended to attack, as well as numerous other guns, including long-range rifled artillery, along the line capable of raking an attacking army.

The Rebel lines opened ranks to pass their now-quiet batteries and swept on into the shallow valley between the two famous ridges. A gasp arose from Cemetery Ridge as the two long gray lines, a hundred fifty yards apart, came into sight. It was three o'clock, the hottest time of a scorching day, and forty thousand Union soldiers were in position to directly contest the hopeless Confederate assault. Many defenders were sheltered by stone walls or wooden fences. Their awe at the impressive parade coming their way must have been mixed with an understandable fear of battle and a confidence in the strength of their numbers and position.

Their brave Rebel counterparts must have had increasing fear and decreasing confidence with every step they took toward the stronghold on Cemetery Ridge.[102] Their forty-seven regiments (including nineteen from Virginia and fourteen from North Carolina) initially traversed the undulating landscape in absolute silence except for the clunking of their wooden canteens. Although a couple of swales provided temporary shelter from most Union view and rifle fire, the Confederates were under constant observation from Little Round Top to the southeast. Long-range artillery fire began tearing holes in the Confederate lines, which approached and turned slightly left to cross the Emmitsburg Pike. Having marched into the middle of a Union semicircle of rifles and cannon, they attempted to maintain their perfect parade order, but all hell broke loose as Federal cannon firing short-range round-shot exploded along the entire ridge line—from Cemetery Hill on the north to Little Round Top on the south.

As the attackers came closer, Union cannons' double loads of canister (pieces of iron) and Minié balls from thousands of Union rifles decimated their front ranks. The slaughter was indescribable, but the courageous Rebels closed ranks and marched on. Taking tremendous losses, they started up the final rise toward the copse that was their objective. They had come so far that they were viciously assaulted from the front, both their flanks and even their rear. Especially devastating was the point-blank rifle fire from Brigadier General George J. Stannard's advanced Vermont brigade into the Rebel right flank. Gaping holes opened in the Confederates' now-merged lines, and their numbers dwindled to insignificance. The survivors let loose their Rebel yell and charged the trees near the center of Cemetery Ridge. With cries of "Fredericksburg," the men in blue decimated the remaining attackers with canister and Minié balls. General Lewis Armistead led the final surge. He and 150 others crossed the low stone wall, but all of them were killed, wounded, or captured within minutes. Armistead was mortally wounded.

Just as the Union soldiers recognized a Fredericksburg-like scenario, General Lee at long last did so as well. From 1,700 yards away, he watched the death throes of his grand assault, his gray-and-butternut troops disappearing in the all-engulfing smoke on the ridge, and some of them emerging in retreat. Fewer than seven thousand of the original thirteen thousand were able to make their way through the carnage and return to Seminary Ridge. There was no covering fire from Alexander's cannon because he was saving his precious ammunition to repel the expected counter-attack. As the survivors returned to Confederate lines, Lee met them and sobbed, "It's all my fault this time."[103] It was.[104]

Lee and Longstreet tried to console Pickett, who was distraught about the slaughter of his men.[105] Lee told him that their gallantry had earned them a place in history, but Pickett responded: "All the glory in the world could never atone for the widows and orphans this day has made."[106] To his death, Pickett blamed Lee for the "massacre" of his division.[107]

The result of Lee's Day Three strategy was the worst single-charge slaughter of the whole bloody war—with the possible exception of John Bell Hood's suicidal charge at Franklin, Tennessee, the following year. The Confederates suffered 7,500 casualties to the Union's 1,500. More than one thousand of those Rebel casualties were killed—all in a thirty-minute bloodbath. Brigadier General Richard Garnett, whose five Virginia regiments led the assault, was killed, and 950 of his 1,450 men were killed or wounded. The Thirteenth and Forty-seventh North Carolina and Eighteenth Virginia regiments were virtually wiped out on Cemetery Ridge.[108]

AFTERMATH

That night Lee rode alone among his troops. At one point he met Brigadier General John D. Imboden, who said, "General, this has been a hard day on you." Lee responded, "Yes, it has been a sad, sad day to us." He went on to praise Pettigrew's and Pickett's men and then made the puzzling statement, "If they had been supported as they were to have been—but for some reason not fully explained to me were not—we would have held the position and the day would have been ours. Too bad. Too bad. Oh, too bad."[109] General Alexander found Lee's comment inexplicable since Lee was the commanding general and had personally overseen the entire preparation and execution of the disastrous charge.[110] Providing necessary supporting troops was Lee's responsibility.

Even if Lee was nonplussed, his officers had little difficulty seeing the folly of Pickett's Charge and its parallel to the senseless Union charges at Fredericksburg the previous December. Having lost more than half his own 10,500 men in the July 3 charge, Pickett submitted a battle report highly critical of that assault—and probably of Lee. Lee declined to accept the report and ordered him to rewrite it.[111] Pickett never did.

The attack never should have been made. As Allan Nevins observes, "It was a glorious charge, but it was not war. Some thought it glorious that color-bearers of thirty-five regiments were shot down, and that seven Confederate colonels were buried on the battleground.... Yet futile carnage is never glorious."[112] Ernest Furgurson sums up the calamity: "Properly led on the decisive afternoon at Gettysburg, George Pickett's Virginians and Johnston Pettigrew's Carolinians would not have been sent across the killing fields from Seminary to Cemetery Ridge, against the massed Union army. But their bravery at Chancellorsville had persuaded their general that they were invincible, and so he sent them. And so Gettysburg was lost, and so the war."[113]

The only saving grace for Lee's battered army was that General Meade, believing his mission was not to lose, failed to follow up his victory immediately with an infantry counterattack on the stunned and disorganized Confederates. To Lincoln's chagrin, Meade developed a case of the "slows" reminiscent of McClellan's after Antietam and took a total of nine days to pursue and catch Lee, who was burdened by a seventeen-mile ambulance train.[114] Unlike McClellan at Antietam, however, Meade's entire army had been engaged and battered at Gettysburg. After missing his chance for a quick and decisive strike, Meade wisely did not attack Lee's strongly entrenched position at Williamsport, Maryland, on the Potomac River after Meade had caught up with him. As the Confederates waited to cross, Confederate officers hoped for a Union assault: "Now we have Meade where we want him. If he attacks us here, we will pay him back for Gettysburg. But the Old Fox is too cunning."[115] Alexander likewise recalled the moment: "oh! how we all did wish that the enemy would come out in the open & attack us, as we had done them at Gettysburg. But they had had their lesson, in that sort of game, at [Fredericksburg] & did not care for another."[116] Lee's army crossed the receding river and returned ignominiously to Virginia.[117]

CONCLUSIONS

Who lost Gettysburg? Robert E. Lee bore primary responsibility for a demoralizing Confederate triple disaster in the summer of

1863—Gettysburg, Vicksburg, and Tullahoma. Confederate morale and prospects fell to a new low and never recovered. Confederate Chief of Ordnance Josiah Gorgas, on July 28, bemoaned the rapid change of Rebel fortunes resulting from its defeats at Gettysburg and Vicksburg:

> Lee failed at Gettysburg, and has recrossed the Potomac & resumed the position of two months ago, covering Richmond. Alas! he has lost fifteen thousand men and twenty-five thousand stands of arms. Vicksburg and Port Hudson [down the Mississippi from Vicksburg] capitulated, surrendering thirty five thousand men and forty-five thousand arms. It seems incredible that human power could effect such a change in so brief a space. Yesterday we rode on the pinnacle of success—to-day absolute ruin seems to be our portion. The Confederacy totters to its destruction.[118]

Longstreet was unfairly made a scapegoat for Gettysburg to remove blame from Lee, who protected his own reputation by suppressing Pickett's battle report.[119] Longstreet's role in the battle and campaign seems rather insignificant, and his advice was consistently and mistakenly ignored by Lee. Even before the campaign, Lee had convinced Davis to ignore Longstreet's recommendation that the bulk of Longstreet's troops be sent to another theater. Longstreet's troops might have been used to reinforce, directly or indirectly, the Western Theater Rebels in Mississippi under Lieutenant General John Pemberton, who were opposing Grant's campaign against Vicksburg, or to reinforce the outmanned Middle Theater Confederate forces under General Braxton Bragg in east-central Tennessee and thereby prevent them from being driven out of Tennessee by the numerically superior Union Army of the Cumberland commanded by Major General William Rosecrans. Because Lee kept Longstreet from going west, the Gettysburg disaster was coupled with twin defeats in other theaters. He helped ensure that Grant would capture Vicksburg and Pemberton's army, and he kept Bragg so shorthanded that his army was maneuvered back into Georgia from Tennessee in the virtually bloodless Tullahoma Campaign.[120]

Lee's strategic and tactical performance was filled with blunders. The *Charleston Mercury* assessed the Gettysburg Campaign accurately: "It is impossible for an invasion to have been more foolish and disastrous. It was opportune neither in time nor circumstance." In a July 26 diary entry, Robert G. H. Kean of the Confederate War Department called Gettysburg "the worst disaster which has ever befallen our arms.... To fight an enemy superior in numbers at such terrible disadvantage of position in the heart of his own territory, when the freedom of movement gave him the advantage of selecting his own time and place for accepting battle, seems to have been a great military blunder.... Gettysburg has shaken my faith in Lee as a general."[121]

Confederate General Alexander concluded, "Then perhaps in taking the aggressive at all at Gettysburg in 1863 & certainly in the place & dispositions for the assault on the Third day, I think, it will undoubtedly be held that [Lee] unnecessarily took the most desperate chances & the bloodiest road."[122]

William C. Davis, generally supportive of Lee's war effort, provides this insight into some specifics of Lee's performance at Gettysburg:

> Confronted with a battle he did not want in ground not of his choosing, Lee exercised minimal control before he reached the field late on July 1. While struggling to concentrate the army, he could have sent staff to impose instructions on Hill and Ewell, but he did not, and left them to it. When he directed Ewell to take the key to the Union line on Cemetery Hill, he used the discretionary caveat "if practicable," an unproductive phrase with a mercurial general like Ewell. Once he established his headquarters on the field, Lee erratically communicated plans to his corps commanders.... Lee gave orders to his corps commanders but sent no staff with them to make certain his wishes were obeyed.[123]

Davis offers this overall appraisal of Lee's Gettysburg efforts:

> He forfeited any long- or midrange tactical reconnaissance Stuart might have provided, and as a result had no grasp of the overall battlescape. He learned of Union movements too late to react, and never identified Meade's center of gravity in order to direct his own efforts to best effect. He let Hill bring on a major engagement despite instructions not to do so, and then gave orders too imprecise and discretionary to be effective. Five years later Lee offered two reasons for defeat: Stuart's absence left him blind; and he could not deliver the "one determined and united blow" that he believed would have assured victory.... What he did not say was that he was ultimately responsible. He let Stuart go, and his own laissez-faire management helped bungle the attacks on July 1 and 2.... Every general has his worst battle. Gettysburg was Lee's.[124]

After the war, Lee provided his rationale for having attacked on the second and third days at Gettysburg:

> It had not been intended to deliver a general battle so far from our base unless attacked, but coming unexpectedly upon the whole Federal army, to withdraw through the mountains with our extensive trains would have been difficult and dangerous. At the same time we were unable to await an attack, as the country was unfavorable for collecting supplies in the presence of the enemy who could restrain our foraging parties by holding the mountain passes with local and other troops. A battle had therefore become, in a measure, unavoidable, and the success already gained gave hope of a favorable issue.[125]

Lee, in fact, had *not* come upon "the whole Federal army." That whole army was not on the battlefield until late on the second day of the Gettysburg struggle. Later, even after suffering three days of terrible losses, Lee in fact *was* able to retreat safely through the mountains after the battle, and his army managed to live off the country north of the Potomac for nine more days. Lee's rationale justifies neither his series of frontal attacks on the second day nor the suicidal charge on the third day.[126]

Furthermore, Lee's strategic campaign into the North had come to its inevitable conclusion: the appearance of defeat and an unforeseen actual military defeat. Rhode Island's Elisha Hunt Rhodes's diary entry for July 9 typified the North's elation over Gettysburg: "I wonder what the South thinks of us Yankees now. I think Gettysburg will cure the Rebels of any desire to invade the North again."[127] Archer Jones provides this analysis: "Lee...suffered a costly defeat in a three-day battle at Gettysburg. With Lee's loss of twenty-eight thousand men (killed, wounded, missing, and captured) to the North's twenty-three thousand, the battle became a disaster of depletion for the Confederate army. His inevitable retreat to Virginia, seemingly the result of the battle rather than his inability to forage, made it a serious political defeat also."[128]

Considering the nearly equal number of combatants at Gettysburg, Lee's losses were staggering in both absolute and relative terms. Of the seventy-five thousand Confederates, 22,600 (30 percent) were killed or injured. The toll of general officers was appalling: six dead, eight wounded, and three captured. Just as significantly, the Southern field grade officers (majors and above) suffered high casualties, and their absence would be felt for the duration of the war. Of the 83,300 Union troops at Gettysburg, 17,700 (21 percent) were killed or wounded.[129] Although his losses were higher, absolutely and proportionally, Lee told Davis, "Our loss has been very heavy, that of the enemy's is proportionally so."[130]

The Richmond newspapers, and therefore many others in the South, initially reported Gettysburg as a grand Confederate victory,[131] so Southerners did not at first realize the extent of their losses in Pennsylvania. By July 31 Lee had deluded himself into calling the campaign a "general success."[132] A Virginia private who had fought at Gettysburg wrote his sister with a different view: "We got a bad whiping.... they are awhiping us...at every point...I hope they would make peace so that we that is alive yet would get home agane...but I supose Jef Davis and lee dont care if all is killed."[133]

It became apparent that Lee had used the same approach he had taken in his prior thirteen months in command. He attacked too frequently and relied too much on frontal assaults. British Colonel Arthur Fremantle discussed the flaw of Lee's aggressiveness: "Don't you see your system feeds upon itself? You cannot fill the places of these men. Your troops do wonders, but every time at a cost you cannot afford."[134] Lee's offensive strategy and tactics were causing irreplaceable losses at an unsustainable rate—a casualty rate far greater than that of his stronger opponent. Gettysburg was the epitome of Lee's flawed approach.[135]

Allen Guelzo concludes his authoritative analysis of Gettysburg with a summary of Lee's role in the Confederate defeat: "It can be said, then, that Lee lost a battle he should have won, and lost it because (a) he began the battle without completely concentrating his forces, (b) he proved unable to coordinate the attacks of the forces he did have available, and (c) he failed to reckon with how tenaciously the Army of the Potomac...would hold its ground under direct infantry attack on July 3."[136]

Gettysburg featured many blunders by Lee and demonstrated all of his weaknesses. He initiated an unnecessary strategic offensive that, because of his army's inevitable return to Virginia, would be perceived as a retreat and thus a defeat. He rejected alternative uses for Longstreet's corps that might have avoided or mitigated critical losses of the Mississippi River (including Vicksburg and then Port Hudson, Louisiana) or middle and southeastern Tennessee (including Chattanooga). After making his army more important than all other Rebel armies, he misused it offensively. His tactics were inexcusably and fatally aggressive on Days Two and Three, he failed to take charge of the battlefield on any of the three days, his battle plans were ineffective, and his orders, especially to Stuart and Ewell, were vague and too discretionary. Lee had the freedom of movement to choose the time and place of battle, but he allowed chance and a compulsion for attacking to pick it for him. Gettysburg was Lee at his worst.

CHICKAMAUGA AND CHATTANOOGA

DAVIS, LEE, AND BRAGG FAIL TO DESTROY A UNION ARMY AND TO KEEP CHATTANOOGA IN REBEL HANDS

WHO BLUNDERED?

Confederate President Jefferson Davis and
Generals Robert E. Lee and Braxton Bragg

HOW?

They delayed sending Longstreet's troops to Chickamauga, missed a
chance virtually to destroy a Union army at or immediately after
Chickamauga, conducted an ineffective partial siege at Chattanooga,
and moved Longstreet's troops away from Chattanooga, ensuring
Union victory there.

CONSEQUENCES?

The results were that William Rosecrans's army survived
Chickamauga and the siege, Ulysses S. Grant was able to unite three
armies and drive the Rebels away from Chattanooga, and the stage
was set for Sherman's 1864 Atlanta Campaign.

In late 1863, Jefferson Davis, assisted by many of his leading generals, committed a series of blunders and missed the chance to trap and destroy as many as three Union armies at Chattanooga after the major Confederate victory at Chickamauga. Robert E. Lee started the blunders by delaying Longstreet's reinforcement of Bragg on the eve of the battle of Chickamauga and throughout the engagement, which was fought September 18–20. Other Rebel failures included Braxton Bragg's failure to attack the isolated Union Army of the Cumberland, which had fled to Chattanooga and was desperately short of supplies. Then, after numerous Union reinforcements reached Chattanooga, Davis, Lee, and Bragg combined to transfer Longstreet's fifteen-thousand-man corps away from Chattanooga, opening the door for Union success at Missionary Ridge and missing the opportunity to bottle up Grant's forces in the Chattanooga Valley. These blunders were compounded by Lee's refusal to send additional reinforcements to what was the most critical point in the national struggle. The loss of that crucial ground opened the door for Sherman's game-changing Atlanta Campaign of 1864.

Major General William Rosecrans's Army of the Cumberland incurred substantial losses at the bloody two-and-a half-day battle of Chickamauga in northern Georgia. Braxton Bragg's Army of Tennessee, belatedly reinforced by General James Longstreet with troops from Virginia, attacked Rosecrans's army. While George Thomas—"the Rock of Chickamauga"—prevented the loss of the Union army by a heroic holding action, Rosecrans led a hasty retreat of the rest of his army to Chattanooga, Tennessee. Chickamauga had cost Rosecrans more than sixteen thousand casualties and Bragg an astounding eighteen thousand-plus. More importantly, the Confederates had missed the opportunity for an even greater victory—perhaps even the surrender of Rosecrans's army.[1]

The missteps began in Richmond. Although politically weakened by his Gettysburg defeat, General Robert E. Lee still had enough influence to delay Longstreet's movement out of the Virginia Theater. In mid-August, Longstreet had pressed Secretary of War Seddon and Lee to send many of his troops west.[2] Beginning August 21 Bragg warned Richmond of a massive offensive by Rosecrans and Major General Ambrose Burnside and requested reinforcements. On August 24 Lee was summoned to Richmond to discuss the situation in Tennessee and Georgia. During the last week of August, Davis began discussing with Lee the possibility of Lee's providing reinforcements to Bragg. Lee, who usually argued that Union reinforcements on his front precluded transfers from his army, now argued that transfers away from Meade, facing Lee in Virginia, made Meade's army vulnerable to an offensive by Lee's full army.[3] In fact, on August 31 Lee even ordered Longstreet to prepare for such an offensive.[4]

While Davis and Lee dithered, the situation in the West radically changed. Burnside and the Ninth Corps marched into Knoxville in northeastern Tennessee on September 3 and cut the direct rail link (the East Tennessee & Virginia and the East Tennessee & Georgia railroads) from Virginia to Chattanooga. After finally agreeing on September 5 to the movement of Longstreet's troops, Lee and Davis took three more days to finalize the details. Longstreet's two divisions, which did not begin to leave Orange Court House in central Virginia until September 9, had to take a thousand-mile route to Chattanooga on ten railroads through the Carolinas instead of traveling only five hundred rail miles by way of Knoxville, which was then in Union hands.[5]

Each of Longstreet's units took eight to ten days to reach Chickamauga. Thus, none of those transferred soldiers fought in any but the last day of the two-and-a half-day battle. Only five thousand of them, without artillery, wagons, or horses, had a hand in breaking Rosecrans's Union lines on the last day of the battle, September 20, and driving the Northerners back into Chattanooga. More or most of Longstreet's fifteen thousand troops, as well as his artillery and horses, would have arrived in time to fight and contest the Yankee retreat if Lee's reluctance to part with any troops had not caused a delay of more than two weeks.[6]

On September 20 at Chickamauga, George Thomas and Major General Gordon Granger, barely able to hold Horseshoe Ridge and Snodgrass Hill against Rebel assaults that continued all afternoon and into the evening, conducted an orderly retreat to join Rosecrans. It is doubtful they could have held off a full-blown assault that included *all* of Longstreet's troops with their artillery and horses. Thousands more

Union soldiers would have been killed, wounded, captured, or forced into a disorderly retreat instead of protecting Rosecrans's retreat and then making an orderly retreat themselves to Chattanooga. Further, the Rebels would have had the manpower, firepower, and momentum to follow up their victory with an immediate assault on Rosecrans's reeling army in Chattanooga. The outcome at Chickamauga and even Chattanooga probably would have been quite different, therefore, if Davis and Lee had not blundered in delaying reinforcements.

Bragg himself compounded their blunders by failing to pursue and attack the reeling Yankees immediately after Chickamauga. Peter Cozzens writes, "Obviously, Bragg had had his best chance to crush the Army of the Cumberland and reverse the tide of war in the West—perhaps irrevocably, given the deepening war weariness in the North—during the first hours following the Federal flight into Chattanooga."[7] James McDonough concurs: "[Bragg] failed to take advantage of the disorganized union army when its soldiers were despondent in defeat. Instead of attacking and maintaining momentum, Bragg elected to pursue a siege operation in which his enemy's supplies were never completely cut off."[8] The Rebel Army of Tennessee's failure to pursue and conquer Rosecrans's army led to a debilitating struggle among Bragg and his subordinates about who was to blame.[9]

Chattanooga was a critical crossroads for land, rail, and river transportation between the Deep South and Virginia, between the Mississippi River and the Carolinas, and between Nashville and the industrial center of Atlanta. After Chickamauga, Bragg's army occupied the high ground to the east and southwest of Chattanooga, trapping the Union forces and reducing their supply line to a single, mountainous, sixty-mile wagon-road from the railhead at Bridgeport, Alabama. Rations were cut, animals were dying, and starvation threatened the Federal troops.[10]

Recognizing the gravity of Rosecrans's position in Chattanooga, Lincoln, Stanton, and Halleck looked to Grant to resolve the crisis. In an October 3 dispatch, Halleck told Grant to proceed to Cairo, Illinois, and report by telegraph. Arriving there on October 16, Grant immediately telegraphed Halleck and was ordered to proceed to Louisville to meet "an officer of the War Department." Grant's train was flagged down at Indianapolis, where he was joined by none other than Secretary of War Stanton, who accompanied him the rest of the way to Louisville and explained the desperate situation in Chattanooga. Stanton named Grant the commander of a new Military Division of the Mississippi, which included the Departments (and Armies) of the Ohio (Burnside), the Cumberland (Rosecrans), and the Tennessee (Grant), and all territory between the Mississippi and the Alleghenies north of Major General Nathaniel Banks in Louisiana.[11]

Grant's top priority now became saving Chattanooga. His first action was to replace Rosecrans as commander of the Army of the Cumberland with George Thomas, the hero of Chickamauga, to whom he wired: "I will be there as soon as possible. Please inform me how long your present supplies will last, and the prospect for keeping them up." Thomas replied that he and his troops would hold "until we starve."[12]

Meanwhile, Lincoln, Stanton, Halleck, and senior staff held a midnight meeting to discuss the crisis in Chattanooga, which they realized was a key to victory in the war. Authorized to send badly needed reinforcements, Stanton ordered twenty thousand troops from the Army of the Potomac under Major General Joseph ("Fighting Joe") Hooker to proceed by rail from Virginia to the Chattanooga area. Major General Oliver O. Howard's Eleventh Corps and Major General Henry W. Slocum's Twelfth Corps, along with ten artillery batteries, embarked the next day on the twelve-hundred-mile journey over seven railroads through Virginia, Maryland, West Virginia, Ohio, Indiana, Kentucky, and Tennessee, all the way to Bridgeport, Alabama, covering the distance in an astonishing fifteen days. Their three thousand horses and transport vehicles followed within about a week.[13]

While the Union high command appreciated the surpassing importance of the confrontation at Chattanooga, the Confederates did not. As we have seen, Lee and Davis had delayed Longstreet's movement to Chickamauga—a delay that likely had serious consequences for both

Chickamauga and Chattanooga. Yielding to Lee's opposition, Davis declined to send additional troops to Chattanooga after the Confederates learned that two Union corps had been moved out of Lee's theater. Lee's Virginia-centric myopia, combined with Davis's acquiescence, haunted the Confederates throughout the Chattanooga Campaign.

Recently injured, Grant arrived by rail at Bridgeport and immediately began the painful and arduous sixty-mile horseback ride over the mountains to Chattanooga. He had to be carried part of the way because sections of the road were unfit for riding horses. The animal-loving Grant must have been dismayed by the sight of thousands of horse and mule carcasses and the wreckage of numerous wagons—all evidence of the need to open a better supply route into Chattanooga. Arriving on October 23, he asked Halleck to promote Sherman to Grant's old command of the Army of the Tennessee, and Halleck complied.[14]

Grant immediately conferred with Thomas and his staff, including General William F. "Baldy" Smith, chief engineer of the Army of the Cumberland. After scouting the area with Thomas and Smith the next day, Grant approved Smith's creative plan to open an adequate supply line to the town. Three nights later, under the cover of darkness and fog, eighteen hundred Union troops in sixty pontoon boats floated downriver from Chattanooga around Moccasin Bend to Brown's Ferry, where they quickly overcame the surprised Confederate guards and ferried across another brigade of waiting troops. Coordinating with the first of Hooker's Eleventh and Twelfth Corps soldiers coming north through Lookout Valley from Bridgeport, they repelled a Rebel counterattack and had a bridge built across the river by 4:30 the next afternoon. This virtually bloodless operation gave Grant's forces control of Lookout Valley and the Tennessee River below (and west of) Chattanooga, opening the "Cracker Line" by which massive quantities of rations and supplies could be brought directly and efficiently from Bridgeport to Chattanooga. Grant's troops in Chattanooga celebrated as the first barges carrying four hundred thousand rations and thirty-nine thousand pounds of forage arrived behind the steamer *Chattanooga*,[15] but they remained short of full rations and adequate fodder for weeks.[16]

Grant received the troops' praise for their sudden change of fortune, though he gave credit for the breakthrough to Thomas and Smith in his dispatches to Washington. But Grant deserved and received credit for the new atmosphere among the troops at Chattanooga. As the recently-arrived General Howard wrote later that fall, "This department was completely 'out of joint' when we first arrived.... I cannot be too thankful for the policy that placed these three Depts. under Grant." Years later a veteran said, "You have no conception of the change in the army when Grant came. He opened up the cracker line and got a steamer through. We began to see things move. We felt that everything came from a plan. He came into the army quietly, no splendor, no airs, no staff. He used to go about alone. He began the campaign the moment he reached the field."[17]

Bragg's Confederates must have been shocked by the suddenness and ease with which Grant altered the situation at Chattanooga. Instead of being bottled up and starving, the Union forces had a supply line that promised adequate food, rations, forage, clothing, ammunition, and other provisions in the near future—as well as a route for reinforcements from both the East and West. Grant himself would summarize the reversal of fortunes in his memoirs:

> In five days from my arrival in Chattanooga the way was open to Bridgeport and, with the aid of steamers and Hooker's teams, in a week the troops were receiving full rations. It is hard for any one not an eye-witness to realize the relief this brought. The men were soon reclothed and also well fed; an abundance of ammunition was brought up, and a cheerfulness prevailed not before enjoyed in many weeks.... I do not know what the effect was on the other side, but assume it must have been correspondingly depressing. [Jefferson] Davis had visited Bragg but a short time before, and must have perceived our condition to be about as Bragg described it in his subsequent report. "These dispositions," he said "faithfully sustained, insured the enemy's speedy evacuation of Chattanooga for

want of food and forage. Possessed of the shortest route to his depot, and the one by which reinforcements must reach him, we held him at our mercy, and his destruction was only a question of time."[18]

In desperation, the rattled Confederates counterattacked the second night following the surprise Union assault on Brown's Ferry. Longstreet's men came down from Lookout Mountain to attack Hooker's troops in Lookout Valley. Union Brigadier General John W. Geary was badly outnumbered at the Battle of Wauhatchie but held his position. Moving to the rescue from Brown's Ferry, Howard engaged Confederates attacking from a foothill of Lookout Mountain, drove them back, and captured the hill. The attack on Geary, meanwhile, was broken up when his horses and mules stampeded toward the attackers, who mistook the stampede for a cavalry charge on the pitch-black night. The Union victory at Wauhatchie, which kept Lookout Valley open and guaranteed the Cracker Line's security, came at a minimal cost. There were no further Confederate attempts to impede the supply and reinforcement route Grant had so easily opened. Grant had saved a trapped army and opened and defended a practical supply and reinforcement route to Chattanooga. Soon he would pose a serious threat to Bragg's encircling army.[19] On the other hand, Bragg and Longstreet had failed to deploy adequate forces in the Lookout Valley either to hold or to recover that area so critical to an effective siege.[20]

In the following days, Grant made a one-man reconnaissance of the situation along the Chattanooga Creek west of Chattanooga and near the base of Lookout Mountain. When he approached the Union pickets on his side of the creek, one of them recognized him and called out, "Turn out the guard for the commanding general." Grant dismissed the Union pickets who turned out—but not in time to keep the Confederates across the creek from learning what was happening. Thus, a Confederate picket called out, "Turn out the guard for the commanding general, General Grant." The line of Confederate pickets saluted Grant, and he returned their salute.[21]

Chattanooga, TN. View of Army camp. *Courtesy of the Library of Congress*

Having improved the supply situation, Grant spent the next month gathering his reinforcements, assembling an army of eighty thousand, and planning an assault on the six-mile Confederate line half encircling Chattanooga. The presence of Hooker's twenty thousand troops and Sherman's two corps from Mississippi swelled Grant's army, demonstrating Lincoln's, Stanton's, and Grant's grasp of the importance of Chattanooga to their national strategy.

Lee and Davis not only prevented a reciprocal increase of Bragg's force but actually reduced it. Anxious to get back the bulk of Longstreet's corps, which Davis had belatedly pried loose from Lee and sent to Chickamauga, Lee persistently lobbied Davis for Longstreet's return. He started before Longstreet had even left Virginia. On September 11, writing to Davis that Longstreet should have reached Richmond the prior evening on his way south, Lee closed with the plea, "The blow at Rosecrans should be made promptly and Longstreet returned."[22] Just three days later, he raised the ante: "I begin to fear that we have lost the use of troops here where they are much needed, and that they have gone where they will do no good.... And it is a matter worthy of consideration whether Genl Longstreet's corps will reach Genl Bragg in time and condition to be of any advantage to him...." (Whose fault was that, we may ask.) "Should Genl Longstreet reach Genl Bragg in time to aid him in winning a victory *and return to this army*, it will be well, but should he be detained there without being able to do any good, it will result in evil."[23]

A week later Lee came up with a specific proposal for the president to consider. If Major General Simon Bolivar Buckner could join Bragg (which he did at Chickamauga), then, "Longstreet can successfully move to E Tennessee, open that country, where [Major General] Sam Jones can unite with him, *& thence rejoin me*. No time ought to be lost or wasted. Everything should be done that can be done at once, *so that the troops may be speedily returned to this department*."[24] On October 29 while visiting Bragg's army, Davis passed Lee's suggestion to Bragg, whom Davis had just retained in command despite requests from Longstreet and virtually all of Bragg's other generals that he be removed.[25]

According to Peter Cozzens, "Davis's suggestion [which was originally Lee's] that Bragg detach Longstreet was quixotic, reflecting both his lack of appreciation of the Union buildup at Chattanooga and the degree to which he was swayed by Robert E. Lee."[26] James McDonough agrees that Davis "was apparently unaware of either strategic or tactical reality" and "seemed oblivious to the Federal concentration of forces at Chattanooga," which left Bragg outnumbered by about two to one.[27]

Ignoring the Union buildup, Bragg went along with Lee's and Davis's recommendation. He knew that Longstreet had aggravated the discontent among Bragg's generals and suspected—probably correctly—that Longstreet wanted his command. On November 3, Bragg convened his corps commanders and bluntly ordered Longstreet to move toward Knoxville and drive Burnside out of Tennessee. Two days later Longstreet took at least fifteen thousand troops away to the northeast.[28] This gambit reduced Bragg's strength to thirty-six thousand against Grant's eventual eighty thousand and deprived Bragg of a reserve in the event of a Union breakthrough—which Lee, Davis, and Bragg seemed determined to make feasible.[29] In the words of Peter Cozzens, "Bragg had committed the most egregious error of his checkered career. In all too typical fashion, he had allowed rancor [toward Longstreet] to crowd out rational thought. Without a coherent plan or even the desire for close coordination between the two segments, he had divided his army in the face of a now numerically superior foe who was about to receive even more reinforcements."[30]

Grant's battle plan for a breakthrough at Chattanooga sent Sherman against the Confederate right (north) wing all the way to the railroad in Bragg's rear (the pathway to Knoxville and Atlanta), sent Hooker against the Confederate left at Lookout Mountain, and had Thomas pressure the Confederate center to keep reinforcements from going to either flank. Grant did not foresee that the arrival of Sherman's troops would cause Bragg to think they were headed toward Knoxville and to order eleven thousand more of his troops to proceed there. They were on their way, further weakening Bragg's army, before being recalled when Grant attacked at Chattanooga.[31]

The first Union advance, on November 23, was a one-mile movement by Thomas's troops against the center of the Confederate line, in which he turned what looked like a drill into a takeover of the advance Confederate lines and a prominent hill called Orchard Knob. That night, to the north, thousands of Sherman's men crossed the river in pontoon boats, established a beachhead, and built a pontoon bridge for the men behind them. The next day Grant ordered Hooker to take Lookout Mountain, the twelve-hundred-foot landmark dominating the Tennessee River southwest of Chattanooga. His three divisions crossed Lookout Creek and proceeded to take control of the thinly-manned mountain in a daylong "Battle above the Clouds." The fighting on the upper half of the mountain was visible to cheering Union troops in the Tennessee River Valley and to Grant and other generals on Orchard Knob in the center of the Union lines. After taking more than twelve hundred casualties, Bragg ordered the mountain abandoned that night, ending a sixty-three-day occupation. Hooker's success cleared the way for an all-out assault on the remaining Confederates threatening Chattanooga.[32]

Grant ordered Sherman and his troops, who had marched more than six hundred miles from Vicksburg before crossing the Tennessee north of town, to attack Tunnel Mountain on the north end of Missionary Ridge, the Confederate heights overlooking Chattanooga from the east.[33] Grant simultaneously ordered Hooker to drive from Lookout Mountain through Lookout Valley to threaten the south end of Missionary Ridge. Grant held George Thomas's troops in reserve between Sherman and Hooker to reinforce any breakthrough made by either of them. Sherman's planned offensive made little progress on November 24, but a full eclipse of the moon that evening seemed to auger significant developments the next day.

Sherman continued to encounter serious problems on the twenty-fifth, however. Tunnel Hill turned out to be a couple of ridges beyond where he expected it to be—and behind a ravine. A frustrated Sherman sent small portions of his troops into deadly frontal assaults on defensive positions well conceived by Confederate Major General Patrick R. Cleburne.

Sherman's frustration was matched on the other end of the line, where Hooker was having difficulty crossing the now bridgeless Chattanooga Creek in Lookout Valley. From his outpost on Orchard Knob between Chattanooga and Missionary Ridge, Grant became concerned about Sherman after observing Confederate reinforcements shifting to deal with Sherman's attack on the north.[34]

The commanding general approached his old West Point roommate Brigadier General Thomas J. Wood and said, "General Sherman seems to be having a hard time." "Yes, General," Wood responded, "he does seem to be in a warm place." Sensing that neither of his primary options was working, the hands-on Grant then ordered Wood and Major General Philip H. Sheridan, under Thomas's command, to "advance your divisions to the foot of the ridge and there halt.... [I]t will menace Bragg's forces so as to relieve Sherman." Preparing to do so, Wood said, "I think we can carry the entrenchments at the base of the ridge."[35]

Thomas assembled twenty-three thousand infantrymen for the assault on the rifle pits at the base of Missionary Ridge. To Confederates in the pits, in positions halfway up the ridge, and atop the ridge, there appeared to be fifty thousand advancing troops. Bragg was foolish to place about 30 percent of the Rebels in such a vulnerable position. They could not expect to hold the rifle pits and inevitably had to flee to the top of the ridge, where their exhaustion impeded their fighting ability. The "Rebel effort was poorly conceived, poorly engineered, and poorly coordinated."[36]

The attackers moved out in good order and, despite some defensive fire, quickly made their way to the base of Missionary Ridge, where the defending Rebels fled uphill. Thomas's men, however, soon realized they were in a no-man's land where they were under fire from numerous Confederate riflemen and some artillery on the side and top of the ridge. A Union infantryman, Fred Knefler of the Seventy-ninth Indiana, described the situation: "Nothing could live in or about the captured line of field works; a few minutes of such terrific, telling fire would quickly convert them into untenable hideous slaughter pens. There was no time or opportunity for deliberations. Something must be done and it must be done quickly." Given the option of retreating, dying, or continuing the assault, they scrambled up the ridge to attack the source of the killing rifle fire.[37]

Many officers at the base of the hill, moreover, apparently thought they had orders to continue the assault. Wood's division quickly began climbing the ridge. Sheridan reputedly yelled, "As soon as you get your wind, men, we will go straight to the top of that hill," and his division immediately followed. Others reported that Sheridan's men and others went up the ridge without orders and that Sheridan himself went with them before he could receive an answer to his inquiry about whether to stop at the rifle pits. When the diminutive Sheridan raised a silver whiskey flask in salute to the Rebel gunners, he was just missed by an artillery shell and then retorted, "That's damn ungenerous! I shall take those guns for that!"[38]

Back at Orchard Knob, Grant and numerous generals watched in astonishment as Thomas's men scrambled up the ridge. Grant accusingly asked Thomas, "Who ordered those men up the ridge?" After Thomas denied knowledge, Grant turned to Thomas's deputy Granger, and asked, "Did you order them up, Granger?" He said he had not and explained,

"When those fellows get started, all hell can't stop them." Grant mumbled that someone would "catch it" if the attack failed.[39]

Thomas's men had three things going for them—each one a result of Confederate incompetence. First, with Longstreet's fifteen thousand men having been sent away and most Confederates defending their flanks, Bragg did not have the numbers to withstand such a massive assault at the center of his line. Cozzens stresses this blunder: "Had President Davis not suggested and Bragg not acceded to sending Longstreet off on his quixotic expedition toward Knoxville, Bragg could have disposed of his forces...so as to have such a reserve. Even allowing for the acrimony between Bragg and Longstreet, it is inconceivable that the two or three brigades needed to break the initial, tentative Federal foothold on the crest of Missionary Ridge would not have been on hand."[40]

Second, the Confederates had placed their artillery at the geologic, instead of the military, crest of the ridge, and most of their guns therefore were too far back from the slope to fire at the thousands of men desperately heading their way.

Third, the wasteful and foolish placement of a substantial number of Confederate troops in indefensible positions at the base and on the side of the ridge, from which they were compelled to retreat if they survived the initial assault, compounded the other two blunders.[41]

Hundreds and then thousands of Thomas's troops reached the summit, where they wreaked havoc on fleeing Confederates. Shouting "Chickamauga! Chickamauga!" they avenged the embarrassing defeat and retreat of the previous September. General Wood, General Granger, or both humorously addressed the Union troops: "Soldiers, you ought to be court-martialed, every man of you. I ordered you to take the rifle pits and you scaled the mountain."[42] "They did what they sensed had to be done, and coupled with the numerous Confederate blunders, the effort resulted in a decisive Union triumph."[43]

As the center of the Confederate line collapsed, troops from all sectors of that line abandoned their positions and fled toward Georgia. Bragg, their unpopular commander, rode among his troops in a vain attempt to stop the retreat. To his cries of "Here is your commander!" they responded, "Here's your mule!" Bragg had completely lost control over his men, many of whom were captured, and thousands threw away their weapons. They abandoned forty-one guns, one-third of their army's total, and seven thousand firearms. By seven o'clock that evening, Bragg had reached Chickamauga Station and telegraphed news of the debacle to Richmond. Despite Phil Sheridan's immediate pursuit and the later pursuit by Hooker, Cleburne saved the army with an effective rear-guard defense at strong defensive positions—especially near Ringgold, Georgia.[44]

The Battle of Chattanooga was not fought and won as Grant had planned. "Baldy" Smith provided an excellent summary of its planning and execution: "The original plan contemplated the turning of Bragg's right flank, which was not done. The secondary plan of Thomas looked toward following up the success of Hooker at Lookout Mountain by turning the left flank of Bragg [through Rossville Gap], and then an attack by Thomas along his entire front. The Rossville Gap was not carried in time to be of more than secondary importance in the battle. The assault on the center before either flank was turned was never seriously contemplated, and was made without plan, without orders ...."[45] The victory was the result of Grant's aggressive use of all his forces to keep the pressure on the enemy at all points.

Davis and Lee, of course, helped. In October, Lee had stymied a Confederate plan to reinforce Chattanooga with twenty-five thousand of Lee's troops from Virginia and ten thousand of Johnston's from Mississippi. That same month, Davis proposed sending more troops to Chattanooga from Lee's command—especially in light of the Union's transfer of two corps away from his theater. But Lee refused to provide any more than those previously sent under Longstreet. Davis chose not to override Lee again. Their shared miscalculations—belatedly sending Longstreet and then declining to send additional troops—showed they did not appreciate the importance of the Western Theater, where, according to many historians, the Civil War was decided.

Consistent with Lincoln's direction to "Remember Burnside," immediately after his Chattanooga victory Grant sent a relief expedition and supplies toward Knoxville. Before that expedition, six thousand of

Burnside's troops had avoided being trapped, beaten Longstreet's troops to Campbell's Station on the road to Knoxville, held them back in a daylong battle there on November 16, and retreated to Knoxville.[46] Later Burnside thwarted Longstreet's poorly executed assault on Knoxville, and the threat of the relief column drove Longstreet into the Tennessee mountains twenty miles east of Knoxville, where his troops spent a hard winter. The heart of eastern Tennessee was now in Union hands.[47] With both Chattanooga and Knoxville secure, Lincoln finally tendered Grant "and all under your command, my more than thanks—my profoundest gratitude—for the skill, courage, and perseverance with which you and they, over so great difficulties, have effected that important object."[48]

Having achieved his objectives in eastern Tennessee, Grant issued a congratulatory order to his troops on December 10:

> In a short time, you have recovered from the enemy the con-
> trol of the Tennessee River from Bridgeport to Knoxville. You
> dislodged him from Chattanooga Valley, wrested from his
> determined grasp the possession of Mission[ary] Ridge,
> repelled with heavy loss to him his repeated assaults upon
> Knoxville, forcing him to raise the siege there, driving him at
> all points, utterly routed and discomfited, beyond the limits
> of the state. By your noble heroism and determined courage,
> you have most effectually defeated the plans of the enemy for
> regaining possession of the states of Kentucky and Tennessee.
> You have secured positions from which no rebellious power
> can drive or dislodge you.[49]

In Georgia, a retreating Rebel officer observed, "Captain, this is the death knell of the Confederacy. If we cannot cope with those fellows with the advantages we had on this line, there is not a line between here and the Atlantic Ocean where we can stop them." His captain responded, "Hush, Lieutenant. That is treason you are talking."[50]

More evidence of the despondency Grant's successes at Chattanooga had induced among the Confederate troops is found in a letter that a surgeon in the Army of Tennessee, John T. Farris, wrote from winter quarters at Dalton, Georgia, on the day after Christmas 1863:

> [O]ur cause is lost, certain, and I would just now say that I do not know but it will be as well. I am of the opinion that, should we gain independence, that we would have a totering [sic] of aristocrat government, and many are of this opinion. From what I can learn, this whole army was yesterday and night before last in the same condition as our Brigade. All drunk, and shame forever. I also understand that one Major and four privates were killed dead by accident shots of drunken rowdys. God knows, you can have no idea of what took place yesterday last night and the night before.... I am troubled at the way everyting [sic] is going. If I had known at the beginning of the war what I now know, I today would have been in Canida [sic] making an honest living. God knows I wish I was there now.[51]

That Confederate despair reached all the way to Richmond, where President Davis reluctantly accepted the resignation of his friend Bragg as commander of the Army of Tennessee and even more reluctantly replaced him with their common adversary, Joseph Johnston.[52]

James McDonough spells out what might have happened but for the errors of Davis, Lee, and Bragg: "The Federal army might have been destroyed at Chickamauga, or starved into surrender at Chattanooga, or flanked out of Chattanooga and forced either to retreat or to fight under undesirable circumstances."[53] To recap, those fatal Confederate blunders were:

1. Delaying the transfer of Longstreet and his troops from Virginia to Chickamauga;
2. Failing to pursue and attack the fleeing Union army immediately after Chickamauga;
3. Failing to seal off Chattanooga from resupply and reinforcement;

4. Failing to attack the demoralized and weakened Union army in Chattanooga before it was resupplied and reinforced;

5. Leaving Bragg in command of an army many of whose commanders and soldiers hated and disrespected him;

6. Sending Longstreet and his troops away from Chattanooga as Union forces were increasing to almost eighty thousand; and

7. Placing thousands of troops in vulnerable rifle pits at the base and on the side of Missionary Ridge.

These blunders, Allan Nevins explains, were catastrophic because "[i]t had been highly important for the Union army to take and hold Chattanooga.... Had it lost its grip upon the city and been forced back toward Nashville, a heavy depression would have settled upon the Northwest. Now a sense of elation pervaded the great area from Ohio to Kansas."[54] Instead depression fell on the South. According to Bruce Catton, "the Confederacy had passed the last of the great might-have-beens of the war. Its supreme attempt to restore the lost balance had failed."[55]

Peter Cozzens paints a dreary picture: "That they had lost not only a battle but the war in the West was evident to most of the stunned Southern soldiers who shuffled along the trails winding away from the battlefield on the night of 25 November."[56] A series of presidential and command blunders had put them on the road to final defeat.

7

MOBILE, ALABAMA

ABRAHAM LINCOLN AND HENRY HALLECK FAIL TO ATTACK OR CAPTURE MOBILE IN 1863 OR EARLY 1864

WHO BLUNDERED?

U.S. President Abraham Lincoln and
Union Major General Henry W. Halleck

HOW?

They rejected General Ulysses S. Grant's recommendations
in 1863 and 1864 to seize Mobile.

CONSEQUENCES?

Mobile remained open for blockade runners for an extra year
and was not utilized to attack the Confederacy's soft underbelly
in those years.

After his victory at Vicksburg in mid-1863 and again during the winter of 1863–1864, Ulysses S. Grant urged a campaign against Mobile, Alabama, the soft underbelly of the Confederacy and its last major port still open on the Gulf of Mexico.[1] Capturing Mobile at either time would have cut off a flow of imported goods and destroyed the city's manufacturing capability. A massive attack there would have enabled Union forces to invade Georgia earlier and more effectively than they eventually did. Moving into Alabama would have had even broader ramifications because by mid-1863 Richmond and Lee's nearby army were obtaining most of their food from Alabama and Georgia.[2]

On July 12, 1863, only eight days after the Confederates' surrender to Grant at Vicksburg, Sherman proposed a Mobile campaign to Grant. He telegraphed, "Mobile should be attacked…from the direction of New Orleans, and when it is taken we can move on to Selma [a Confederate industrial stronghold in Alabama]."[3] Even the less-than-stalwart Major General Nathaniel Banks realized Mobile's importance at about the same time. On July 18, he wrote to Grant, "The Corps you propose to send me [for Texas coastal operations] will be of infinite assistance. It is my belief that [Joseph] Johnston when defeated by you [in central Mississippi], as I am confident he will be, will fall back upon Mobile—Such is also the expectation of the Rebels. The capture of Mobile, is of importance, second only in the history of the war, to the opening of the Mississippi. I hope that you will be able to follow him. I can aid you somewhat by land & sea, if that shall be your destination—Mobile is the last stronghold in the west and southwest No pains shd. be spared to effects its reduction."[4]

On the same day that Banks wrote, Grant first recommended a Mobile campaign to General in Chief Halleck: "It seems to me now that Mobile should be captured, the Expedition starting from some point on lake Ponchetrain [sic]."[5] He clearly saw Mobile as the logical next target for his large Army of the Tennessee. Halleck, however, definitively rejected Grant's proposal only four days later, preferring other uses for Grant's troops: "Before attempting Mobile, I think it will be best to clean up a little." Specifically, he wanted Johnston defeated in Mississippi,

Confederate troops cleared out of the Trans-Mississippi near the Arkansas River, Vicksburg and Port Hudson remodeled to accommodate small garrisons, and Banks assisted in cleaning out western Louisiana. Halleck concluded, "When these things are accomplished, there will be a large available force to operate either on Mobile or Texas. The navy is not ready for co-operation."[6] As Grant later complained in his *Memoirs*, Halleck was repeating the error he made after Corinth, breaking up Grant's army and sending it where it "would do the least good."[7]

Grant, whose dominant trait was persistence, wasted no time in reiterating his recommendation, bringing it up in a long letter to Halleck two days later: "It seems to me that Mobile is the point deserving the most immediate attention. It could not be taken from here [Vicksburg] at this season of the year. The country through which an army would have to pass is poor and water scares [sic]. The only present route it seems to me would be from some point on Lake Ponchertrain [sic]. I have not studied this matter however it being out of my Department."[8] On August 1, the determined Grant, referring to a Confederate withdrawal in Louisiana, tried to allay Halleck's concerns about demands on the navy: "Mobile can be taken from the Gulf department, with only one or two gunboats to protect the debarkation. I can send the necessary force, with your leave—I would like to visit New Orleans, particularly if the movement against Mobile is authorized."[9]

While Halleck was concerned about "cleaning-up" operations, Grant was trying to focus the general in chief's attention on the inviting target of Mobile, even though that city would not be in Grant's official purview until a few months later. Grant even conferred with Banks on August 1 about plans for a Mobile expedition, and in early August he received a spy report on Confederate fortifications at Mobile.[10]

But Halleck, and apparently Lincoln, had other plans. As early as July 24, Halleck was telling Banks to prepare for a Texas venture: "[Y]our next operations must depend very much upon the condition of affairs. Texas and Mobile will present themselves to your attention. The navy are very anxious for an attack upon the latter place, but I think Texas the most important.... While your army is engaged in cleaning out Southwestern Louisiana, every preparation should be made for an expedition into Texas." He said that Grant would probably be able to send him "considerable reinforcements."[11]

On July 30, Halleck ordered Grant to transfer a corps of ten to twelve thousand men to Banks. Their role was clarified by an order Halleck sent to Grant on August 6 for conveyance to Banks: "There are important reasons why our flag should be restored in some point of Texas with the least possible delay. Do this by land, at Galveston, at Indianola, or at any other point you may deem preferable. If by sea Admiral Farragut will cooperate. There are reasons why the movement should be as prompt as possible."[12] It was becoming clear that a decision had been made in Washington to establish a Union presence in Texas and to defer any movement on Mobile. On August 3, Halleck told Grant, "It will be well to keep up the impression in your army that Mobile will be the next point of attack,"[13] making it clear that any plan to attack Mobile would be a mere bluff.

Giving up on Halleck, Grant proposed a Mobile campaign to Assistant Secretary of War Charles A. Dana, who had become a good friend, writing to him on August 5, "I am very anxious to take Mobile while I think it can be done with comparative ease. But this would have to be done from Pascagoula [Mississippi], or even a point further along on the coast, and through Bank's Dept. [of the Gulf]. He has not the troops to do it. I am sending one army corps, Ord's, to Natchez so that if authorized they can be sent under Banks's direction on this enterprise."[14] Despite his considerable influence, Dana did not change Washington's opposition to a Mobile campaign.

It soon became evident that the decision was actually President Lincoln's. He explained to Banks, "Recent events in Mexico, I think, render early action in Texas more important than ever."[15] On August 9, Lincoln explained his rationale to Grant: "I see by a despatch of yours that you incline quite strongly toward an expedition against Mobile. This would appear tempting to me also, were it not that in view of recent events in Mexico, I am greatly impressed with the importance of re-establishing the national authority in Western Texas as soon as possible."[16] The president added a curious note—"I am not making an order, however. That I leave, for the present at least, to the General-in-Chief."[17] It is doubtful that Lincoln was leaving this decision up to Halleck, but he appears to have been trying to escape full responsibility for the decision against a Mobile campaign. Concerned about France's installation of the puppet dictator Maximilian in Mexico, he wanted a movement toward or into Texas to discourage a Franco-Mexican campaign in that direction.[18]

Grant was as deferential as ever to the president. From Cairo, Illinois, on August 23, he responded: "After the fall of Vicksburg, I did incline very much to an immediate move on Mobile. I believed that the place could be taken with but little effort, and with the rivers debouching there, in our possession, we would have such a base to operate from on the very center of the Confederacy as would make them abandon entirely the states bound West by the Miss. I see however the importance of a movement into Texas just at this time."[19]

Two decades later, in his *Memoirs*, which were generally hostile to Halleck, Grant downplayed Lincoln's role in this decision:

> I suggested to the General-in-chief the idea of a campaign against Mobile, starting from Lake Pontchartrain. Halleck preferred another course. The possession of the trans-Mississippi by the Union forces seemed to possess more importance in his mind than almost any campaign east of the Mississippi. I am well aware that the President was very anxious to have a foothold in Texas, to stop the clamor of some of the foreign governments which seemed to be seeking a pretext to interfere in the war.... This, however, could have been easily done without wasting troops in western Louisiana and eastern Texas, by sending a garrison at once to Brownsville on the Rio Grande.
>
> Halleck disapproved of my proposition to go against Mobile.... It would have been an easy thing to capture Mobile at the time I proposed to go there. Having that as a base of operations, troops could have been thrown into the interior

to operate against General Bragg's [Army of Tennessee]. This would necessarily have compelled Bragg to detach in order to meet this fire in his rear. If he had not done this the troops from Mobile could have inflicted inestimable damage upon much of the country from which his army and Lee's were yet receiving their supplies. I was so much impressed with this idea that I renewed my request letter late in July and again about the First of August, and proposed sending all the troops necessary, asking only the assistance of the navy to protect the debarkation of troops at or near Mobile.[20]

Whether the decision was that of Lincoln, Halleck, or both, the fact is that Grant's recommendation of a movement against Mobile soon after his brilliant Vicksburg Campaign was rejected in Washington. This was a serious blunder. Murray and Hsieh write, "Whatever the consequences of the French intervention in Mexico, it made little sense to put Grant on the shelf.... Had Washington followed Grant's advice to take Mobile after Vicksburg, the war might well have ended in 1864, with the Confederate military position collapsing in its crucial interior, whatever tactical successes Lee might score in Virginia." They add, "[Halleck's] contemptuous dismissal, a dismissal buttressed by Lincoln and Stanton, of Grant's proposal for a move against Mobile after Vicksburg's surrender...prevented a move that would have forced the Confederates to divide their attention between southern Alabama and Rosecrans's move against Chattanooga."[21]

Not surprisingly, the incompetent Banks's foray into Texas produced little. His attempts to land troops at Sabine Pass, near the Louisiana border, on September 8 were repelled by a small Confederate artillery battery, the Davis Guard of the First Texas Heavy Artillery, in one of the war's more farcical engagements. Two of the four Union gunboats trying to clear the way for a five-thousand-man landing force were hit, disabled, and surrendered. Fearing phantom Rebel reinforcements, the Union fleet retreated—having suffered three hundred eighty casualties to the Confederates' none![22]

Banks's one success was occupying the Gulf coast north from Brownsville to Matagorda and the Rio Grande northwest to Laredo during the fall and winter. On November 2, six thousand Union troops took over Brazos Santiago on the Gulf, twenty-four miles from Brownsville, an occupation that interfered with Confederate blockade running in South Texas for a few months. Confederates recovered the Rio Grande Valley in March 1864 and Brownsville itself the following July. Thereafter, they resumed their cross-border trading of valuable cotton for sorely needed medicines and munitions that had been exported from Europe to Mexico.[23]

All in all, Banks spent the better part of a year obtaining skimpy results on the fringes of the Confederacy, while Mobile and most of Alabama, at its heart, went unmolested. Lincoln and Halleck mistakenly had rejected Grant's strategic recommendation for a much more vital mission.

Meanwhile, from September 18 through 20 in the Battle of Chickamauga in northern Georgia, Rosecrans's Army of the Cumberland was attacked by Bragg's Army of Tennessee belatedly augmented by some of James Longstreet's corps from Virginia. Although the attackers took more casualties, they forced Rosecrans to retreat to Chattanooga and semi-encircled his army while controlling the high ground south and east of the town.[24] Rosecrans was trapped, and the call went out for help.

Actually, Rosecrans had realized a few days earlier that he had overextended his army into Georgia and that reinforcements likely would be needed. As a result, Halleck called upon Grant to send troops to Rosecrans's aid.[25] On September 22, from Vicksburg, Grant advised Halleck that he was sending two divisions to Rosecrans and that he would therefore be unable to provide Banks with an additional division he had requested.[26] Sherman, who was losing some troops in the shuffle, advised Grant, through Grant's chief of staff, John Rawlins, of his own thoughts on the matter: "The easiest way to relieve pressure on Rosecrans would be for that Texas expedition to be directed on Mobile & all our available forces…with the new orleans force. Or in other words leave the trans Mississippi alone…& using the interior to attack the line of the Alabama destroying in passing the Mobile & Ohio Road. This would force Joe

Johnston to make very heavy detachments from Bragg[.] I doubt if our reinforcements to Rosecrans can reach him in time to do good...."[27] It is unclear whether Grant had advised Sherman of Lincoln's focus on Texas for international diplomatic reasons.

Perhaps not. Grant himself was not letting go of the issue. On September 25, less than a month after telling Lincoln he understood his concerns about Mexico and Texas, Grant advised a member of Halleck's staff that a Mobile campaign would remove the pressure on Rosecrans: "I regret not having a force now to move against Mobile with. I am confident that Mobile could now be taken with a comparatively small force. At least a demonstration in that direction would either result in the abandonment of the city or force the enemy to weaken Braggs army to hold it."[28]

Grant persisted in a letter to Halleck of September 30, which closed, "I regret that I have not got a movable force with which to attack Mobile, or the river above. As I am situated however I must be content with guarding territory already taken from the enemy. I do not say this complainingly but simply regret that advantage cannot be taken of so fine an opportunity of dealing the enemy a heavy blow."[29]

Grant continued lobbying Halleck on October 5, when he signed a letter to him vouching for Union spy Louis Trager, who was to report personally to Halleck on his extremely thorough observations of Confederate military operations throughout the South. Grant referred to an October 1 letter from Major General Stephen A. Hurlbut to Halleck forwarding Trager's written report. That report, which included in-depth information about Mobile's fortifications and guns, concluded with this insight: "I spoke with many men in Mobile who are in official employment; they told me the place could be taken by land, and the sign of it is that they have fortified Chickasaw Bluff on the Alabama River, 25 miles by water and 10 miles by land from Selma, Ala. They are thinking if Mobile is taken by land, the forts [defending Mobile Bay] will be starved out and our fleet could go up the Alabama River to Montgomery...."[30] Halleck therefore had a great deal of information about the feasibility and usefulness of taking Mobile. But events at Chattanooga would foreclose such a campaign for the time being.

General Henry W. Halleck. *Courtesy of the Library of Congress*

Responding to Grant's September 30 letter, Halleck wrote obliquely on October 11 that a decision had been made in Washington to use Grant for something other than a Mobile campaign: "I regret equally with yourself that you could not have forces to move on Mobile; but there were certain reasons, which I cannot now explain which precluded such an attempt. You need not fear being left idle. The moment you are well enough to take the field you will have abundant occupation."[31]

Grant, who had been injured when his spooked horse fell on him in New Orleans, reported his recovery to Halleck and soon received a major new assignment. Lincoln, Stanton, and Halleck sent Grant to Chattanooga to rescue Rosecrans's army. Rosecrans's personal fate was left in Grant's hands. Assuming command of the Military Division of the West, which included three armies, and relieving Rosecrans of command, Grant traveled to Chattanooga, where he saved the Union army with a victory that forced Bragg's army back into northern Georgia. With his victory at Chattanooga on November 25, Grant once again became a national hero.[32]

The Union lost the Southern winter campaign season for advancing on the Confederates because Halleck continued to deny Grant's renewed recommendation to attack Mobile and then move on to Montgomery and Atlanta.[33] By late 1863, after his successes at Vicksburg and Chattanooga, Grant took a greater interest in a national strategy that would finally end the war. Bruce Catton explains, "[Grant] had at last reached the point where he could see that final triumph for the Union depended on crowding a beaten foe without respite, permitting no breathing spell in which the weaker antagonist could regain his balance and repair damages—using the superior power of the North, in short, to apply unrelenting pressure of a sort the Confederacy had not the resources to resist."[34]

So Grant looked again toward Mobile. He persuaded Charles Dana of the desirability of a Mobile campaign, and on November 29, after the crushing victory at Missionary Ridge only hours before, Dana wrote to Stanton from Chattanooga about Grant's plans for a winter campaign. He reported that Grant wanted to use thirty-five thousand "surplus" troops from his armies for "an offensive campaign against Mobile and the interior of Alabama." Grant would move from New Orleans or Pascagoula Bay. Dana outlined the proposal and endorsed it:

> Investing Mobile, [Grant] will leave a sufficient force to hold his lines and keep the garrison imprisoned without any unnecessary fighting, while with the mass of his army he operates in the interior against Montgomery, Selma, or whatsoever

point invites attention. He has asked me to lay this plan before you, and to ask for it the approbation of the Government. He will himself write to General Halleck on the subject, and perhaps also to yourself. I earnestly hope that you will agree to his design, and as soon as may be give your assent to its execution. A winter campaign may be made there with little if any difficulty. I can see nothing to condemn, but everything to approve, in the scheme.[35]

On December 1, Grant shared his plans for such an offensive with his friend and subordinate Major General James B. McPherson. Although Grant believed that Washington (Halleck?) expected no action until spring, he was eager to gather troops from specific scattered locations at Pascagoula, Mississippi, from which he would launch a Mobile campaign. He added, "To get ready for this it will take fully to the middle of January before we could leave New Orleans [for Pascagoula] if the authority is promptly granted. I write this merely to let you know what to expect."[36]

On December 7, a week after encouraging Dana to soften up Stanton, Grant followed military protocol and wrote to Halleck recommending the Mobile campaign. First, he pointed out that a winter campaign would occupy otherwise idle troops, harass the enemy, interrupt their reorganization, and "go far towards breaking down the Rebellion before Spring." Second, Grant argued that the imminent rainy season would prevent any large-scale Rebel return to Tennessee. Third, he laid out the specifics of his plan:

> ... I propose, with the concurrence of higher authority, to move by way of New Orleans and Pascagoula on Mobile. I would hope to secure that place, or its investment, by the last of January. Should the enemy make an obstinate resistence [sic] at Mobile I would fortify outside and leave a garrison sufficient to hold the garrison of the town and with the balance of the Army make a campaign into the interior

of Alabama, and, possibly, Georgia. The campaign of course would be suggested by the movements of the enemy.—It seems to me this move would secure the entire states of Alabama & Mississippi, and a part of Georgia or force Lee to abandon Virginia & North Carolina. Without his force the enemy have not got Army enough to resist the Army I can take.

Grant closed with an expression of hope for an early reply by telegraph.[37]

Clearly Grant was eager to put his plan into action as soon as possible. As Catton indicates, he was considering the national ramifications of such a campaign. Grant perceived that it could give the Union control of the remainder of the Deep South, putting pressure on the keystone state of Georgia and perhaps even affecting the Virginia (Eastern) Theater. Here was a national military strategy that could win the war, a strategy that would prove too daring for those responsible for national strategy at that time—Lincoln, Stanton, and Halleck.

Those Washington strategists were not so enthusiastic about Grant's plan. The first harbinger of rejection came in Halleck's response on December 17, in which he promised to bring the plan to the attention of Lincoln and of Stanton, who knew from Dana what Grant wanted to do. Halleck mentioned the need to drive the enemy from eastern Tennessee (near Knoxville), protect eastern and middle Tennessee from invasion, and repair and secure supply lines in those areas. He agreed that surplus troops could be used effectively in the wintry South but ominously added, "Genl Banks will need all the assistance you can give him just now on the lower Mississippi & in Louisiana...." Halleck said he would reply fully after learning the wishes of the War Department (Stanton) and the president.[38]

That fuller, and negative, answer came on December 21 in a wire from Halleck to Grant setting preconditions to any Mobile campaign: expelling Longstreet from eastern Tennessee and preventing his return, forcing the Rebels farther back into Georgia or preventing their return into Tennessee toward Chattanooga, and cleaning out western Tennessee. In classic Halleckian language, the general in chief added, "It is thought that the [Mobile campaign] should not be definitely determined upon till the [above missions] are accomplished, or their accomplishment made reasonably certain." Although these preconditions effectively precluded a Mobile campaign, the general in chief added forebodingly that if Grant's forces reached the lower Mississippi in a Mobile campaign, they might be needed in the West, in which case the Mobile campaign would be changed or delayed.[39]

Dana also wrote to Grant on December 17, reporting on his discussions with Lincoln, Stanton, and Halleck about Grant's proposal. Dana tried to be encouraging by explaining that the three decision-makers greatly favored the planned campaign itself. Stanton had even said, "If it succeed, Bragg's army become prisoners of war without our having the trouble of providing for them." Stanton certainly understood the plan's potential, but Dana explained that there were concerns and concluded that Halleck's worries about Longstreet's lingering in eastern Tennessee weighed against a Mobile campaign. When Dana had suggested that the best way to get Longstreet out of eastern Tennessee was to involve the Army of the Potomac, he was told that nothing could be expected under its current commander, Major General George Meade.[40] Since Lincoln's perennial concern—perhaps over-concern—about eastern Tennessee's Unionists was well known, it is likely that the president himself was vetoing Grant's plan until he was absolutely sure that Longstreet no longer posed a threat to them. Grant temporarily yielded to that decision in a letter to Halleck of December 23.[41]

Grant's smashing victory at Chattanooga in late November, in contrast with Meade's inaction in the East, resulted in pressure from Congress and the press for his elevation to lieutenant general and general in chief. Nevertheless, early 1864 saw no change in high-level Union military planning, and a Mobile campaign continued to be discouraged. On January 8, 1864, Halleck wrote a long letter to Grant explaining the decisions of the past year and forecasting more of the same for 1864. Banks's operations in Texas, he repeated, had been ordered for political and foreign policy, not military, reasons and therefore could not be judged on purely military grounds. Ominously, Halleck made it clear that Banks's operations against Texas would have to continue that winter. He concluded, "[I]t is to be considered whether it will not be better to direct our efforts for the present to the entire breaking up of the rebel forces west of the Mississippi river, rather than to divide them by also operating against Mobile and Alabama."[42] Whether he was speaking for Lincoln or himself, Halleck indicated that Banks's forces would not be available for a Mobile campaign and that perhaps Grant's own troops should be used west of the Mississippi rather than against Mobile.

Grant brushed off the suggestion that his troops be used west of the Mississippi by responding that the Red River and other Trans-Mississippi waterways were too low for navigation. He was therefore sending Sherman with twenty thousand troops toward Meridian, Mississippi, to destroy the railroads in the center of the state, which were key Confederate supply lines. Sherman, he wrote, "will then return unless the opportunity of going into Mobile with the force he has appears perfectly plain," slipping in a reiteration of his strategic preference. Painting a larger picture, Grant explained that he thought the next line he should secure was from Chattanooga to Atlanta to Montgomery to Mobile, arguing that a separate army under Sherman or McPherson could be trusted to undertake a Mobile-to-Montgomery campaign in conjunction with his own (later Sherman's) army moving from Chattanooga to Atlanta.[43] In early 1864, therefore, the persistent Grant was again proposing a two-pronged attack against Georgia with the added benefit of first destroying or neutralizing Rebel resources in Mississippi and Alabama.

Although Halleck did not respond directly to Grant's recommendation, events in northeastern Tennessee intervened. There was growing concern about, even fear of, a possible offensive by Longstreet, who had wintered in far northeastern Tennessee. Lincoln did not want to risk a Confederate re-conquest of eastern Tennessee, a region generally friendly to the Union and dear to the president's heart throughout the war.[44] Halleck explained to Grant, "As I have before remarked, the holding of that country is regarded by the President and Secretary of War of the very greatest importance, both in a political and a military point of view, and no effort must be spared to accomplish that effort." He therefore directed that maximum supplies be gathered at Chattanooga and lines of transportation reinforced from Nashville to Chattanooga to Knoxville.[45]

A disappointed Grant saw that Longstreet's threat foreclosed a full-scale Mobile campaign any time soon. As he wrote to George Thomas on January 19, 1864, "Owing to the presence of Longstreet in East Tennessee it will be impossible to attempt any movement from present positions whilst he remains." Nevertheless, he informed Thomas, Sherman would still be able to gather and use twenty thousand Mississippi Valley troops for his Meridian Campaign—"and if possible will throw troops as far east as Selma, or, if he finds Mobile so far unguarded as to make his force sufficient for the enterprise, will go there." Perhaps sensing that Sherman would not be able to move on to Mobile, Grant stressed to Thomas the desirability of an early spring campaign to secure the Chattanooga-to-Mobile line, as he had recommended to Halleck.[46]

Indeed, although the Meridian Campaign of February 3 to March 4 achieved much, it did not produce an opportunity to attack Mobile. Sherman's twenty thousand moved east from Jackson, Mississippi, drove Confederate forces away from Meridian, wreaked havoc on Meridian's rail and supply facilities, and destroyed 115 miles of railroad track in every direction from the town. But Brigadier General William Sooy Smith, who was supposed to augment Sherman's force with seven thousand cavalry from the West, started late and never showed up at Meridian. Without his cavalry arm, Sherman had no chance of launching a campaign against Mobile.

On March 4, 1864, Grant became Union general in chief and immediately named Sherman to replace him in Chattanooga. From there Sherman would embark on the Atlanta Campaign with his three armies. In March and April, Grant planned a comprehensive nationwide campaign to end the war before the presidential election in November. Banks's role was to capture Mobile and then coordinate with Sherman's Atlanta Campaign. Union forces were expected then to command the railroad running between Atlanta and Mobile—a critical Confederate supply and transportation route.[47] A Mobile campaign also would have engaged Confederate troops in that city and prevented them from moving to Georgia to reinforce Joseph Johnston in the Atlanta Campaign.

Lincoln, however, had already undermined Grant's plans and instead ordered Banks to undertake the Red River Campaign in northern Louisiana. His intention again was to send a message to France that its involvement in Mexico would not be tolerated and to Mexico that any reacquisition of former Mexican lands was out of the question. Union success would interrupt the flow of supplies through Shreveport, Louisiana, to Texas.

In mid-March, the new general in chief tried to salvage his plans for a Mobile campaign by expediting the newly begun Red River Campaign. A spring campaign involving all the Union armies required the swift completion of the Red River Campaign, he informed Banks. When Sherman had sent ten thousand of his men under Brigadier General A. J. Smith to assist Banks, he had stipulated that they should return to the Mississippi thirty days from when they entered the Red River. Grant urged that Shreveport be taken as soon as possible so they could meet Sherman's deadline.[48] If seizing Shreveport would take more than ten to fifteen days after that date, Sherman's troops were to be returned "even if it leads to the abandonment of the main object of your expedition." Explaining the rush, Grant informed Banks: "It may be part of the plan for the Spring campaign to move against Mobile. It certainly will be if troops enough can be obtained to make it without embarrassing other movements. In this case New Orleans will be the point of departure for such an expedition."[49] Grant and Sherman thus tried to encourage a short campaign by Banks that would not interfere with a Mobile campaign. But their efforts would be in vain.

As of March 25, Grant was still optimistic. He advised Halleck, "I sent a letter to Genl Banks before leaving Nashville directing him to finish his present expedition and assemble all his available force at New Orleans as soon as possible and prepare to receive orders for the taking of Mobile." He outlined plans to use Banks's army, eight thousand other troops from west of the Mississippi, and some of Sherman's, if needed, to ensure a successful campaign against Mobile.[50] Halleck let Grant know that Admiral Farragut thought he could take Mobile with his fleet and two or three ironclads if a land force could be sent to hold it.[51] That land force, of course, was the problem.

Meanwhile, Grant continued planning for a Mobile campaign. Hopeful but well aware of Banks's weaknesses, Grant told Halleck that when the Mobile campaign started, "it is important to have someone near Banks who can issue orders to him and see that they are obeyed."[52] On March 31, Grant gave Banks additional instructions on how and when to organize the Mobile mission. If he succeeded against Shreveport, he was to turn over the defense of the Red River to General Frederick Steele and the navy, leaving only four thousand troops in Texas and reducing his force on the Mississippi to ten thousand. Calculating that these steps would give Banks a force of thirty thousand—with another five thousand from Missouri—to operate against Mobile, Grant concluded that Banks should gather at least twenty-five thousand soldiers and then "lose no time in making a demonstration to be followed by an attack, upon Mobile." This movement, he explained, would be in conjunction with others, and he urged Banks that "you cannot now start too soon."[53]

Under Banks's incompetent "leadership," the Red River Campaign was a failure and almost a catastrophe. In Grant's words, "Banks was not ready in time for the part assigned to him" in the national scheme because he had not completed "the campaign which he been ordered upon before my appointment to the command of all the armies...."[54] Banks's Red River Campaign of March 14–May 20, 1864, was one of the great fiascoes of the entire war. The Confederates repelled his upriver assault and nearly captured his army and the accompanying navy vessels. Banks started late, operated ineptly, and began retreating after losing the Battle of Mansfield on April 8. He almost lost all of Rear Admiral David D. Porter's fleet. The most serious consequence was that the conquest of Mobile itself was delayed for about a year because Banks's army, Sherman's ten thousand troops, and another eight thousand Trans-Mississippi Union soldiers were used up or otherwise unavailable for a Mobile campaign. Steven Woodworth agrees that Banks's conduct of the Red River Campaign was a major blunder and adds: "One can hardly improve on Sherman's assessment of this wretched expedition as 'one d— blunder from beginning to end.' The troops it diverted might have shortened the war significantly if employed as Grant had intended."[55]

Grant came to realize he was not going to receive any timely, meaningful support from Banks. In mid-April, Grant told Banks, "I would much rather the Red River expedition had never been began [sic] than that you should be detained one day after the First of May in commencing your movement East of the Miss."[56] Major General David Hunter, sent to check on Banks, reported back on April 28 that the campaign was a disaster, adding, "Why this expedition was ordered I can not imagine. Gen. Banks assures me it was undertaken against his opinion and earnest protest. The result is certainly a sad one."[57] Four days later Hunter added, "General Banks has not certainly the confidence of his army."[58]

On the cusp of his Overland Campaign in Virginia in the spring of 1864, Grant advised Halleck that Banks was proposing to keep Smith's troops with him "to give him sufficient strength to operate against Mobile. It is now too late for Smith's force to return to be of any use in the Spring Campaign but I do think it is a waste of strength to trust Gen Banks with a large command or an important expedition." With that, Grant told Halleck, "I will have to leave the affairs West entirely with you."[59] For the time being, Grant washed his hands of the mess Lincoln and Halleck had caused by ignoring his persistent pleas for a campaign against Mobile.

Craig Symonds concludes, "On the Union side, the greatest strategic error [of the war] may have been the decision to allow Nathaniel P. Banks to carry out the Red River expedition, which led nowhere and nearly ended in disaster."[60] Banks's failure and the consequent elimination of a threat to Mobile and Montgomery enabled the Confederates to transfer Lieutenant General Leonidas Polk's fourteen-thousand-man corps from Alabama to Georgia, where it reinforced Johnston against Sherman.[61]

Because of Lincoln's decisions, with Halleck's characteristically feeble contribution, Mobile itself, the last rail connection between the Confederate East and West, was not occupied by Union troops until April 1865. Union troops did not occupy the railroad from Mobile to Atlanta, did not prevent the transfer of Confederate troops in Alabama to Johnston in Georgia, and did not move against the Rebel industrial center at Selma, Alabama, until 1865. Mobile's role as a blockade-running port, however, ended with Admiral Farragut's "Damn the torpedoes—full speed ahead" charge into Mobile Bay with his fleet on August 5, 1864, and the capture on August 23 of Fort Morgan, which controlled the bay's entrance.

Steven Newton theorizes, "Confederate resistance in Georgia and the Gulf would arguably have collapsed during the late spring or early summer of 1864 had there been another 25–30,000 men advancing on Mobile or through central Mississippi."[62] Lincoln's and Halleck's failures to approve Grant's repeated recommendations of a Mobile campaign constituted major blunders and missed strategic opportunities to shorten the war.

SNAKE CREEK GAP

WILLIAM T. SHERMAN MISSES THE CHANCE FOR A GAME-CHANGING VICTORY EARLY IN THE ATLANTA CAMPAIGN

WHO BLUNDERED?

Union Major General William T. Sherman

HOW?

He failed to exploit Snake Creek Gap near Resaca, Georgia, as a means for quickly using the bulk of his army to outflank and get in the rear of General Joseph Johnston's Army of Tennessee at the start of the 1864 Atlanta Campaign.

CONSEQUENCES?

This blunder extended Sherman's campaign and delayed the fall of Atlanta by two or more months, caused thousands of additional Union casualties, contributed to a crisis of morale in the summer of 1864, and delayed the end of the war by two or more months.

In early May 1864 William T. Sherman began his famous campaign toward Atlanta from Chattanooga, Tennessee, and northern Georgia. He commanded George Thomas's large Army of the Cumberland (sixty-one thousand men), James McPherson's medium-size Army of the Tennessee (twenty-four thousand), and John Schofield's small Army of the Ohio (thirteen thousand). Their Confederate opponents, General Joseph Johnston's Army of Tennessee (forty-seven thousand men) occupied a strong defensive position along Rocky Face Ridge about five miles northwest of Dalton, Georgia. The Rebels planned to delay Sherman's offensive and impose heavy casualties on any Union forces attempting to attack their strong position.[1]

About thirteen miles south of Dalton, athwart the strategically important Western & Atlantic (W&A) Railroad, close to the railroad bridge over the Oostanaula River, lay the small town of Resaca, Georgia. The destruction or capture of the railroad and bridges at Resaca would cut Johnston's line of supply and possible retreat and isolate his army north of that point. Resaca was vulnerable to a flanking attack from the west because it was only five miles east of the mouth of Snake Creek Gap, through which Union troops could surreptitiously approach the town.

In late February 1864, before Ulysses S. Grant had been promoted to general in chief, Thomas, in the course of making some minor attacks and probing the Confederate defenses, "discovered that Snake Creek Gap south of Dalton lay unguarded and offered a hidden way to Johnston's rear," as the historian Benson Bobrick notes. "This was a discovery of vast importance, and, if properly exploited, promised to save thousands of lives in a swift, smart campaign."[2]

A surprise flanking attack would bypass Johnston's strong defensive position and possibly trap his army well north of Atlanta in the earliest stages of Sherman's Atlanta Campaign. It would at least cause Johnston to abandon his strong defensive position. Thomas proposed a flanking attack in a wire to Grant on February 28.[3]

Thomas later testified before the Joint Committee on Conduct of the War that he had proposed "a strong demonstration against Buzzard's

Roost [on the northern end of Rocky Face Ridge], attracting Johnston's whole attention to that point," while throwing "the main body of my infantry and cavalry through Snake Creek Gap upon his communications, which I had ascertained from scouts he had up to that time neglected to observe or guard." Thomas already had asked for return to him of Major General Gordon Granger's troops and his cavalry from eastern Tennessee so he could execute the maneuver.[4]

With such a move, Thomas's army most likely would have seized the railroad and wagon bridges at Resaca and cut Johnston's line of communication and supply. In his study of Sherman's cavalry in the Atlanta Campaign, David Evans comments, "Faced with the loss of this railroad, Johnston would have no choice but to quit Rocky Face and retreat southward, only to find Thomas's men planted squarely across his front and McPherson and Schofield closing in from behind."[5]

After Grant's promotion and Sherman's arrival in Chattanooga in late March to take command of the Union armies and the Atlanta Campaign, Thomas renewed his proposal. He recommended to Sherman that a large force—specifically, Thomas's own Army of the Cumberland—be sent around the left (west) flank of Johnston to sneak through Snake Creek Gap, capture Resaca, and get behind Johnston. In Thomas's own words to the Joint Committee:

> I proposed to General Sherman that if he would use McPherson's and Schofield's armies to demonstrate on the enemy's position at Dalton...I would throw my whole force through Snake Creek Gap, which I knew to be unguarded, fall upon the enemy's communications between Dalton and Resaca, thereby turning his position completely; and force him either to retreat toward the east...or attack me, in which latter event I felt confident that my army was sufficiently strong to beat him.... General Sherman objected to this plan for the reason that he desired my army to form the reserve of the united armies, and to serve as a rallying point for the two wings.[6]

John Scales concludes, "Modern commentators believe that if Thomas—who originally suggested Snake Creek Gap to [Grant and then] Sherman—had made this attack with his entire Army of the Cumberland, it would have succeeded."[7]

When Sherman finally decided that he liked the idea of using Snake Creek Gap to get around and behind Johnston's army, he declined to give the assignment to Thomas and his sixty-one-thousand-man Army of the Cumberland. Instead, Sherman selected McPherson and the much smaller twenty-four-thousand-man Army of the Tennessee, which until recently Sherman had commanded. James McDonough asserts that Sherman liked Thomas's idea but believed that Thomas's army was "too large and unwieldy for the assignment." McDonough also points out that "[f]or whatever reason," Sherman did not give Thomas any credit for the Snake Creek Gap proposal.[8]

Sherman justified his decision, writes Brian Steel Wills, on the grounds that "[t]he Army of the Tennessee are better marchers than the Army of the Cumberland and I am going to send McPherson." The spurned Thomas remarked to an aide, "I saw the game was up." Wills concludes that Sherman's selection of his fellow Ohioan McPherson reflected a lack of trust in Thomas and the "symbiotic relationship" between Sherman and McPherson.[9]

In any event, the choice of McPherson meant that the surprise attack might not be carried out by a sufficiently large force and thus would fail. Thomas's cavalry alone numbered 3,800 troopers to McPherson's mere six hundred, an important figure because Johnston's only manpower advantage was in cavalry; he had seven thousand cavalrymen to Sherman's six thousand.[10]

Sherman was clearly unwilling to go all-out to flank and get in Johnston's rear even though he outnumbered the Confederates ninety-nine thousand to fifty-five thousand.[11] In fact, his initial plan was to send McPherson even farther south to cut Johnston's supply line at Rome, Georgia. In a letter to Grant from April 10, Sherman wrote that McPherson would have nine divisions of the Army of the Tennessee, and his total lack of cavalry would be corrected by sending, from Thomas's army,

Brigadier General Kenner Garrard's six-thousand-man division, which was far away and "mounting[,] equipping and preparing."[12] Snake Creek Gap and Resaca were not mentioned. Ultimately, McPherson would have only two of the nine envisioned divisions at Resaca and the promised cavalry would not arrive in time to help.

Sherman canceled the Rome plan when he belatedly realized that four of McPherson's divisions and his cavalry were not yet on scene. So, changing the target, Sherman sent the undermanned McPherson down the still unguarded Lafayette-Villanow-Snake Creek Gap route to approach Resaca from the northwest. He failed to provide sufficient cavalry support to McPherson and his mission, however. The commanding general arranged Thomas's and Schofield's armies in a long line from north to southwest of Dalton. Sherman also placed one division of cavalry on each end of this line, leaving no independent cavalry to be assigned to McPherson.[13]

Sherman's specific orders to McPherson of May 5 told him of Thomas's and Schofield's much shorter movements and then stated:

> As these are in progress I want you to move...to Villanow; then to Snake [Creek] Gap, secure it and from it make a bold attack on the enemy's flank or his railroad at any point between Tilton [north of Resaca] and Resaca. I am in hopes that Garrard's cavalry [on loan from Thomas] will be at Villanow as soon as you, for, you know, I have sent General Corse to meet him at Shellmound and conduct him across the mountain to La Fayette [sic] and to you. But, in any event, his movement will cover your right rear and enable you to leave all incumbrances either at Ship's Gap or Villanow, as you deem best. I hope the enemy will fight at Dalton, in which case he can have no force there that can interfere with you. But, should his policy be to fall back along the railroad, you will hit him in flank. Do not fail in that event to make the most of the opportunity by the most vigorous attack possible.... In either event you may be sure the forces north

of you will prevent his turning on you alone. In the event of hearing the sound of heavy battle about Dalton, the greater necessity for your rapid movement on the railroad. It once broken to an extent that would take them days to repair, you can withdraw to Snake [Creek] Gap and come to us or await the development according to your judgment or information you may receive....[14]

Johnston, concerned about where he was likely to be attacked, was dealt a blow by one of his own corps commanders, John Bell Hood, who was beginning a months-long campaign to undermine Johnston. That campaign would succeed by mid-July, when Johnston was relieved of command and Hood became the army commander. On May 4 Hood wrote to Confederate cavalry commander Joseph Wheeler asking him to ascertain the location of a particular Union division because, "I am anxious to move, but fear General J will abandon the idea." Thus, while Johnston desperately needed information on any Union movements beyond the hills to his left (west), Hood was contemplating a movement of his own and diverting the Confederate cavalry from their major scouting mission. The diversion flew in the face of Johnston's orders to Wheeler over the next three days to conduct reconnaissance on the Rebels' left flank. Wheeler never carried out the scouting missions ordered by Johnston. Robert Jenkins concludes that "Wheeler spent the balance of May 4–8 in front of Hood's position maintaining a close connection with the federals advancing on Tunnel Hill [near the northernmost extension of Johnston's army], doing precisely what Hood had asked for, rather than scouting the Federals to the west as Johnston had ordered."[15]

Although Hood and Wheeler undermined Johnston's reconnaissance efforts, Richard McMurry insists that Johnston himself must bear responsibility for their failure: "[Johnston] did not insist that his cavalry commander make better use of his horsemen, and he seems not to have had much interest in events on his left. As a result, he did not get the vital intelligence he needed." McMurry concludes that Johnston's "fixed conviction" that McPherson would move on Rome (southwest of Resaca)

Major General George H. Thomas. *Courtesy of the Library of Congress*

"blinded him to other possible meanings" of scouting reports about McPherson's movements to his west and southwest.[16]

Late on May 7, Thomas's Twentieth Corps commander, Major General Joseph Hooker, called Sherman's attention "to the importance of seizing and holding Snake Creek Gap, having no knowledge of his [Sherman's] intended movements."[17] Sherman's chief of staff, Brigadier General William D. Whipple, assured Hooker that "the Snake Creek Gap will or ought to be occupied to-morrow by McPherson's troops."[18]

So Hooker was belatedly made aware of the plan for McPherson to move into that gap, which was immediately south of Hooker's position. Sherman's failure to coordinate had serious consequences, contributing mightily to a shortage of cavalry at Snake Creek Gap.

On May 7–8, Thomas captured Tunnel Hill and its vital railroad tunnel northwest of Dalton, enabling Sherman to supply his armies by way of the W&A Railroad for the balance of his campaign. The Confederates' failure to destroy the tunnel, however difficult a task, is inexplicable—especially since they had so many months to do so. Sherman then moved south to Mill Creek Gap, west-northwest of Dalton, and Dug Gap, west-southwest of Dalton. Fighting at those gaps, especially the latter, was costly to Sherman (about four hundred casualties) but provided cover for McPherson's movement farther south toward Snake Creek Gap and Resaca. At Dug Gap, Rebel cavalry from Colonel J. Warren Grisby's Kentucky brigade and two regiments of Arkansas troops occupied a steep and virtually impregnable position. They held off the Union assault until two brigades of Confederate infantry under Major General Patrick Cleburne arrived to end any hope of a Union breakthrough. Grisby's cavalrymen were then ordered south to protect Resaca.[19]

During the diversionary fighting at Dug Gap, McPherson made his way toward the northwestern entrance to Snake Creek Gap. At 7:30 a.m. on May 7, Union cavalry commander Brigadier General Judson Kilpatrick arrived at the village of Villanow and announced that McPherson's army was marching in his direction.[20] By the evening of May 8, McPherson's troops had reached Villanow and camped a mere ten miles from Resaca. They were unopposed and unseen.

McPherson, however, faced a serious problem. Although Hooker to his immediate north had cavalry to use for reconnaissance,[21] McPherson had virtually none. The single cavalry division assigned to his army, under Garrard's command, had not arrived. In fact, it lagged so far behind, that during the night Sherman ordered cavalry commander Kilpatrick to join McPherson with one of his brigades. The order, however, was way too late. McPherson was left with only his puny cavalry escort, the Ninth Illinois Mounted Infantry, for support as he made his final move on Resaca. This oversight attests to the inadequacy of the forces Sherman had tardily assigned to this critical mission and to his failure to coordinate the McPherson gambit with Hooker, the adjoining army commander.[22]

Nevertheless, the diversionary Union attacks to the east, northeast, and then north of McPherson's moving army, combined with Johnston's failure to realize the threat McPherson posed to Resaca and Johnston's army, allowed McPherson's army to reach Snake Creek Gap by the evening of May 8. His leading units, the Ninth Illinois Mounted Infantry and the Thirty-ninth Iowa Infantry, had found the gap, in McMurry's words, "unoccupied, unguarded, unobstructed, and unobserved. McPherson had completed one of the great strategic marches of the war. In retrospect, we can see that, in all likelihood, his seizure of the gap determined the outcome of the campaign."[23]

Awaiting him at Resaca was Colonel James Nisbet's Sixty-sixth Georgia, which had arrived on May 1 and been assigned to guard the Oostanaula River bridge. Expecting little action, Nisbet's deputy commented, "Well, Nisbet, what would our leader, Stonewall [Jackson], think of us? Going eighteen miles to the rear to guard a bridge, at the beginning of a campaign? Let's beat our swords into Ploughshares and pruning hooks and make a garden; the opportunity seem[s] to be favorable." The soldiers had a dilapidated battery in an old fort by the bridge for defense, and a company of cavalry was scouting the area roads.[24]

On May 7 they had been augmented by two thousand men of James Cantey's brigade, the vanguard of a large contingent of reinforcements under Lieutenant General Leonidas Polk moving from Alabama to Johnston in Georgia. Demonstrating his ignorance of McPherson's threat, Johnston on the morning of May 8 ordered Cantey to move from Resaca to Dalton. By 12:10 Johnston had countermanded that order and directed Cantey to be ready to move by rail to Dalton while watching the approaches to his west. Finally, on the evening of May 8, Grigsby's cavalry brigade arrived from its Dug Gap engagement—not expecting to engage Union infantry once again.[25]

But Nisbet had previously learned from a Negro girl brought in by the roving cavalry that Yankee soldiers had taken her horse along the Snake Creek Gap Road. He had passed this information on to Johnston, who, because of Wheeler's failure to carry out his mission and Johnston's belief that any threat was to Rome, was unaware of the threat to his rear at Resaca. When Grigsby arrived at Resaca, he was immediately ordered toward the mouth of Snake Creek Gap. Early the next morning, May 9, Grigsby's advancing men encountered the leading edge of McPherson's army, briefly engaged them in a firefight, and then retreated. As Jenkins writes, "The way to Resaca was open, but McPherson's column had been discovered."[26]

McPherson had approached Resaca with fewer than ten thousand troops and his cavalry escort. His manpower represented a small portion of Sherman's ninety-nine-thousand-man army. As his men proceeded from the mouth of Snake Creek Gap toward Resaca on the morning of May 9, McPherson had no idea of the Confederates' strength. Grenville Dodge's Sixteenth Corps took the lead, and John "Black Jack" Logan's Fifteenth Corps followed. At 12:30 p.m., about five miles from Resaca, McPherson sent a dispatch advising Sherman that Dodge's forward troops "must be within" two miles of the town. He said he could not determine if there was a large force of infantry at Resaca but would know soon. He added that the terrain and foliage prevented signals communications with Hooker. McPherson's most critical statement was not optimistic: "I propose to cut the railroad, if possible, and then fall back and take a strong position near the gorge on this [side] of the mountain and await your orders."[27]

When the commanding general received that dispatch, he interpreted it over-optimistically and exalted, "I've got Joe Johnston dead."[28] Sherman later said he immediately renewed his orders to army commanders Thomas and Schofield to be prepared to pursue "what I expected to be a broken and disordered army, forced to retreat by roads to the east of Resaca, which were known to be very rough and impracticable."[29] But Sherman's hopes would soon be quashed—primarily because he had failed to provide McPherson with sorely needed cavalry.

Around midday on May 9, 4,800 of Dodge's men approached within two miles of Resaca before they came under fire from Grigsby's cavalry, which then retreated. As the afternoon proceeded, the Union troops occupied a bald hill, brought up artillery, and fired into the town—now only a mile away. Blocking the Union advance was a stronger line manned by the collection of four thousand rebels, including a few Georgia Military Institute cadets. McPherson, however, had no idea of their strength.[30]

About 2,400 Union troops, despite a volley from the cadets, advanced on the second Confederate line of defense, which was a mere half-mile from Resaca. McMurry describes the situation: "McPherson, with the lead units, saw to his front the Rebel fortifications at Resaca and to his left (north) good roads running south from Dalton. Isolated from other Federal units, not knowing how many Secessionists were at Resaca...and fearing that Johnston might have sent troops from Dalton south to strike the left flank of his column, McPherson decided that the risk was too great. He would preserve what he had gained." So he called off the attack and ordered a retreat back to Snake Creek Gap. At the gap, he fortified his position and then notified Sherman of his withdrawal.[31] Steven Newton writes that McPherson did so because he was "paralyzed" by Resaca's defense, Rebel cavalry's awareness of his presence, and the threat that Johnston might overwhelm his exposed command.[32] In his message to Sherman, McPherson stressed his continuing lack of cavalry and reported that his cavalry commander Garrard wanted to stay back at Lafayette because of fatigued horses and a shortage of fodder.[33]

Sherman sent a message to Hooker on the *evening* of May 9 directing him to send a division that night "through Snake Creek Gap to its southern terminus, with orders to watch well all avenues of approach from the direction of Dalton. This will leave McPherson full freedom for his operations without danger to his rear."[34] Not only was this order about two days too late and sent *after* McPherson's Resaca attack, but it failed to address McPherson's lack of *cavalry*. Sherman wrote he was ordering Kilpatrick's cavalry "to operate between Villanow and Snake Creek Gap until Garrard is up, which surely will be during the day [May 10]."[35] A similar order went to Kilpatrick.[36] By the evening of May 9,

Kilpatrick reported that McPherson's wagons had arrived at Snake Creek Gap and were being guarded by infantry and artillery (not cavalry). He also reported on the non-arrival of Garrard and his own willingness to attack: "General Garrard is still at La Fayette [sic]. My command is in good condition, fully supplied with rations, forage, and ammunition, and is ready and anxious for an order to strike the enemy."[37] Sherman seems to have fixated on Garrard, and even after McPherson's attack he had not ordered other on-scene cavalry to proceed into and through Snake Creek Gap in aid of McPherson.

On the morning of May 10, Sherman prematurely reported to General in Chief Halleck that he believed McPherson had destroyed Resaca.[38] But that evening he informed Halleck that McPherson "reached Resaca, but found the place strongly fortified and guarded, and did not break the road. According to his instructions, he drew back to the debouches of the gorge, where he has a strong defensive position...."[39] McPherson made no further effort to cut the railroad on May 10 even though he had been re-provisioned, Kilpatrick's cavalry had arrived, another Union division had reached him, and he had twenty thousand troops at his disposal. He was convinced that Johnston's entire army was about to pounce on him.[40]

Sherman was disappointed that McPherson had not achieved complete success and realized that the now obvious threat to Johnston's rear would cause him to retreat from Dalton through Resaca. Johnston did retreat southward toward Resaca before his army could be trapped north of that town. By gaining a foothold in Snake Creek Gap, however, McPherson had provided a pathway for Sherman's entire army group to bypass Rocky Face Ridge and attack Johnston's flank as he retreated. So Sherman subsequently moved virtually his whole force through the gap, and the opposing sides engaged in battle at Resaca before Johnston safely retreated across the Oostanaula and continued his retreating campaign toward Atlanta. The Union opportunity to trap his army above Resaca had been missed.

The trap had been set but never sprung. The failed Union attempt to take Resaca and trap Johnston's army raises three questions: (1) Why did

Johnston present this golden opportunity to Sherman by leaving Snake Creek Gap undefended? (2) Did McPherson adequately carry out his assigned mission? (3) Does the ultimate blame for Union failure rest on Sherman's shoulders?

On the first question, Major General Patrick Cleburne wrote in his campaign report:

> How this gap, which opened upon our rear and line of communication, from which it was distant at Resaca only five miles, was neglected I cannot imagine. General [William] Mackall, Johnston's chief of staff, told me it was the result of a flagrant disobedience of orders, by whom he did not say. Certainly the commanding general never could have failed to appreciate its importance. Its loss exposed us in the outset of the campaign to a terrible danger, and on the left forced us to retreat from a position where, if he adhered to his attack, we might have detained the enemy for months....[41]

Any disobedience on the Confederate side, writes Jenkins, most likely came from Wheeler, who repeatedly failed to execute Johnston's orders to patrol an area in which he would have discovered McPherson's advance.[42] John Scales contends that Snake Creek Gap could have been defended by a small force and that Johnston bears responsibility for not doing so because he failed to perform proper reconnaissance earlier in the year or because his orders to Wheeler were too vague or not followed up.[43] Jenkins concludes that Johnston's failure to censure or replace Wheeler indicates that "Johnston simply failed to consider the gap as a threat regardless of the reason."[44]

Stephen Davis points out that Johnston's biographers agree with Cleburne's exculpatory remarks but that other historians, such as Edwin C. Bearss and Thomas L. Connelly, have faulted Johnston for ignoring the vulnerability of Snake Creek Gap.[45] After fixing part of McPherson's army at Lafayette on May 7, writes Davis, Johnston seemed to ignore McPherson's army or to assume that Polk's arriving troops would adequately protect Rome, which Johnston assumed would be McPherson's main target.[46]

In McMurry's view, Johnston was fortunate to have avoided "a calamitous defeat" after he had guessed wrong in two respects: placing and keeping too many troops in the Dalton area and fixating on the possible threat to Rome while overlooking the threat to Resaca. For example, Johnston had shifted to Dalton cavalry brigades that would have been useful to Cantey in discovering any threat to Resaca, particularly through Snake Creek Gap. Also, Johnston's off-and-on orders to Cantey on May 7 and 8 first to move his infantry from Resaca to Dalton and later to be prepared to move to Dalton by rail distracted Cantey's attention from the gap. In summary, writes McMurry,

> [Johnston] had left Snake Creek Gap completely open and his defenses at Resaca were suited for protecting the bridges there from a cavalry raid, not for holding off a major attack by a large force. The place to have defended Resaca from such a force as Sherman sent against it from the northwest was Snake Creek Gap. Johnston's failure to guard that passage was one of the great mistakes of the war.... Clearly, Johnston did not grasp the importance of the gap or understand the objective of Sherman's movements.[47]

The second and third questions boil down to placing primary responsibility on McPherson or Sherman for the Federals' failure to trap Johnston. Cleburne, somewhat ambiguously, blamed McPherson: "As it was, if McPherson had hotly pressed his advantage, Sherman supporting him strongly with the bulk of his army, it is impossible to say what the enemy might not have achieved—more than probable a complete victory."[48] But did Sherman support him strongly with the bulk of his army? And, in any event, did McPherson do all his orders required?

In his often self-serving memoirs, Sherman succeeded in placing the blame, at least in many historians' minds, for the failure at Resaca on McPherson. Sherman wrote:

I had no intention to attack the [strong Confederate position northwest of Dalton] seriously in front, but depended on McPherson to capture and hold the railroad to its rear, which would force Johnston to detach largely against him, or rather, as I expected, to evacuate his position at Dalton altogether.****

McPherson had startled Johnston in his fancied security, but had not done the full measure of his work. He had in hand twenty-three thousand of the best men of the army, and could have walked into Resaca (then held only by a small brigade), or he could have placed his whole force astride the railroad above Resaca, and there have easily withstood the attack of all of Johnston's army, with the knowledge that Thomas and Schofield were on his heels. Had he done so, I am certain that Johnston would not have ventured to attack him in position, but would have retreated eastward by Spring Place, and we should have captured half his army and all his artillery and wagons at the very beginning of the campaign. Such an opportunity does not occur twice in a single life, but at the critical moment McPherson seems to have been a little cautious.[49]

Examples abound of Sherman's influence on the placement of blame for this missed opportunity. For one, the *West Point Atlas of American Wars* concludes, "[McPherson] withdrew to the gap (a move sanctioned by his discretionary orders), feeling that he was not strong enough to cut the Confederate supply line—thus, through overcaution, abandoning an excellent opportunity to bring on the defeat of Johnston's army."[50]

Similarly, the *Oxford Atlas of American Military History* states, "McPherson attempted a turning movement through Snake Creek Gap that would have put his force in Johnston's rear, but he stopped too soon, allowing Johnston to evacuate his positions around Dalton on 12 May and pull back safely to Resaca the next day."[51] The same story is told in the *Civil War Battlefield Guide*: "McPherson neither seized Resaca, which was held by several Confederate brigades behind strong earthworks, nor managed to cut the railroad, missing, as Sherman later told him, the opportunity of his life."[52] Even the usually neutral *Generals in Blue* finds fault with McPherson: "[T]he affair at Snake Creek Gap, which might have dispersed Joseph E. Johnston's Confederates, came to nothing because of seemingly excessive caution by McPherson, and the handling of his troops thereafter was largely directed by Sherman himself."[53]

Even a Civil War dictionary blames McPherson: "McPherson began his move on May 7 while the two armies were engaged at Rocky Face Ridge. [On May 9, after pushing Grigsby's brigade aside, he] sent [troops ahead] to cut the vital railroad north of Resaca. At this critical moment, when it appeared success was at hand, McPherson became overly cautious. Surprised to learn that Confederate infantry were in Resaca, he was afraid of being attacked and cut off, and on May 10 withdrew into Snake Creek Gap and entrenched. The Confederates at Resaca actually were only James Cantey's brigade.... Sherman was very disappointed at McPherson's failure and remarked to his friend that he had lost the opportunity of a lifetime."[54]

John Scales, in one place,[55] comes down hard on McPherson, asserting that his failure to boldly execute his orders lost the opportunity for a "truly decisive battle" on terms that would have favored Sherman's army. He also mentions McPherson's "timidity."[56] James McDonough concurs: "The strike through Snake Creek Gap was McPherson's first significant assignment as an army commander.... Perhaps with greater experience, McPherson would have acted more aggressively, and Sherman's turning maneuver would have brought an unqualified triumph at the inception of the campaign.... The overly cautious action of McPherson, who graduated first in his West Point class, was not foreseeable, and Sherman should not be faulted for something no one could have prophesized."[57]

Other historical accounts seem to blame but then excuse McPherson. Mixing up some dates, David S. and Jeanne T. Heidler write in their *Encyclopedia of the American Civil War*, "The inherent cautiousness of McPherson can be observed in his slow advance against Johnston's Army of Tennessee at Dalton (8–9 May 1864 [sic]), allowing the

General William T. Sherman. *Courtesy of the Library of Congress*

Confederate army to escape. At Resaca (13–15 May [sic]), again
McPherson failed to entrap the Rebel army. In McPherson's defense, he
did not have the numbers to successfully carry out his assignment."[58]
Stephen Davis concludes, "McPherson had lost his nerve," but he cites
McPherson's explanation that he had too few cavalry to test the Rebel
flanks or break the railroad.[59]

Another school of thought holds that Sherman, not McPherson, was primarily responsible for the missed opportunity to trap Johnston's army at Resaca. Philip Secrist concludes, "In a very real sense, the escape of the Confederate army from the trap at Resaca was a major strategic defeat for Sherman."[60] Brian Wills reiterates Sherman's statement to McPherson, "Well, Mac, you have missed the great opportunity of your life," and then astutely adds, "Left unsaid was the notion that by relying on that general [instead of Thomas] Sherman might have missed his, too."[61]

Benson Bobrick emphatically finds Sherman culpable, pointing out that while Sherman included his own messages to McPherson in his memoirs, he stated that McPherson's "to me were mere notes in pencil, not retained." It appears that Sherman suppressed McPherson's communications to him but failed to destroy all copies of them. Bobrick writes, "[T]hey were found in the archives of the War Department, some proved to be of great length, and showed that Sherman, not McPherson, had been the one at fault. McPherson's instructions had not been to hold the railroad but to cut it and then withdraw to Snake Creek Gap. From there, he was to strike Johnston's army in retreat. Sherman thought that with his supply line cut Johnston would have to retreat, and that McPherson would be waiting for him as Thomas and Schofield pursued."[62] Since McPherson was killed within two months of the Resaca affair, Sherman apparently believed he could paint his own picture of the events without fear of rebuttal. But the discovery and contents of McPherson's surviving communications show that Sherman's description of them as "mere notes in pencil not retained" was false, casting doubt on Sherman's credibility.

Bobrick asserts that McPherson's communications (including his message of May 9 at 10:30 p.m.) show that Sherman, not McPherson, was at fault. McPherson was ordered to cut, not hold, the railroad in Johnston's rear. That is a key issue. In support of his position, Bobrick quotes part of Sherman's May 10 status report to Halleck: "General McPherson reached Resaca, but found the place strongly fortified and guarded.... According to his instructions, he drew back to the debouches of the gorge, where he has a strong defensive position, and guards the only pass into the valley of the Oostanaula available to us."[63] Tellingly perhaps, Sherman said nothing about McPherson's not accomplishing his assigned mission but instead stated that McPherson's drawing back into Snake Creek Gap was "[a]ccording to his instructions."

A little more than a month later Sherman was telling a different story. In a private letter of June 18 to his friend Grant, Sherman wrote:

> If our movemt has been slower than you calculated I can explain the reasons though I know you believe me too earnest, and impatient to be behind time. My first movemt against Johnston was really fine, and now I believe I would have disposed of him at one blow if McPherson had crushed Resacca, as he might have done, for then it was garrisonned only by a small Brigade, but Mc was a little over Cautious lest Johnston still at Dalton might move against him alone, but the truth was I got all of McPhersons army 23,000, eighteen miles to Johnstons rear before he knew they had left Huntsville. With that single exception McPherson has done very well.[64]

Sherman took all the credit and none of the blame for the well-conceived (by Thomas) but ultimately unsuccessful movement on Resaca.

Bobrick quotes at length, but incompletely, from an appendix to Sherman's memoirs describing Sherman's actions on May 9. This document, a letter of William Warner of Sherman's staff to Mrs. Sherman, tells how Sherman reacted so positively when he received McPherson's first communiqué of that day. Sherman took him outside, he writes, gestured vehemently, and said, "I have got Joe Johnston dead. This letter is from McPherson. At one o'clock today he was within one and a half mile of the railroad. He must be on it now. I want to go over and see Tom [George Thomas]." Warner describes Sherman meeting with Thomas to discuss Johnston's inevitable retreat, noting "that Thomas and Schofield must push him hard in the morning to crush him and to prevent his crushing McPherson."[65]

Warner continues:

> Late that night word came from McPherson that he had failed
> to seize the railroad, and had fallen back to the mouth of the
> gap and fortified.... All the members of the staff will remem-
> ber how disappointed and excited the general was on receipt
> of the news, and how cross he was the next day.... We all
> thought he might relieve McPherson of his command. I was
> present when General Sherman and McPherson first met after
> this.... His first remark was, "Well, Mac, you have missed
> the great opportunity of your life."[66]

Unfortunately, Bobrick omits some language from the original that
could be construed as more critical of McPherson. The full passage from
Warner's letter (with the text that Bobrick cuts in italics) reads:

> Late that night word came from McPherson that he had failed
> to seize the railroad, and had fallen back to the mouth of the
> gap and fortified. I think that all the members of the staff will
> remember how disappointed and excited the general was on
> receipt of this news, and how cross he was the next day, and
> that we all thought he might relieve McPherson of his com-
> mand, *though the general gave no intimation of such intent—
> to me, at least. We simply inferred it from McPherson's failure
> to execute the work expected of him.*
>
> I was present when General Sherman and McPherson first
> met after this, and well remember that General Sherman's
> manner toward McPherson was one of sadness rather than
> anger, and that his first remark was, "Well, Mac, you have
> missed the great opportunity of your life." *General Adkins
> and Colonel Hickenlooper, both of whom were in good posi-
> tion to know the truth, express, I think, the general judgment
> of the Army of the Tennessee—that if certain other division*

commanders had been in the lead, the railroad would have been seized and held, and Johnston ruined.

That the failure to do this was by far the most grievous disappointment which General Sherman met with during the Atlanta campaign, will, I think, be admitted by all who participated in it, and were familiar with the history.[67]

Warner clearly condemns McPherson's performance. Nevertheless, what else would one expect in a letter from a staffer to Sherman's wife that Sherman chose to include in his own memoirs? Warner's letter is perfectly consistent with Sherman's efforts to absolve himself of responsibility for the missed opportunity at Resaca by casting blame on the long-dead McPherson.

In his memoirs, John Schofield came to the defense of McPherson, his fellow army commander and 1853 West Point classmate, asserting that McPherson's army was "entirely too small for the work assigned it" and that Sherman should have had a corps of Thomas's army in close support of McPherson's movement.[68]

McMurry firmly defends McPherson against what he calls Sherman's typical and ungracious attempts to blame someone else—in this case the charge that McPherson was timid and lacked vigor—and points out that McPherson had neither adequate manpower nor sufficient cavalry to carry out his assigned mission. As McPherson neared the Resaca fortifications, his "column, originally scheduled to consist of nine divisions, then reduced to seven, then to five, had been whittled down to one as its advance closed on its objective." Two of his divisions had been delayed in Illinois, and two others had been detailed to Nathaniel Banks's disastrous Red River Campaign. Also, he had been ordered or compelled to leave division after division behind to cover his flanks and rear—in part because he had totally inadequate cavalry to determine the extent of any enemy presence. A not insignificant part of the Union armies' problem was that Sherman had rejected Thomas's proposal that his large army go through Snake Creek Gap and occupy the railroad at Resaca and instead had sent a smaller and reduced army merely to cut the railroad and fall back.[69]

In a synopsis of Sherman's major blunders in this missed opportunity, McMurry concludes:

> In truth, the failure rested squarely on Sherman. He had chosen to send a relatively weak column to Snake Creek Gap. (Any one of Thomas's three massive infantry corps was almost as strong as McPherson's total force.) Sherman had not provided McPherson with adequate cavalry. As a result, the column often had to halt while infantrymen performed scouting duties that should have been handled by mounted units.... [T]here was no good reason why at least some of the mounted units on Hooker's right in the valley north of Villanow could not have joined McPherson's once he cleared Taylor's Ridge [west of Snake Creek Gap], thereby providing him with the horsemen he needed. Sherman's failure to strengthen McPherson is even more puzzling because as early as May 6 the Federals knew that Polk's troops were moving from Alabama to Georgia [and thus posed a threat to McPherson].[70]

His point is that Sherman failed to provide the resources for McPherson to "make a bold attack."

Scales agrees with McMurry's criticism of Sherman but concludes that both Sherman and McPherson were to blame:

> McPherson could have cut Johnston's supply line easily, trapping the Confederate army and possibly sealing its fate. However, he had no cavalry and only a small mounted infantry unit to reconnoiter to the north—the direction of the bulk of Johnston's army—because Garrard's cavalry was not yet up. McPherson was very concerned about the strong infantry resistance at Resaca and about the potential of the entire Confederate army attacking him from the north, cutting him

off from the gap and Sherman. Such an attack could possibly destroy the Army of the Tennessee before Sherman could rescue him. It was McPherson's first experience at the army level...and he was cautious.... Sherman, although greatly disappointed by the outcome, agreed that McPherson had acted within his orders. McPherson, listening to the voice of caution, missed the opportunity of a lifetime.[71]

Elsewhere, Scales more pithily writes, "Sherman's plan stood an excellent chance of destroying Johnston's army. However, he did not give his turning movement adequate strength (particularly in cavalry) and his subordinate McPherson, made cautious by this lack and by his relative inexperience, did not press his advantage."[72] The shortage of cavalry at Snake Creek Gap caused McPherson to proceed cautiously because he could not send cavalry to the north of Resaca to screen his movements or, most importantly, to determine whether Johnston was sending large numbers of troops in his direction. There certainly was good reason to find fault with both generals.

Somewhat puzzling is that Sherman and most later commenters have said that McPherson acted within his orders when he withdrew to the gap. But his orders had authorized him to withdraw to the gap once he had broken the railroad "to an extent that would take [the Confederates] days to repair." He retreated without having broken the railroad at all. Sherman also had ordered McPherson to "make a bold attack on the enemy's flank or his railroad," but McPherson called off his attack after suffering only fifty casualties.[73] That hardly seems to have been a bold attack. Does Sherman's generous initial appraisal of McPherson's alleged compliance with his orders reflect his friendship for McPherson? Had there been verbal orders or discussions that gave McPherson more latitude than his written orders? Was it that McPherson was still alive? Or perhaps Sherman realized that he had provided McPherson with inadequate resources? We are unlikely ever to know.

Regardless of who was to blame, Sherman's army blundered in failing to trap and substantially damage the major Confederate army in its theater at the very beginning of the vital Atlanta Campaign. If the Snake Creek Gap gambit had been successful, Johnston's army probably would have been badly damaged and Atlanta might have fallen long before September. Such a series of events also would likely have reduced Sherman's casualties during the campaign and would have at least ameliorated the malaise that beset the North during the summer of 1864. Finally, it likely would have shortened the war by several months.

PETERSBURG

ULYSSES S. GRANT AND A BEVY OF UNION GENERALS FAIL TO END THE WAR BY CAPTURING PETERSBURG IN JUNE 1864

WHO BLUNDERED?

Union Generals Ulysses S. Grant, George Meade, Benjamin Butler, William "Baldy" Smith, Ambrose Burnside, Gouverneur Warren, and Winfield Scott Hancock

HOW?

After the Army of the Potomac's brilliant surprise crossing of the James River just after the Overland Campaign of 1864, these generals failed to capture lightly defended Petersburg and thus deprive Lee's army of its critical supply route to Richmond.

CONSEQUENCES?

Lee's Army of Northern Virginia was able to hold Richmond and Petersburg and to extend the war for another ten months—at the cost of tens of thousands of additional Union and Confederate casualties.

After his disastrous assaults at Cold Harbor, Virginia, from May 31 to June 12, 1864, Ulysses S. Grant determined to restore the morale of his soldiers and to threaten Richmond and Petersburg by making surreptitious crossings of the Chickahominy and James Rivers east of those cities. "For Grant, Cold Harbor had been a setback, not a defeat," observes his biographer Jean Edward Smith.[1] Petersburg, a key transportation hub twenty miles south of Richmond,[2] became Grant's initial target because its fall would cut off food and supplies to Lee's army at Richmond, forcing it to abandon the Confederate capital and engage Grant's armies in the open. Even before beginning the Overland Campaign, which ran from May 4 to June 12, Grant had foreseen this possible river-crossing assault. On April 15, he had ordered Brigadier General Henry W. Benham's Volunteer Engineer Brigade at Fort Monroe in Hampton Roads to ready "sufficient water transport to tow necessary quantities of bridge-building materials to span the James." On June 4, Grant ordered 155 pontoon boats and their bridging equipment to proceed to Bermuda Hundred—the peninsula between the James and Appomattox Rivers—where they were joined by bridge trains from Grant's lines.[3]

Grant revealed his plans to Halleck the next day: "My idea from the start has been to beat Lee's Army, if possible, north of Richmond, then after destroying his lines of communication North of the James river to transfer the Army to the South side and besiege Lee in Richmond, or follow him South if he should retreat."[4] Bypassing the heavily fortified Rebel army, he believed, was necessary to avoid "a greater sacrifice of human life" than Grant was willing to make.[5] His plan to move through hostile territory, extracting his army from contact with enemy lines and crossing two rivers undetected, was extremely risky, and the Confederates had a strong flotilla, including several ironclads, on the upper James River. "If Lee were to detect this movement and strike the Federal columns while they were astride either river," writes Vincent Esposito, "a disastrous defeat could hardly be avoided."[6]

As a prelude to his secret move, Grant on June 6 sent Major General Phil Sheridan on his "Second Raid" to destroy much of the Virginia

Central Railroad, a key supply connection between Richmond and the Shenandoah Valley, and to meet up with Major General David Hunter, whose troops were to destroy the James River Canal at Lynchburg. Both Sheridan and Hunter failed. Confederate cavalry commanded by Major General Wade Hampton kept Sheridan from reaching his critical goal of Gordonsville and drove him into retreat at the Battle of Trevilian Station on June 11 and 12. Lieutenant General Jubal Early and the Second Corps arrived from Richmond in time to save Lynchburg from the dawdling Hunter, whom they drove back into West Virginia. The only benefit of Sheridan's expedition was depriving Lee of the eyes of Hampton's cavalry at a critical period when Grant again moved his army.[7]

UNION RIVER CROSSINGS

Back at Cold Harbor, Grant planned for and then began his secret back-door assault on Petersburg across the Chickahominy and the James. On June 5, he requested more vessels from Washington and ordered Colonels Horace Porter and Cyrus Comstock of his staff to locate a suitable place to cross the James. At two o'clock in the morning on June 12, they reported that they had found a crossing "which will give the Army of the Potomac as short a line of march as practicable, and which at the same time be far enough downstream [from] Lee's army to prevent the chances of our being attacked successfully while in the act of crossing." They had selected the narrowest point downstream from City Point, where the Appomattox flows into the James.[8]

Grant, in the meantime, had sent Major General William F. "Baldy" Smith's Eighteenth Corps east from Cold Harbor to White House on the Pamunkey River, where they embarked on vessels for the trip back to Butler's command in the Bermuda Hundred area between Richmond and Petersburg. The vessels carried them down the Pamunkey and York Rivers, south on the Chesapeake Bay, through Hampton Roads, and then up the James to Bermuda Hundred, which they reached on the fourteenth.[9]

On the evening of June 12, Grant evacuated his seven-mile Cold Harbor line one corps at a time, loud band music masking their noise.

Major General Gouverneur Warren's Fifth Corps led the way, marching east along the north bank of the Chickahominy River, crossing on a newly built 1,200-foot pontoon bridge at Long Bridge. Turning back west toward Richmond, they provided a screen for the rest of the army by occupying a five-mile line from White Oak Swamp on the Chickahominy to Malvern Hill on the James, a position that suggested an attack on Richmond from between the two rivers.[10] All the other corps moved out undetected from Cold Harbor, crossing the Chickahominy at three different spots—two fixed bridges and a pontoon bridge.

The next day, when Lee discovered that Grant's army was south of the Chickahominy, he sent his own army over the river in pursuit. According to the *West Point Atlas of American Wars*, Lee thought he had caught Grant in "another one of those short-range attempts to envelop the [Rebel] right flank that the Federal commander had been trying ever since the Wilderness."[11] Lee's troops tested the lines of Warren's Fifth Corps between the Chickahominy and the James but made only a tentative attack with sharpshooters from Hill's Corps. "Nightfall brought a halt to the Confederate attack and saved Warren, who faced Lee's entire army with no support within miles. Lee, however, failed to grasp Warren's perilous situation and contented himself with probing the Fifth Corps line."[12]

The Rebels, Porter Alexander would later reflect, could have pounced on the isolated Fifth Corps that afternoon of June 13: "The only trouble about that was that we were entirely ignorant of the fact that it was isolated. On the contrary… Warren's corps had taken up its line so near to Riddell's Shop as to give us the idea that it was the advance corps of Grant's whole army pushing toward Richmond on the road from Long Bridge."[13] As Jean Edward Smith observes, "[t]he Army of the Potomac—115,000 men—had marched away so quietly that Confederate pickets had not observed its departure."[14] Overnight, Lee discovered that Warren's corps was isolated and ordered Hill to attack. When Hill did so on the morning of the fourteenth, however, Warren was gone.

That same morning, Major General Winfield Scott Hancock's Second Corps began crossing the James by boat from Wilcox's Landing and established a bridgehead around Windmill Point on the south shore, clearing the way for construction of what was then the world's longest pontoon bridge. Most of the infantry of the Second, Fifth, and Sixth Corps then began crossing the James by ferry, a sixty-two-hour operation that might have taken one-fourth the time if the pontoon bridge had been available.[15] This crossing coincided with the arrival of Smith's Eighteenth Corps after a roundabout water journey.

Union engineers built the pontoon bridge in an amazing seven hours, completing their work before midnight on the fourteenth. The rest of Grant's army—in particular its animals and supply train—crossed on June 15, 16, and 17. Although the bridge was operational at 1:00 a.m. on the fifteenth and Meade had ordered Burnside's Ninth Corps to cross immediately, that corps did not start crossing until 6:00 a.m. Fifty hours later the crossing was completed, the bridge was torn up, and its components were moved upriver to Bermuda Hundred and City Point to facilitate the crossings of the Appomattox and the James. Crossing the river was a mammoth undertaking that involved 115,000 soldiers and their artillery and trains, including thousands of wagons and two or three thousand cattle.[16]

Grant boldly gambled that he would be able to detach his large army from Lee's, cross two rivers, ferry many of his troops across the James, construct and use a 2,170-foot bridge across a river with a four-foot tide, and cross that river with the rest of his army without being attacked while his army was split on two sides of the river. As the crossing succeeded, Assistant War Secretary Dana wired Stanton, "All goes on like a miracle."

Federal cavalry and Warren's corps had prevented prying Southern eyes from learning of this massive movement and kept Lee baffled as to where Grant would strike next. On the thirteenth, he knew that Grant's army had moved away from his Cold Harbor front, but he did not know its whereabouts. At midday on the fourteenth, he speculated that Grant's army might occupy the Harrison's Landing fortifications on the James, which would be easy to defend with the aid of Union gunboats.[17] Grant had stolen a march on Lee, and a prompt, competent attack on Petersburg by the relocated army would have cost Lee both Petersburg and Richmond, which was dependent on rail supply through Petersburg.

That successful, deceptive movement contrasts sharply with the campaign's disappointing, actually tragic, outcome. Although the Army of the Potomac ultimately failed to achieve the critical goal of capturing Petersburg to isolate Richmond, it apparently had recovered from the Cold Harbor disaster in carrying out the well-conceived and surreptitious crossing of the James and deceiving Lee as to its whereabouts. As Colonel Theodore Lyman of Meade's staff later recalled, "If General Grant erred in his battle at Cold Harbor, he corrected his error in the brilliant operation of transferring the army to the south bank of the James; and General Meade, the immediate commander of that army, deserves the highest praise for his admirable execution of the order."[18]

DILATORY CONFEDERATE RESPONSE

The Confederate reaction was slow but, in the nick of time, effective. General P. G. T. Beauregard was the Confederate commander south of Richmond. By the sixteenth, while continuing to plead with Lee for reinforcements, he had consolidated his Bermuda Hundred line between Richmond and Petersburg and sent more troops south to Petersburg. Beauregard's skimpy force at Petersburg gave ground but was able to hold off rather half-hearted attacks by the Eighteenth, Second, and newly-arrived Ninth Corps. Yet another corps, the Fifth, arrived at Petersburg by the seventeenth, but the uncoordinated union attacks still were ineffective. That night Beauregard, realizing the extreme danger of his forward position, withdrew to a new fortified line.

While Grant was moving his entire army toward Petersburg, Lee was totally in the dark.[19] His ignorance of Grant's massive movement is clear from a telegram he sent to Beauregard on the seventeenth: "Fifth Corps [Warren's] crossed Chickahominy at Long Bridge on 13th; was driven from Riddell's Shop by General Hill, leaving many dead and prisoners on our hands. That night it marched to Westover.... Have not heard of it since."[20] In contrast, Beauregard had predicted Grant's movement in dispatches of June 7 and 9 to Braxton Bragg, who was serving in Richmond as Jefferson Davis's chief of staff.[21]

On the night of the fourteenth, after a visit from one of Beauregard's staff officers, Lee decided to improve his options by moving Robert Hoke's division of Beauregard's own army south from Drewry's Bluff on the James and by moving some of Lee's own troops early the next morning in the direction of Petersburg. Thus, some of Lee's men marched on the fifteenth toward the Rebel pontoon bridge over the James between Chaffin's and Drewry's Bluffs. Nevertheless, Lee halted even that movement because of the presence of Union cavalry in the vicinity of Malvern Hill north of the James—cavalry that in fact was just checking to make sure Lee was still there. As of midday on the fifteenth, Lee was advising both Davis and Bragg that he was maintaining the bulk of his troops in place north of the James because the enemy's plans seemed or appeared "to be unsettled."[22]

Lee continued to doubt Beauregard's assessment, sending the following telegrams to Beauregard in the days *after* Grant's troops had begun attacking Petersburg:

> June 16 at 10:30 a.m.: "I do not know the position of Grant's army, and cannot strip north bank of James River. Have you not force sufficient?"[23]
>
> June 16 at 4:00 p.m.: "The transports you mention have probably returned Butler's troops. Has Grant been seen crossing James River?"[24]
>
> June 17 at 6:00 a.m.: "Can you ascertain anything of Grant's movements?"[25]
>
> June 17 at noon: "Until I can get more definite information of Grant's movements, I do not think it prudent to draw more troops to this [south] side of the river."[26]
>
> June 17 at 4:30 p.m.: "Have no information of Grant's crossing James River, but upon your report have ordered troops up to Chaffin's Bluff [still north of the James]."[27]

Finally, at 6:40 in the evening of the seventeenth, Beauregard began getting Lee's attention with a dispatch of desperation: "The increasing number of enemy in my front, & inadequacy of my force to defend the already much too extended lines, will compel me to fall within a shorter one, which I will attempt tonight. This I shall hold as long as practicable, but without reinforcements, I may have to evacuate the city very shortly."[28]

His telegraphed pleas having been ignored for days, Beauregard resorted to extraordinary means of getting Lee's attention after he had been compelled by overwhelming force to retreat to inner lines on the night of the seventeenth. He sent three emissaries in succession. By 2:00 a.m. on the eighteenth, Lee had told the first of these, Lieutenant A. R. Chisolm, that he doubted any significant part of Grant's forces had crossed the James. The second, Lieutenant Colonel Alfred Roman, was turned away by Lee's aides. The last, Major Giles B. Cooke, finally convinced Lee after three o'clock in the morning that the broad representation of three Union corps among captured prisoners demonstrated that Grant indeed had crossed the James in strength.[29]

Realizing that he had been duped and was in danger of losing Petersburg, Richmond, and the war, Lee sent an urgent message to the superintendent of the Richmond and Petersburg Railroad at 3:30 asking whether trains could run to Petersburg, directing that cars be sent for troops wherever they could be picked up, and concluding, "It is important to get troops to Petersburg without delay."[30]

FAILED UNION ATTACKS

As a result of Lee's three-day delay, Grant's army needed only competence and aggressiveness to break through at Petersburg and virtually end the war. Grant and his generals, however, demonstrated neither. The Union assaults on Petersburg from June 15 to 18 were so inept and tepid that Lee's belated reinforcements reached Beauregard and repelled the assaults.[31]

Although Grant knew what he wanted to do—quickly occupy Petersburg—he appears to have failed to convey that urgent message clearly to Meade and all corps commanders. A few days earlier, on June 9, Grant

Area of the Appomattox River where Baldy Smith crossed on his way to Petersburg, by William Waud. *Courtesy of the Library of Congress*

had ordered Ben Butler to attack Petersburg from Bermuda Hundred, where Butler had been bottled up for a month. Butler sent a division under Major General Quincy Gilmore, but it was repelled by outnumbered Rebels, many of them old men and boys.[32] On June 14, as the James crossing started, Grant advised Halleck, "The Enemy show no signs of yet having brought troops to south side of Richmond. I will have Petersburg secured if possible before they get there in much force."[33]

The movement across the river took a toll on Grant's troops, who had been on campaign since May 4. On June 14, Lieutenant Colonel Elisha Hunt Rhodes, Second Rhode Island Volunteers, described in his diary his Sixth Corps' itinerary. They had moved from Cold Harbor beginning on the night of June 12, crossed the Chickahominy on June 13, and resumed their march toward the James on June 14. "The men are used up by the intense heat and fatigue of the past week," he wrote. "As soon as my tent was pitched I lay down and slept for four hours. It is said that we are to cross the James River and attack Richmond from the south side. Either side suits me if we can only win." Rhodes's unit and the rest of the Sixth Corps crossed the James on the night of June 16–17 and marched twenty-five miles to Petersburg, but they were too late to join the Union attacks.[34]

The four corps that had crossed or come up the James before the Sixth Corps crossed it ended up conducting a series of tardy, timid, uncoordinated, unfocused, and unsuccessful attacks on Petersburg from June 15 to 18—a failed effort that was one of the major blunders of the entire war.[35] Their commanders Grant and Meade were not without fault. Grant had decided to accompany Meade's army in the field, but the joint presence of Grant and Meade produced confusion. Who was in charge, the general in chief or the army commander? Major General John Gibbon explained: "Gen. Meade occupied a peculiar position at the head of the [A]rmy [of the Potomac]. He was a commander directly under a commander, a position at best and under the most favorable circumstances, not a very satisfactory one to fill.... [H]e must be necessarily shackled and sensible of the fact that he is deprived of that independence and untrammeled authority so necessary to every army commander."[36] Further complicating matters was the presence of the separate Union Army of Virginia under the command of the incompetent Butler. Grant had authority over him, but Meade did not.

On June 14, without sharing his plans with Meade or Hancock,[37] Grant left Meade in charge of the James crossing and went to tell Butler of his plan to capture Petersburg the next day. Baldy Smith's Eighteenth Corps, part of Butler's command, had arrived, and Hancock's Second Corps was crossing the James. Those two corps had thirty-five to forty thousand troops. Smith was to move out of Bermuda Hundred and take the lead. Hancock supposedly had been ordered to bring up his Second Corps to support Smith.[38] They were to take Petersburg before Rebel reinforcements arrived. Smith's problems began on the fourteenth when he kept changing the disembarkation orders for his troops. While Smith's soldiers were still getting straightened out early on the fifteenth, Union screening cavalry arrived late. "In his meeting with Butler the prior day," writes Thomas Howe, "Grant had envisioned an organized march taking place before dawn on the 15th, followed by an early-morning attack on the city. The plan to take Petersburg was already awry."[39]

In part because of the Union cavalry's delay, Smith's march was slowed by Rebel cavalry, which he had to drive off at Baylor's Farm. Further, the usually aggressive Smith, perhaps remembering the slaughter at Cold Harbor and concerned that Butler's assurances to him about light Confederate opposition were unreliable, decided he needed more time to reconnoiter the area in his front. That time was well spent, for he discovered that the enemy's Dimmock Line was lightly manned, and he identified certain ravines through which Confederate strongpoints were vulnerable to attack.[40]

So with Lee twenty-five miles away, Smith spent hours conducting critical reconnaissance before attacking. Between six and seven o'clock on the evening of June 15, Smith's fourteen to seventeen thousand attackers, greatly outnumbering the approximately five thousand defenders Beauregard had assembled, suddenly emerged from the ravines and captured key redans (small forts containing artillery batteries) from behind. Forcing the defenders to flee a mile or more back, Smith captured numerous trenches, forts, and guns. After overwhelming redans Five and Six, Smith's troops rolled up the Confederates, captured redans Three through Eleven, and opened a three-mile gap in the center of Beauregard's line. Skirmishers accomplished all of this before much of the Federal battle line even formed.[41]

Looking back ruefully, Porter Alexander believed that Smith's attack could have been another disaster like Cold Harbor for Grant, but "General Lee did not have a soldier there to meet him! Grant had gotten away from US completely & was fighting *Beauregard*. The Army of Northern Virginia had lost him, & was sucking its thumbs by the roadside 25 miles away, & wondering where he could be!!!"[42]

But with Petersburg open for the taking, Smith hesitated. One reason for his hesitation was Beauregard's repeat performance of what he had done to Henry Halleck at Corinth.[43] Murray and Hsieh write that he "put on a wonderful show: troops appeared to be marching into the fortifications that surrounded Petersburg—and then snuck out to be seen moving into other parts of the fortifications; whistles blew again and again along with clouds of steam from the few locomotives in the Petersburg station."[44] More importantly, between six and nine o'clock p.m. Butler's signal station north of Petersburg advised that trains with fifty cars plus two additional trains apparently were rushing reinforcements to Petersburg and that others were moving by road.[45] Smith decided he had done all he could that day and decided to await Hancock's Second Corps.[46] No further attack occurred on the fifteenth, when Petersburg was virtually undefended.

Smith has often been blamed for not continuing his attack that night. Beauregard later wrote, "Petersburg at that hour was clearly at the mercy of the Federal commander, who had all but captured it."[47] Thomas Howe concludes, "In one of the greatest command blunders [of] the war, Smith chose to go no farther than the lines just taken."[48] But there is more to the story. Butler, worried by the signal station reports, ordered Smith to entrench and hold his position. Those reports and his corps commander's orders make Smith's failure to resume his attack after nine o'clock understandable—especially since he expected to be reinforced by Hancock's Second Corps.[49]

What happened to Hancock that day is inexplicable. Uninformed of his intended role, suffering from the wound he received at Gettysburg, relying on an inaccurate map, and concerned about missing rations he had been promised, Hancock spent the fifteenth moving only slowly in the direction of Petersburg.[50] According to Howe, "Grant failed, almost unbelievably, to inform either Meade or Hancock of the forthcoming attempt to take Petersburg. Neither of these key officers had moved with celerity on the morning of June 15 simply because they were ignorant of the Second Corps' duty to support Smith."[51] Furthermore, since Butler had not told Smith of Hancock's intended role, Smith did not know of Hancock's availability until four o'clock that afternoon, when a courier finally arrived from Grant.[52] It was eleven o'clock before Smith met with Hancock to ask for help and Hancock's men moved into position with Smith's.[53]

Having spent most of the morning fruitlessly awaiting rations, Hancock set out at 10:30 a.m., moving at a deliberate pace until about 5:00 p.m., when he finally received an order from Grant and a message from

Smith indicating that he was supposed to move toward Petersburg with all possible speed to support Smith.[54] In his memoirs, Grant excused Hancock's tardiness: "This seems to have been the first information that General Hancock had received of the fact that he was to go to Petersburg, or that anything in particular was expected of him. Otherwise he would have been there by four o'clock in the afternoon."[55] As the historian Diane Smith observes, "Grant does not explain why neither Meade nor Hancock knew what else Grant expected of them."[56] Certainly the general in chief bears responsibility for failing to ensure that Hancock knew what was expected of him. Meade, the Army of the Potomac's titular head, was likewise uninformed by Grant, learning about Smith's attack only as he sat down to dinner at 6:30.[57]

Shortly after arriving at Petersburg, Hancock relieved some of Smith's men at Smith's request, but the two left unresolved who was in command. Although Hancock's belated arrival on the night of June 15–16 increased Union strength to thirty-five thousand against perhaps seven thousand Rebels, he and Smith merely had their men switch places. They both failed to take advantage of their five-to-one superiority and the three-mile gap in the Rebel line by sweeping into Petersburg. Both Smith and Assistant Secretary of War Charles Dana, who was on the scene, believed the Yankees had Petersburg under their control or within their grasp, but many Union soldiers wondered why there was no attack on that moonlit night to finish the job.[58]

Just after midnight on the sixteenth, Hancock directed Major Generals John Gibbon and David Birney to attack with their divisions at dawn. At the appointed hour, however, they merely started their reconnaissance, which consumed the whole morning. Although Gibbon and Birney did some attacking, their progress was minimal.[59] Something was lacking in the Army of the Potomac. The Overland Campaign had wiped out many of their leaders. Lieutenants were leading regiments in place of dead or wounded colonels and majors. Many soldiers were awaiting their enlistment expirations, and others were untrained fresh arrivals, including heavy artillerymen recently moved out of the forts defending Washington.[60]

Confusion reigned, and the on-site commanders dithered. On the morning of the sixteenth, when every man should have been thrown into an aggressive assault on Petersburg, Grant from City Point inexplicably authorized some of Smith's soldiers to be withdrawn as a reserve. That action conflicted with overnight orders Smith had received from Butler to attack immediately. By mid-morning Grant finally came to the scene of action and was astounded at the strength of the Rebel positions that had been so easily taken. That observation should have reinforced reports about the small number of Rebel defenders. Nevertheless, he ordered Meade to come take charge and did not order an immediate assault. He and Meade were content to wait for Burnside's Ninth Corps to arrive and augment their forces, and Grant ordered Meade to lead an attack at 6:00 p.m.[61]

Beauregard, meanwhile, had reinforced his weak Petersburg line with troops that had been facing the Bermuda Hundred peninsula between Petersburg and Richmond, leaving that critical stretch of rail and road undefended. Butler briefly occupied that area to block any reinforcements from Lee, but he quickly backed off as soon as he was challenged.[62]

Grant telegraphed Meade to order Gouverneur Warren to move his Fifth Corps to Petersburg as backup for the three corps already there or arriving. Warren did so in his usual deliberate manner, slowed down by Confederate skirmishers whom he believed were part of a larger force. Hancock's Gettysburg wound was so painful that he had to be relieved by Birney on the afternoon of the sixteenth. By the time of the attack at six o'clock that evening, almost another full day had been wasted.

Although Beauregard had brought his force up to fourteen thousand, the Union army was able to muster fifty thousand against them. Many of the Yankee troops, especially Burnside's, were not properly coordinated in the assault, attacking well-manned defensive lines instead of undefended lines to the south, and the evening and night attack failed. By four o'clock the next morning, Meade called off the moonlit assault.[63] In Howe's words, "That Petersburg did not fall on June 16 seems nearly unbelievable." The Federals were more numerous, more experienced, and better trained and armed. He blames the "lack of imaginative leadership," pointing out that Meade attacked where Beauregard was strongest and did so with less than his full force. Union fatigue was noted by all, and "Grant remained curiously detached from the fighting of June 16" as he remained back at City Point.[64]

In the words of David Alan Johnson, "Nothing seemed to be going right. Orders were bungled or sometimes missed altogether. A little bit of drive and determination by any of the corps commanders would have gone a long way. But the memory of Cold Harbor was still fresh in everyone's mind and had effectively curbed all thoughts of another frontal attack on the Confederate lines. The combined effects of Cold Harbor, the heat and exhaustion, and almost continual marching and fighting since May 4, had stalled the offensive just as effectively as any Confederate counterattack could have done."[65]

June 17 would be the last full day when Petersburg was only lightly defended. Still unsure of Grant's position, Lee continued to hold back possible reinforcements. Grant ordered an all-out assault by Smith, Birney, and Burnside, with Warren coming to their assistance. Warren came up late, and Beauregard aggressively counterattacked in the early morning as he was skillfully developing a new inner line of defense. Although initially achieving some early morning success, the costly series of Union attacks, with feeble participation by Smith, were partial, uncoordinated, and unsupported by artillery. Some attacks were misdirected, and others were ordered into murderous enemy fire. Meade failed to order Warren's fresh Fifth Corps to assault the relatively weak Rebel southern flank; his twenty thousand troops were wasted.[66]

The failures of June 17 were similar to those of the prior two days. Despite overwhelming numerical superiority, the piecemeal, uncoordinated attacks failed because of fierce Confederate resistance, poor reconnaissance and resupply staff-work, and minimal use of cavalry. Tentative and defensive, Meade failed to launch coordinated attacks, and he never effectively used the Fifth Corps. His corps commanders, especially

Warren and Burnside, failed him by not aggressively attacking as ordered. For yet another day, Grant passively allowed the less competent army commanders, Meade and Butler, to direct activities in the most vital area of his theater and never took decisive, hands-on command in the critical culmination of his six-week campaign.[67]

The ineffective Union attacks of the seventeenth were followed by another assault the following morning. By then, however, reinforcements were arriving from Lee, and the opportunity to capture Petersburg had been lost.[68] At dawn on the eighteenth, with the newly arrived Sixth Corps further bolstering their strength, the Federals launched a seventy-thousand-man, five-corps assault on Petersburg. They overran the recently abandoned Confederate outer lines and seriously threatened to take the town at last. As at Spotsylvania Court House in early May, Lee's troops appeared on the scene just in time to stop a Federal advance and save the day. Four hours after Lee began arranging for their transportation from north of Richmond, Confederates began pouring into their comrades' Petersburg defensive lines at 7:30 that morning, continuing to do so until 11:00 a.m. Miraculously, Lee's reinforcements from north of the James River arrived just in time to repulse the attack.

At noon Major General David B. Birney launched an unsupported attack and was beaten back. That afternoon a frustrated Meade issued an order to his corps commanders: "Finding it impossible to effect cooperation by appointing an hour for attack, I have sent an order to each corps commander to attack at all hazards and without reference to each other."[69] But he was a day or two late in decisively taking charge. All along the Union lines, officers were waving their swords and ordering attacks, but seasoned soldiers remained on the ground and refused to obey. Virtually no one attacked. There was one tragic exception. At 4:00 p.m. one of Birney's regiments, the green First Maine Heavy Artillery, attacked alone. Its 950 men suffered 632 casualties (including 115 killed), an extremely high 66.5 percent casualty rate. Later that afternoon a frustrated Grant called off the attacks. The multi-day assault on Petersburg had failed—a disappointing result after the brilliant, surreptitious crossing of the James.[70]

SUMMARY

Grant and his corps commanders had missed a golden opportunity presented to them by Lee to capture a virtually undefended Petersburg. Although Lee had been deprived of maneuverability and forced into a semi-siege situation, which he had said ensured that defeat "would be a mere question of time," Grant and his generals had failed to capture the transportation hub critical to Richmond's survival. Not until April 2 of the next year would Grant order another frontal assault. In the interim, he expressly prohibited such assaults.[71] Siege warfare would commence.

What had gone wrong?[72] Grant, in his memoirs, blamed the calamity on the failure to communicate in a timely manner to Hancock his orders to promptly proceed to Petersburg after crossing the James. He asserted that the usually prompt Hancock would have reached Petersburg by 4:00 p.m. on the fifteenth and that the long days would have permitted an attack before dark. In that event, wrote Grant, "I do not think there is any doubt that Petersburg itself could have been carried without much loss; or, at least, if protected by inner detached works, that a line could have been established very much in rear of the one then occupied by the enemy. This would have given us control of both the Weldon and Southside railroads."[73]

If this criticism is aimed at the Army of the Potomac's commander, George Meade, it overlooks Grant's personal direction of many of the army's field operations, which led to gaps, oversights, and other missteps. It also raises the question whether Meade himself and all involved corps commanders had been appropriately briefed or had received clear orders about their primary responsibility after crossing the James—capturing Petersburg before Lee could reinforce it. The absence of any evidence of such a briefing or orders indicates a serious oversight. Grant was responsible for Meade's and Hancock's not knowing Hancock's intended role. Yet even without specific orders, what else might Hancock have thought he was supposed to be doing south of the James besides promptly attacking Petersburg?

There are more comprehensive explanations than that offered by Grant. Unfortunately for the Union, Grant, his staff, and his corps commanders had so focused on the challenging river crossings that they lost sight of their strategic objective: the capture of Petersburg. A search of the *Official Records* reveals a concentration on Union corps' movements and supply but a dearth of urgency about actually capturing Petersburg before it was reinforced by Lee. One after another, the Union corps delayed, dawdled, and approached Petersburg with timidity. The Union orders focused on position, supply, and movement but lacked any compelling language such as "Defeat Beauregard and occupy Petersburg immediately and at all costs." In addition, it appears that the memory of the recent Cold Harbor slaughter may have caused Union generals and foot soldiers alike to avoid aggressively attacking the formidable but weakly manned Petersburg defenses.

The Union command structure may have been part of the problem. Two union armies were present, and Grant failed to coordinate their actions. With neither Grant nor Meade personally coordinating the multi-corps attacks, chaos reigned. Although Meade was the titular commander of the Army of the Potomac, Grant was by his side all the way once the Overland Campaign started. Whenever he grew concerned about what was occurring—beginning on Day One at the Wilderness— or deemed the situation of critical importance, Grant jumped in. The problem that continued to dog that army was uncertainty about who was in charge. This dual leadership inevitably resulted in overlaps and, most dangerously, gaps. Until the afternoon of June 18, when it was too late, there is little indication of a clear, sweeping, top-down mandate from either Grant or Meade—possibly because each thought the other was in charge of the situation. The involvement of another army, Butler's Army of Virginia, in the Petersburg assault posed an additional problem for the command structure.

Personalities also played a role. By mid-June, Grant and Meade apparently were barely speaking to each other, which would explain why Grant did not advise Meade, and thus Hancock, of the role Grant intended Hancock to play on June 15. Similarly, Butler and Smith were both strong-willed, uncooperative, and non-communicative, with the result that Butler failed to tell Smith about Hancock's intended supporting role. According to Gordon Rhea, an expert on the Overland Campaign, "The Union high command resembled a dysfunctional family, of which the Petersburg fiasco of June 15 was a prime exhibit."[74] Grant's failure to coordinate the activities of the two involved Union armies and to issue written orders to the critical commanders constituted the paramount blunder of this failed effort.

Finally, one must remember that Grant's troops had been marching and fighting continuously for six weeks in Virginia's summer heat, suffering sixty thousand casualties. Colonel Horace Porter wrote that the army, having "been engaged in skirmishing or in giving battle from the 4th of May to the 18th of June," lacked the vigor it had displayed in the "Wilderness [Overland] campaign."[75] Grant's persistent aggressiveness, says David Alan Johnson, may eventually have deflated his own army's morale.[76]

In summary, the lack of compelling orders from the top of the Union command, the timidity of the field commanders and troops approaching Petersburg, and the organization and condition of the Union forces resulted in failure at Petersburg. The outcome was a major missed opportunity to end the war many months earlier than actually occurred. The capture of Petersburg would have ensured the evacuation of Richmond and shortened the war by as much as ten months, thereby avoiding tens of thousands of casualties on both sides.

ATLANTA AND SAVANNAH

WILLIAM T. SHERMAN FAILS TO CAPTURE ENEMY ARMIES AND SHORTEN THE WAR

WHO BLUNDERED?

Union Major General William T. Sherman

HOW?

When capturing the cities of Atlanta and Savannah in late 1864, Sherman allowed two Confederate armies to escape.

CONSEQUENCES?

The Rebel soldiers who escaped fought again and inflicted numerous Union casualties at Franklin and Nashville, Tennessee, and while opposing Sherman's 1865 campaign through the Carolinas, extending the war by many months.

Union generals have frequently been criticized for failing to pursue the enemy after a fight. We have already considered Henry Halleck's failure to pursue Beauregard after capturing Corinth, Mississippi, in 1862 and McClellan's inactivity after the battle of Antietam. A more debatable instance was Meade's unsuccessful attempt to trap Lee's army north of the Potomac River after Gettysburg.

Often overlooked, however, is William T. Sherman's failure to pursue, engage, or capture two Rebel armies after he had captured Atlanta and Savannah in late 1864. Sherman is noted for his successes in Georgia and the Carolinas in 1864 and 1865, which played a major role in the Union's victory over the Confederacy. His occupation of Atlanta on September 2, 1864, is widely regarded as having secured the reelection of President Lincoln two months later.

But many historians have overlooked—as Lincoln and Grant did—Sherman's apparent satisfaction with the capture of Atlanta, after which he allowed General John Bell Hood and his Army of Tennessee to escape and remain a threat for another four months. Sherman's orders had been to concentrate on that army. On April 4, 1864, Grant wrote to Sherman, "You I propose to move against Johnston's army [the Army of Tennessee], to break it up and to get into the interior of the enemy's country as far as you can, inflicting all the damage you can against their War resources."[1] Sherman responded, "I will not let side issues draw me off from your main plan in which I am to Knock Joe Johnston, and do as much damage to the resources of the Enemy as possible.... I would ever bear in mind that Johnston is at all times to be kept so busy that he cannot in any event send any part of his command against you or [Nathaniel] Banks."[2] In failing at Atlanta and Savannah to destroy the Confederate armies in his theater, Sherman deviated from his orders and missed two opportunities to shorten the war by eliminating the only Rebel armies of consequence other than Lee's before the end of 1864.

On July 18, 1864, in the midst of Sherman's four-month Atlanta Campaign, Johnston was replaced by General John Bell Hood, whose aggressiveness resulted in three Rebel defeats in late July with irreplaceable casualties, guaranteeing the fall of Atlanta one month later.[3]

Ruins of the Confederate engine house at Atlanta, GA, September 1864. *Courtesy of the National Archives*

Realizing that his army was about to be trapped in Atlanta, Hood began marching his troops out of the city at five o'clock in the afternoon on September 1. They were led by Lieutenant General A. P. Stewart's infantry and guarded at the rear by accompanying cavalry. As they departed, the latter burned or blew up eighty-one freight cars of ammunition, seven locomotives, a steel rolling mill, and large quantities of food and military equipment. As many as five thousand new rifles and three million rounds of ammunition may have been destroyed. The resulting explosions could be heard for miles. Although the Confederate exodus resembled a rout, it provided Hood's weakened army with freedom of movement. The next morning Union patrols encountered the mayor and a delegation from the city asking Union forces to take control.[4]

On the afternoon of August 31, meanwhile, Sherman's superior force was twenty miles south of Atlanta between the forces of Lieutenant General William J. Hardee (at Jonesboro) and the rest of Hood's army. Sherman rejected General George Thomas's request to swing his army south and east to pin down Hardee's troops, preferring to see the enemy's reaction to being separated from Atlanta and to get his own armies together in close order. He planned a September 1 attack on Hardee that depended on swift movement by Major General David Stanley's Fourth Corps. When Stanley was late in coming up, Sherman sent staffers, and finally General Thomas, to hurry them along.[5] Sherman later complained, "Had [Stanley] moved straight on by the flank, or by a slight circuit to his left, he would have inclosed the whole ground occupied by Hardee's...[soldiers], who could not have escaped us; but night came on, and Hardee did escape."[6]

Here at the end of the campaign Sherman again declined to follow Thomas's counsel to be aggressive and pursued a less effective course of action. Instead of being trapped, Hardee escaped with a substantial part of Hood's army. Although Grant, Sherman, and others criticized Thomas—unfairly calling him "Slow-Trot"—for his supposed lack of aggressiveness, Grant and Sherman ignored his advice to be aggressive at the beginning and the end of the Atlanta Campaign. As a result, Snake Creek Gap became a missed opportunity,[7] while Hardee's troops, and then Hood's entire army, escaped as Atlanta fell. It would not be Hardee's last escape from Sherman's clutches.

Early on the afternoon that his troops occupied Atlanta—September 2—General Henry Slocum sent a telegram advising Secretary of War Stanton, "General Sherman has taken Atlanta." Despite hearing the explosions twenty miles away and receiving two unofficial reports that Confederates were fleeing from the city toward McDonough, southeast of Atlanta and of his own position, Sherman did not react. According to Albert Castel, "Meanwhile [Sherman] will continue after Hardee in the hope of overtaking and crushing him before he has time to entrench. There is no evidence that he so much as considers sending a force eastward—the XXIII Corps and units of the IV and XIV corps are available—to block the McDonough road in case the reports that the Confederates are retreating from Atlanta by that route prove true."[8]

After a day of timid and poorly coordinated pursuit and attack, employing only three of his twelve available divisions, Sherman finally

called off the chase when some of his troops encountered hastily con-
structed but effective fortifications and he learned definitively of Atlanta's fall and occupation by Slocum.[9] According to James Donnell,
"Sherman decided that his army was in need of a well-deserved rest, and
pulled back."[10] Hood escaped with forty thousand troops, including
Georgia militia.

An impressive array of historians agree that keeping Sherman's
armies in Atlanta and allowing Hood's army to get away without even
attempting to block the escape route was a major, war-extending blunder.
Evaluating the decision in the context of Sherman's broader mission,
Murray and Hsieh explain the seriousness of his error: "After all, the
campaign's strategic aim was not just to capture Atlanta but to destroy
the Army of Tennessee, as well as to inflict as much economic damage
on the Deep South as possible. By not moving rapidly to attack Hood's
demoralized army as it abandoned Atlanta, Sherman lost the opportunity
to finish off his opponent."[11] The *West Point Atlas of American Wars*
echoes that analysis: "When Sherman occupied Atlanta on 2 September
and left Hood's army at Lovejoy's Station, he had accomplished the
second part of his mission but not the first part—to destroy the Confederate army. Herein lay a real source of embarrassment...."[12]

The perceptive T. Harry Williams points out that "Sherman had
Atlanta but he had not accomplished his primary objective of destroying
the Confederate army, which moved to a position west of the city."[13]
Likewise, Nevins notes that Sherman "had not accomplished all he
desired, for Hood's army, his principal objective, had eluded him."[14] John
Marszalek has more fully explored Sherman's often overlooked blunder:

> Sherman's decision to spare Hood was ignored in the eupho-
> ria over Atlanta's capture. Sherman never doubted that he
> had done the right thing. In his mid-September campaign
> report, he said: "The object of my movement against the
> railroad was therefore already reached and concluded, and
> as it was idle to pursue our enemy in that wooded country
> with a view to his capture, I gave orders on the Fourth for

the army to prepare to move back slowly to Atlanta." It was a mistake. The Confederate army, which had, after all, been his primary objective, was allowed to escape, capable of fighting once more. Clearly Sherman did not want to cause more death and mayhem, satisfied that his capture of Atlanta had given him a major military victory. He was correct, but it was not the military victory he might have achieved. He might have destroyed Hood's force and rendered the entire theater of war defenseless. But Sherman abhorred bloodshed, and Kennesaw showed him in graphic terms how much carnage battle could cause.[15]

Sherman himself admitted to Halleck that "I ought to have reaped larger fruits of victory." But he then proceeded to blame his subordinate generals Thomas, Stanley, and William Hardee. Castel, however, concludes that the responsibility belonged to Sherman: "Six times between August 27 and September 3 he had an opportunity to destroy or to mangle, or, at the very least, to drive Hood's army to the eastern edge of Georgia, thus leaving that state and Alabama at Sherman's mercy. Each time he muffed the opportunity, even when, as happened on one occasion, it was pointed out to him."[16]

Castel explains that Sherman's biggest mistakes in the campaign's final days were wasting days tearing up railroad tracks instead of moving quickly to reach the southern flank and rear of Confederate forces south of Atlanta. He also contends that Sherman once again, to his detriment, rejected astute advice from George Thomas: "Sherman's other mistake— this one major and unforgivable—was his rejection of Thomas's proposal to have the IV and XIV corps move around to Lovejoy's [Station] while Howard pinned down Hardee at Jonesboro [closer to Atlanta]. Had this been done, assuming a modicum of competent management on the Union side, all of the Confederate army, Hardee's Corps included, would have been cut off from Macon, leaving Hood with no rational choice except to withdraw in the direction of Augusta, in effect abandoning Alabama and Georgia."[17]

Sherman reviews his troops in Savannah before pursuing Hardee and invading the Carolinas in January 1865, by William Waud. *Courtesy of the Library of Congress*

Why did Sherman allow Hood's army to escape? Castel shows that from the beginning to the end of his campaign, Sherman intended to capture only Atlanta, not the Army of Tennessee. This fiasco, he concludes, "merely provides another demonstration of Sherman's preference for raiding over fighting, of his penchant for conducting operations on the basis of optimistic preconceptions of what the enemy will do, and of his unwillingness to engage his full force in battle. Thanks to these quirks in his military personality, Hood's army has been able to escape destruction."[18]

It is unlikely that Grant would have allowed a major enemy army to escape. One seeks in vain, however, for a condemnation, let alone criticism, by Grant of his friend Sherman's lapse. Instead, Grant in his memoirs compared the allegedly slow and non-aggressive Thomas with Sherman, concluding that Thomas could not have conducted the Atlanta Campaign as Sherman had done.[19] The evidence, however, indicates that Thomas would have been more aggressive at Snake Creek Gap–Resaca, less aggressive at Kennesaw Mountain, and more aggressive in pursuing Hood's army as Atlanta fell. On all three occasions, Sherman rejected Thomas's astute advice. So in a sense Grant may have been right: Thomas probably would not have conducted the Atlanta Campaign *as Sherman had done*; he would have conducted it *more effectively*.

Because he had allowed Hood's army to escape, Sherman had to send twenty thousand troops off to Tennessee to defend Nashville, and possibly Ohio, against Hood's invading army. The man he put in charge of that important mission was none other than Thomas. By December 16, however, from a distance of hundreds of miles, Sherman was complaining to Grant about Thomas's supposed lack of aggressiveness:

> I myself am somewhat astonished at the attitude of things in Tennessee. I purposely delayed at Kingston until General Thomas assured me that he was all ready, and my last dispatch from him on the 12th of November was full of confidence, in which he promised me that he would ruin Hood if he dared to advance from Florence, urging me to go ahead, and give myself no concern about Hood's army in Tennessee.
>
> Why did he not turn on him at Franklin, after checking and discomfiting him, surpasses my understanding. Indeed, I do not approve of his evacuating Decatur, but think he should have assumed the offensive against Hood from Pulaski, in the direction of Waynesburg. *I know full well that General Thomas is slow in mind and action*; but he is judicious and brave, and the troops feel great confidence in him. I still hope he will outmanoeuvre and destroy Hood.[20]

Back in Georgia, Sherman himself was not through allowing Rebel armies to escape. After the November 4 presidential election, with approval from Lincoln and Grant, he embarked on his famous March to the Sea. For six weeks in November and December, his sixty thousand troops burned a sixty-mile-wide trail of destruction from Atlanta to Savannah. Although few civilians were injured, raped, or killed,[21] the march wreaked economic havoc on the Georgian and Southern econo-mies while demonstrating that the Confederate government could not protect the property of its own people. It is likely that thousands of Confederate soldiers from Georgia deserted, returning home to help their loved ones.

The culmination of Sherman's March was his capture of Fort McAl-lister, where he established connections with the Union naval fleet and its supplies. A week later his army accepted the peaceful surrender of Savannah by the city's leaders, and on December 22 Sherman wired Lincoln, "I beg to present you as a Christmas gift the City of Savannah with 150 heavy guns & plenty of ammunition & also about 25000 bales of cotton."[22]

Once again, however, Sherman allowed a large Confederate force to escape to fight another day. On December 17 Sherman sent to General William Hardee, who had been defending Savannah and was outnum-bered six to one by Sherman's force, a demand that the city be surren-dered. After explaining that he had acquired from the Union fleet large guns and heavy ammunition with which he could bombard the heart of the city, Sherman wrote, "I have for some days held and controlled every avenue by which the people and garrison of Savannah can be supplied, and I am therefore justified in demanding the surrender of the city of Savannah, and its dependent forts...."[23] In refusing Sherman's demands, Hardee, perhaps foolishly, denied that Sherman controlled all avenues into the city, insisting that "I am in free and constant communication with my department."[24]

The next day Sherman assured Grant that Hardee's assertion was false. Sherman's control of the "Union Plank-road on the South Carolina shore" was sufficient to prevent adequate resupply, and Major General John Foster, the commander of the Department of the South, assured him his forces were on that road "so that [railroad] cars no longer run between Charleston and Savannah."[25]

Despite Sherman's assurances, a week after the capture of Fort McAllister (when Sherman told Halleck, "I regard Savannah as already gained"), Hardee and his ten-thousand-man garrison pulled out of the city and escaped across the Savannah River.[26] His nighttime movements were detected by enemy pickets, who sent word up the chain of command, but the Union armies failed to respond, and Hardee's considerable force escaped into South Carolina. Those troops were the foundation of the Rebel forces that opposed Sherman's movements through both Carolinas in the early months of 1865.

In his memoirs, Sherman wrote that he had invested Savannah on the north, west, and south, but "there remained to the enemy, on the east, the use of the old dike or plank-road leading into South Carolina, and I knew that Hardee would have a pontoon-bridge across the river." Although admitting that Union troops could occupy, fortify, and hold the plank-road escape route, Sherman said he declined to do so because Hardee's whole army could have fallen upon the blocking detachment and because he did not want to make a mistake like Ball's Bluff (a Union disaster in 1861) at that point in the war.[27]

So instead of attempting to block the escape route, Sherman on December 18 took a three-day boat trip to Hilton Head, South Carolina, to discuss the situation with Foster. Sherman later asserted ambiguously that he had "represented the matter to General Foster, and he promptly agreed to give his personal attention to it." When Sherman returned from Hilton Head on the evening of December 21, he learned that Hardee had evacuated his army and light artillery across the Savannah River the night before.[28]

To summarize, the supposedly aggressive Sherman may have failed to cut off the escape route of Hardee's army because he feared possible defeat—even though he greatly outnumbered Hardee, who would have had to cross the Savannah River and nearby swamps to attack any blocking Union force. James McDonough provides this rationale for Sherman's inaction: "If Hardee had been trapped in Savannah, Sherman most likely would have attempted to starve the city into submission. He did not want a costly assault, nor the employment of artillery, for he had fond memories of Savannah's homes and gardens."[29] Sherman himself claimed, "I was very much disappointed that Hardee had escaped with his garrison, and had to content myself with the material fruits of victory without the cost of life which would have attended a general assault."[30]

Again, Marszalek offers a different perspective. When Sherman tightened the noose around the city after Hardee's refusal to surrender, "[t]here was one escape route still open to Hardee, and though Sherman talked about closing it, he seemed rather nonchalant about doing so." Marszalek quotes one Union officer who said, "For some reason unknown to me, the General has not pushed a heavy or even a small force across the Savannah River, so as to prevent the rebels from escaping in that direction," and the escape route "remained open to them for at least nine days." Another officer asserted that the army "concluded General Sherman wanted the enemy to leave and not make a fight necessary."[31]

Joining Hardee's soldiers in the Carolinas as part of a reconstituted Army of Tennessee were the remnants of Hood's army that Sherman had allowed to escape from Atlanta. Although Thomas had decimated Hood's army at Franklin and Nashville in late 1864, thousands of Hood's soldiers managed to flee all the way to Alabama and Mississippi. In early 1865 they fought under Joseph Johnston against Sherman as he swept through the Carolinas.

While Sherman was marching to Savannah and allowing Hardee to escape, Thomas, despite harassment by Grant and criticism by Sherman, carried out one of the most effective attacks of the entire war. His two-day assault on Hood's army in December replicated Thomas's battle plans. As Castel writes, "What Thomas, had he had his way, would have done in Georgia in May and again in August has been accomplished by him in December in Tennessee: the elimination of the Army of Tennessee from the war." Elsewhere, he adds that Sherman "was, in short, a general who did not like to fight. Had Thomas's personal relationship with Grant permitted him to command in Georgia in 1864, almost surely the Union victory would have been easier, quicker, and more complete."[32]

In the final four months of 1864, Sherman had committed a pair of blunders, allowing two separate Confederate armies to escape his clutches because he seemed to be satisfied with occupying two Confederate cities.[33] Hood's army of thirty thousand[34] and Hardee's army of ten thousand continued to fight, inflicting thousands of Union casualties and extending the war for eight and four months, respectively. It appears that in their excitement about the capture of Atlanta and Savannah, Lincoln and Grant were willing to overlook these blunders and omit their usual emphasis on eliminating enemy armies.

These dual failures by Sherman provide an appropriate conclusion to this discussion of the ten biggest blunders of the Civil War. But there were many other major blunders in the course of that awful war, several of which I will examine in my next book.

ACKNOWLEDGMENTS

As I did with my previous six books, I have taken advantage of the generosity of almost a dozen friends and professional colleagues who provided their thoughtful input on the "final" working draft of this book. They helped me avoid many mistakes and greatly improved the quality of the text.

Those with the most endurance, who read and commented on the entire text, include longtime *Civil War News* publisher Kay Jorgensen, the country's finest Ulysses Grant historian, John Marszalek, Civil War scholar and author Clint Johnson, Civil War experts and fine attorneys John Foskett and Mike Harrington, and ace editors and wordsmiths Elaine Economides Joost and Steve Farbman.

Richard McMurry, an authority on the Atlanta Campaign and the Army of Tennessee (and a Southern gentleman to boot), provided invaluable insights and corrections for the Snake Creek Gap chapter. Gettysburg scholar John Valori helpfully identified issues in the Gettysburg chapter. Gene Fidell, a Yale Law School Senior Scholar and Visiting Lecturer and an old Coast Guard friend, gave me candid and useful advice.

Once again I owe a debt of gratitude to Regnery History publisher Alex Novak for the opportunity to express my views on the Civil War and to Tom Spence, whose elite editing skills have transformed this work into a lucid and flowing document.

Whatever errors have slipped through the many filters I have tried to use are solely my responsibility.

—Ed Bonekemper

BIBLIOGRAPHY

MEMOIRS, LETTERS, PAPERS, AND OTHER PRIMARY DOCUMENTS AND EVIDENCE

Alexander, Edward Porter. *Fighting for the Confederacy: The Personal Recollections of General Edward Porter Alexander.* Edited by Gary W. Gallagher. Chapel Hill: University of North Carolina Press, 1989.

—————. *The Military Memoirs of a Confederate.* New York: Charles Scribner's Sons, 1907. Much more redacted and less useful than the above publication.

Badeau, Adam. *Military History of Ulysses S. Grant, from April, 1861, to April, 1865.* 3 vols. New York: D. Appleton and Company, 1868.

Basler, Roy P., ed. *The Collected Works of Abraham Lincoln.* 8 vols. New Brunswick: Rutgers University Press, 1953.

Blackford, William Willis. *War Years with Jeb Stuart.* Baton Rouge: Louisiana State University Press, 1945, 1993.

Commager, Henry Steele. *Documents of American History*. New York: Appleton-Century-Crofts, 1958.

Dana, Charles A. *Recollections of the Civil War*. New York: Collier Books, 1893, 1963.

Davis, Jefferson. *The Rise and Fall of the Confederate Government*. 2 vols. New York: Da Capo Press, Inc., 1990. Reprint of 1881 edition. Use skeptically.

Dowdey, Clifford and Manarin, Louis H., eds. *The Wartime Papers of R.E. Lee*. New York: Bramhall House, 1961. Since this volume contains edited versions of Lee's correspondence, try checking other sources to be sure of the exact language of those documents.

Fehrenbacher, Don E. and Fehrenbacher, Virginia, eds., *Recollected Words of Abraham Lincoln*. Stanford: Stanford University Press, 1996. Valuable analysis of oral statements purportedly made by Lincoln.

Freeman, Douglas Southall and Grady McWhiney, eds. *Lee's Dispatches: Unpublished Letters of General Robert E. Lee, C.S.A., to Jefferson Davis and the War Department of the Confederate States of America 1862–65*. Baton Rouge: Louisiana State University Press, 1957, 1994. Update of Freeman's original 1914edition.

Gienapp, William E., ed. *The Civil War and Reconstruction: A Documentary Collection*. New York: W.W. Norton & Company, 2001.

Gorgas, Josiah. *The Civil War Diary of General Josiah Gorgas*. Edited by Frank E. Vandiver and Sarah Woolfolk Wiggins. Birmingham: University of Alabama Press, 1947, 1955.

Grant, Ulysses S. *Memoirs and Selected Letters: Personal Memoirs of U. S. Grant, Selected Letters 1839–1865*. Reprint. New York: Literary Classics of the United States, Inc., 1990. Use skeptically.

Hay, John. *Inside Lincoln's White House: The Complete Civil War Diary of John Hay*. Edited by Michael Burlingame, and John R. Turner Ettlinger. Carbondale: Southern University Press, 1997.

Johnson, Robert Underwood and Buel, Clarence Clough, eds. *Battles and Leaders of the Civil War.* 4 vols. New York: Thomas Yoseloff, Inc., 1956. Reprint of Secaucus, New Jersey: Castle, 1887–88.

Johnston, Joseph E. *Narrative of Military Operations During the Civil War.* New York: Appleton, 1874.

Jones, J. B. *A Rebel War Clerk's Diary at the Confederate States Capital.* 2 vols. Philadelphia: J. B. Lippincott & Co., 1866. 1982 reprint.

Longstreet, James. *From Manassas to Appomattox: Memoirs of the Civil War in America.* New York: Smithmark Publishers, Inc., 1994. Reprint of 1896 edition.

Mackey, Thomas C., ed. *A Documentary History of the American Civil War Era, Vol. II, Political Arguments.* Knoxville: University of Tennessee Press, 2013.

McClellan, George B. *Report of Major General George B. McClellan upon the Organization of the Army of the Potomac, and its campaigns in Virginia and Maryland, from July 26, 1861, to November 7, 1862.* House of Representatives, 38th Congress, 1st Session, Ex. Doc. No. 15. Washington: Government Printing Office, 1864.

Porter, Horace. *Campaigning with Grant.* New York: Smithmark Publishers, Inc., 1994. Reprint.

Rhodes, Robert Hunt, ed. *All for the Union: The Civil War Diary and Letters of Elisha Hunt Rhodes.* New York: Orion Books, 1991. Originally Andrew Mowbray Inc., 1985.

Sears, Stephen W. *The Civil War Papers of George B. McClellan: Selected Correspondence, 1860-1865.* New York: Ticknor & Fields, 1989. Invaluable.

Sherman, William Tecumseh. *Memoirs of General W. T. Sherman.* New York: Literary Classics of the United States, Inc., 1990. Reprint of 1885 second edition.

Simon, John Y., and John F. Marszalek, et al, eds. *The Papers of Ulysses S. Grant*. 34 vols. Carbondale: Southern Illinois University Press, 1967–2015.

Taylor, Walter H. *General Lee: His Campaigns in Virginia 1861–1865 with Personal Reminiscences*. Lincoln: University of Nebraska Press, 1994. Reprint of Norfolk: Nusbaum Books, 1906.

Tower, R. Lockwood, ed. *Lee's Adjutant: The Wartime Letters of Colonel Walter Herron Taylor, 1862–1865*. Columbia: University of South Carolina Press, 1995.

U.S. Congress, Report of the Joint Committee on the Conduct of the War. House of Representatives, 37th Cong., 3rd Sess. 3 vols. Washington: Government Printing Office, 1863.

Ward, Andrew. *The Slaves' War: The Civil War in the Words of Former Slaves*. Boston: Mariner Books, 2008.

The War of the Rebellion: A Compilation of the Official Records of the Union and Confederate Armies. 128 vols. Washington, DC: Government Printing Office, 1880–1901.

Watkins, Sam. R. *"Co. Aytch," Maury Grays, First Tennessee Regiment; or, A Side Show of the Big Show*. Wilmington, NC: Broadfoot Publishing Company, 1987. Reprint of 1952 edition and of Nashville: Cumberland Presbyterian Publishing House, 1882.

Welles, Gideon. *Diary of Gideon Welles*. 3 vols. Boston and New York: Houghton Mifflin Company, 1911.

STATISTICAL ANALYSES

Fox, William F. *Regimental Losses in the American Civil War, 1861–1865: A Treatise on the Extent and Nature of the Mortuary Losses in the Union Regiments, with Full and Exhaustive Statistics Compiled from the Official Records on File in the State Military Bureaus and at Washington.* Dayton: Morningside House, Inc., 1985. Reprint of Albany: Brandow Printing Company, 1898.

Livermore, Thomas L. *Numbers & Losses in the Civil War in America: 1861–1865.* Millwood, NY: Kraus Reprint Co., 1977. Reprint of Bloomington: Indiana University Press, 1957.

Phisterer, Frederick. *Statistical Record: A Treasury of Information about the U.S. Civil War.* Carlisle, PA: John Kallmann Publishers, 1996. Reprint of Statistical Record of the Armies of the United States (1883), a supplementary volume to Scribner's Campaigns of the Civil War series.

———. *Statistical Record of the Armies of the United States.* Edison, New Jersey: Castle Books, 2002. Reprint of 1883 book.

ATLASES, ENCYCLOPEDIAS, OTHER REFERENCE WORKS

Barney, William L. *The Oxford Encyclopedia of the Civil War.* New York: Oxford University Press, 2001, 2011.

Bradford, James C. Bradford, ed. *Oxford Atlas of American Military History.* New York: Oxford University Press, 2003.

Chambers, John Whiteclay II, ed. *The Oxford Companion to American Military History.* Oxford: Oxford University Press, 1999.

Current, Richard N., ed. *Encyclopedia of the Confederacy.* 4 vols. New York: Simon & Schuster, 1993.

Esposito, Vincent J., ed. *The West Point Atlas of American Wars.* 2 vols. New York: Frederick A. Praeger, 1959, 1964.

Garrity, John A., ed. *Encyclopedia of American Biography.* New York: Harper & Row, 1974.

Heidler, David S. and Heidler, Jeanne T., eds. *Encyclopedia of the American Civil War: A Political, Social, and Military History.* New York: W. W. Norton & Company, 2002.

Jones, Terry L. *Historical Dictionary of the Civil War.* Second edition. 2 vols. Lanham, MD: Scarecrow Press, 2011.

Kennedy, Frances H., ed. *The Civil War Battlefield Guide.* Boston: Houghton Mifflin Company, 1990.

The Library of Congress Civil War Desk Reference. Washington: Library of Congress, 2002.

Sifakis, Stewart. *Who Was Who in the Civil War: A Comprehensive, Illustrated Biographical Reference to More Than 2,500 of the Principal Union and Confederate Participants in the War Between the States.* Berwyn Heights, MD: Heritage Books, Inc., 2014.

Symonds, Craig L. *Gettysburg: A Battlefield Atlas.* Baltimore: Nautical & Aviation Publishing Company of America, 1992. Wagner, Margaret E., Gary W. Gallagher, and Paul Finkelman, eds. *The Library of Congress Civil War Desk Reference.* New York: Simon & Schuster, 2002.

Warner, Ezra J. *Generals in Blue: Lives of the Union Commanders.* Baton Rouge: Louisiana State University Press, 1964.

———. *Generals in Gray: Lives of the Confederate Commanders.* Baton Rouge: Louisiana State University Press, 1959.

OTHER BOOKS AND MANUSCRIPTS

Abbazia, Patrick. *The Chickamauga Campaign, December 1862–November 1863.* New York: Wieser & Wieser, Inc., 1988.

Adams, Michael C. C. *Fighting for Defeat: Union Military Failure in the East, 1861–1865.* Lincoln: University of Nebraska Press, 1978, 1992.

———. *Living Hell: The Dark Side of the Civil War.* Baltimore: Johns Hopkins University Press, 2014.

Alexander, Bevin. *How Great Generals Win.* New York: W. W. Norton & Co., 1993.

Ambrose, Stephen E. *Halleck: Lincoln's Chief of Staff.* Baton Rouge: Louisiana State University Press, 1962, 1990.

Arnold, James R. *The Armies of U.S. Grant.* London: Arms and Armour Press, 1995.

Baptist, Edward E. *The Half Has Never Been Told: Slavery and the Making of American Capitalism.* New York: Basic Books, 2014.

Beringer, Richard E. et al. *Why the South Lost the Civil War.* Athens: University of Georgia Press, 1986.

Bobrick, Benson. *Master of War: The Life of General George H. Thomas.* New York: Simon & Schuster, 2009. Use skeptically.

Bonekemper, Edward H., III. *Grant and Lee: Victorious American and Vanquished Virginian.* Washington, DC: Regnery Publishing, 2012.

———. *How Robert E. Lee Lost the Civil War.* Fredericksburg, VA: Sergeant Kirkland's Press, 1998.

———. *Lincoln and Grant: The Westerners Who Won the Civil War.* Washington, DC: Regnery Publishing, 2015.

———. *McClellan and Failure: A Study of Civil War Fear, Incompetence, and Worse.* Jefferson, NC: McFarland & Company, 2007, 2010.

———. *The Myth of the Lost Cause: Why the South Fought the Civil War and Why the North Won.* Washington: Regnery History, 2015.

———. *Ulysses S. Grant: A Victor, Not a Butcher: The Military Genius of the Man Who Won the Civil War.* Washington, DC: Regnery Publishing, 2004.

Boritt, Gabor S., ed. *Lincoln's Generals.* New York: Oxford University Press, 1994.

———. *Lincoln, the War President.* New York: Oxford University Press, 1992.

————, ed. *Why the Confederacy Lost*. New York: Oxford University Press, 1992.

Brown, Kent Masterson. *Lee, Logistics, and the Pennsylvania Campaign*. Chapel Hill: University of North Carolina Press, 2005.

Buell, Thomas B. *The Warrior Generals: Combat Leadership in the Civil War*. New York: Crown Publishers, Inc., 1997.

Cannan, John, ed. *War in the East: Chancellorsville to Gettysburg, 1863*. New York: Gallery Books, 1990.

Carhart, Tom. *Lost Triumph: Lee's Real Plan at Gettysburg and Why It Failed*. New York: G.P. Putnam's Sons, 2005.

Castel, Albert E. *Decision in the West: The Atlanta Campaign of 1864*. Lawrence: University Press of Kansas, 1992.

———— with Brooks D. Simpson. *Victors in Blue: How Union Generals Fought the Confederates, Battled Each Other, and Won the Civil War*. Lawrence: University Press of Kansas, 2011.

Catton, Bruce. *The Army of the Potomac: Glory Road*. Garden City, NY: Doubleday & Company, Inc., 1952.

————. *The Army of the Potomac: Mr. Lincoln's Army*. Garden City, NY: Doubleday & Company, Inc., 1951, 1962.

————. *The Army of the Potomac: A Stillness at Appomattox*. Garden City, NY: Doubleday & Company, Inc., 1953.

————. *Grant Moves South*. Boston: Little, Brown and Company, 1960.

————. *Grant Takes Command*. Boston: Little, Brown and Company, 1969.

————. *Terrible Swift Sword*. Garden City, NY: Doubleday & Company, Inc., 1963.

————. *This Hallowed Ground: The Story of the Union Side of the Civil War*. Garden City, NY: Doubleday & Company, Inc., 1956, 1962.

———. *U.S. Grant and the American Military Tradition.* Boston: Little, Brown and Company, 1954.

Coburn, Mark. *Terrible Innocence: General Sherman at War.* New York: Hippocrene Books, 1993.

Coddington, Edwin B. *The Gettysburg Campaign: A Study in Command.* New York: Charles Scribner's Sons, 1968, 1979.

Conger, Arthur L. *The Rise of U.S. Grant.* New York: Da Capo, 1996. Reprint of New York: Century Co., 1931.

Connelly, Thomas Lawrence. *Army of the Heartland: The Army of Tennessee, 1861–1862.* Baton Rouge: Louisiana State University Press, 1967.

———. *Autumn of Glory: The Army of Tennessee, 1862–1865.* Baton Rouge: Louisiana State University Press, 1971, 1991.

———. *The Marble Man: Robert E. Lee and His Image in American Society.* New York: Alfred A. Knopf, 1977.

——— and Archer Jones. *The Politics of Command: Factions and Ideas in Confederate Strategy.* Baton Rouge: Louisiana State University Press, 1973.

——— and Barbara R. Bellows. *God and General Longstreet: The Lost Cause and the Southern Mind.* Baton Rouge: Louisiana State University Press, 1982.

Cornish, Dudley Taylor. *The Sable Arm: Black Troops in the Union Army, 1861–1865.* Lawrence: University Press of Kansas, 1956, 1987.

Cotham, Edward T., Jr. *Sabine Pass: The Confederacy's Thermopylae.* Austin: University of Texas Press, 2004

Cozzens, Peter. *The Shipwreck of Their Hopes: The Battles for Chattanooga.* Urbana: University of Illinois Press, 1994.

Davis, Stephen. *Atlanta Will Fall: Sherman, Joe Johnston, and the Yankee Heavy Battalions.* Wilmington: Scholarly Resources, Inc., 2001.

Davis, William C. *The Cause Lost: Myths and Realities of the Confederacy*. Lawrence: University Press of Kansas, 1996.

———. *Crucible of Command: Ulysses S. Grant and Robert E. Lee—The War They Fought, the Peace They Forged*. New York: Da Capo, 2015.

———. Jefferson Davis: *The Man and His Hour*. Baton Rouge, Louisiana State University Press, 1991, 1996.

Dickey, Christopher. *Our Man in Charleston: Britain's Secret Agent in the Civil War South*. New York: Crown Publishers, 2015.

Donald, David Herbert, ed. *Why the North Won the Civil War*. New York: Simon & Schuster, 1962, 1996.

———. *Lincoln*. New York: Simon & Schuster, 1995.

Donnell, James. *Atlanta 1864: Sherman Marches South*. New York: Osprey Publishing, 2016.

Doyle, Don H. *The Cause of All Nations: An International History of the American Civil War*. New York: Basic Books, 2015.

Eckenrode, H. J. and Brian Conrad. *George B. McClellan: The Man Who Saved the Union*. Chapel Hill: University of North Carolina Press, 1941.

Eicher, David J. *The Longest Night: A Military History of the Civil War*. New York: Simon & Schuster, 2002.

Evans, David. *Sherman's Horsemen: Union Cavalry Operations in the Atlanta Campaign*. Bloomington: University of Indiana Press, 1996.

Feis, William B. *Grant's Secret Service: The Intelligence War from Belmont to Appomattox*. Lincoln: University of Nebraska Press, 2002.

Fellman, Michael. *Citizen Sherman: A Life of William Tecumseh Sherman*. New York: Random House, 1995.

———. *The Making of Robert E. Lee*. Baltimore: Johns Hopkins University Press, 2000.

Fishel, Edwin C. *The Secret War for the Union: The Untold Story of Military Intelligence in the Civil War.* Boston: Houghton Mifflin, 1996.

Flood, Charles Bracelen. *Grant and Sherman: The Friendship That Won the Civil War.* New York: Farrar, Straus and Giroux, 2005.

Foote, Shelby, ed. *The Civil War: A Narrative.* 3 vols. New York: Random House, 1958–1974.

Freeman, Douglas Southall. *Lee's Lieutenants: A Study in Command.* 3 vols. New York: Charles Scribner's Sons, 1942–44 (1972 reprint).

———. *R. E. Lee.* 4 vols. New York and London: Charles Scribner's Sons, 1934–35.

Fuller, J. F. C. *The Generalship of Ulysses S. Grant.* Bloomington: Indiana University Press, 1958. Reprint of 1929 edition.

———. *Grant and Lee: A Study in Personality and Generalship.* Bloomington: Indiana University Press, 1957. Reprint of 1933 edition.

Furgurson, Ernest B. *Chancellorsville 1863: The Souls of the Brave.* New York: Alfred A. Knopf, 1992.

Gallagher, Gary W., ed. *The Antietam Campaign.* Chapel Hill: University of North Carolina Press, 1999.

———. *Lee and His Generals in War and Memory.* Baton Rouge: Louisiana State University, 1998.

———, ed. *Lee the Soldier.* Lincoln: University of Nebraska Press, 1996.

———, ed. and Alan T. Nolan. *The Myth of the Lost Cause and Civil War History.* Bloomington: University of Indiana Press, 2000, 2010.

———, ed. *The Third Day at Gettysburg & Beyond.* Chapel Hill: University of North Carolina Press, 1994.

Glatthaar, Joseph T. *Partners in Command: The Relationships Between Leaders in the Civil War.* New York: Macmillan, Inc., 1994.

Griffith, Paddy. *Battle Tactics of the Civil War*. New Haven: Yale University Press, 1996.

Guelzo, Allen C. *Gettysburg: The Last Invasion*. New York: Alfred A. Knopf, 2013.

Hagerman, Edward. *The American Civil War and the Origins of Modern Warfare: Ideas, Organization, and Field Command*. Bloomington: Indiana University Press, 1992.

Harsh, Joseph L. *Confederate Tide Rising: Robert E. Lee and the Making of Southern Strategy, 1861–1862*. Kent: Kent State University Press, 1998.

Hassler, Warren W., Jr. *Commanders of the Army of the Potomac*. Baton Rouge: Louisiana State University Press, 1962.

Hattaway, Herman and Archer Jones. *How the North Won: A Military History of the Civil War*. Urbana: University of Illinois Press, 1991. Reprint of 1983 edition.

Hearn, Chester G. *Lincoln, the Cabinet and the Generals*. Baton Rouge: Louisiana State University Press, 2010.

Heleniak, Roman J. and Hewitt, Lawrence L., ed. *The Confederate High Command & Related Topics: The 1988 Deep Delta Civil War Symposium*. Shippensburg, PA: White Mane Publishing Co., Inc., 1990.

Howe, Thomas J. *The Petersburg Campaign: Wasted Valor, June 15–18, 1864*. Lynchburg: H.E. Howard, Inc., 1988.

Hubbell, John T., ed. *Conflict and Command*. Kent, Ohio: Kent State University Press, 2012.

Jewett, Clayton E., ed. *The Battlefield and Beyond: Essays on the American Civil War*. Baton Rouge: Louisiana State University Press, 2012.

Johnson, Clint. *Civil War Blunders*. Winston-Salem: John F. Blair, 1997.

Johnson, David Alan. *Battle of Wills: Ulysses S. Grant, Robert E. Lee, and the Last Year of the Civil War*. Amherst, NY: Prometheus Books, 2016.

Jones, Archer. *Civil War Command & Strategy: The Process of Victory and Defeat.* New York: The Free Press, 1992.

———. *Confederate Strategy from Shiloh to Vicksburg.* Baton Rouge: Louisiana State University Press, 1991.

Jones, R. Steven. *The Right Hand of Command: Use & Disuse of Personal Staffs in the Civil War.* Mechanicsburg, PA: Stackpole Books, 2000.

Jones, Terry L. *Lee's Tigers: The Louisiana Infantry in the Army of Northern Virginia.* Baton Rouge: Louisiana State University Press, 1987.

Katcher, Philip. *The Army of Robert E. Lee.* London: Arms and Armour Press, 1994.

Keegan, John. *The Face of Battle.* New York: Dorset Press, 1986.

———. *The Mask of Command.* New York: Viking, 1987.

Levine, Bruce. *Confederate Emancipation: Southern Plans To Free and Arm Slaves During the Civil War.* Oxford: Oxford University Press, 2006.

Longacre, Edward G. *General John Buford: A Military Biography.* Conshohocken, PA: Combined Books, Inc., 1995.

Lowry, Don. *Fate of the Country: The Civil War from June–September 1864.* New York: Hippocrene Books, 1992.

———. *No Turning Back: The Beginning of the End of the Civil War: March–June, 1864.* New York: Hippocrene Books, 1992.

Luvaas, Jay, and Harold W. Nelson, eds. *The U.S. Army War College Guide to the Battle of Gettysburg.* Carlisle, PA: South Mountain Press, Inc., 1986.

———, eds. *The U.S. Army War College Guide to the Battle of Antietam: The Maryland Campaign of 1862.* Carlisle, PA: South Mountain Press, Inc., 1987.

Marszalek, John F. *Commander of All Lincoln's Armies: A Life of General Henry W. Halleck*. Cambridge, MA: Belknap Press, 2004.

———. *Sherman: A Soldier's Passion for Order*. New York: Macmillan, Inc., 1993.

Marvel, William. *Lincoln's Autocrat: The Life of Edwin Stanton*. Chapel Hill: University of North Carolina Press, 2015.

Matloff, Maurice, ed. *American Military History*. 2 vols. Washington, DC: U.S. Army Center of Military History, 1985.

McDonough, James Lee. *Chattanooga: A Death Grip on the Confederacy*. Knoxville: University of Tennessee Press, 1984.

———. *William Tecumseh Sherman: In the Service of My Country: A Life*. New York: W.W. Norton & Co., 2016.

McKenzie, John D. *Uncertain Glory: Lee's Generalship Re-Examined*. New York: Hippocrene Books, 1997.

McMurry, Richard M. *Two Great Rebel Armies: An Essay in Confederate Military History*. Chapel Hill: University of North Carolina Press, 1989.

McPherson, James M. *Battle Cry of Freedom: The Civil War Era*. New York: Ballantine Books, 1988.

———. *Crossroads of Freedom: Antietam*. Oxford: Oxford University Press, 2002.

———. *Ordeal by Fire*. New York: Knopf, 1982.

———. *The War that Forged a Nation: Why the Civil War Still Matters*. Oxford; Oxford University Press, 2015.

McWhiney, Grady, and Perry D. Jamieson. *Attack and Die: Civil War Military Tactics and the Southern Heritage*. Tuscaloosa: University of Alabama Press, 1982.

Meade, Robert Douthat. *Judah P. Benjamin: Confederate Statesman*. Baton Rouge: Louisiana State University Press, 1943, 2001.

Morris, Roy, Jr. *Sheridan: The Life and Wars of General Phil Sheridan.* New York: Crown Publishers, Inc., 1992.

Murphin, James V. *The Gleam of Bayonets: The Battle of Antietam and the Maryland Campaign of 1862.* Baton Rouge: Louisiana State University Press, 1965.

Nevins, Allan. *Ordeal of the Union.* 8 vols. New York: Charles Scribner's Sons, 1947–50.

Nofi, Albert A. *The Gettysburg Campaign, June and July, 1863.* New York: Wieser & Wieser, Inc., 1986.

Nolan, Alan T. *The Iron Brigade: A Military History.* Bloomington: Indiana University Press, 1961.

———. *Lee Considered: General Robert E. Lee and Civil War History.* Chapel Hill: University of North Carolina Press, 1991.

Osborne, Charles C. *Jubal: The Life and Times of General Jubal A. Early, CSA, Defender of the Lost Cause.* Baton Rouge: Louisiana State University Press, 1992.

Perry, Mark. *Conceived in Liberty: Joshua Chamberlain, William Oates, and the American Civil War.* New York: Viking, 1997.

Pfanz, Donald C. *Richard S. Ewell: A Soldier's Life.* Chapel Hill: University of North Carolina Press, 1998.

Pfanz, Harry W. *Gettysburg—Culp's Hill & Cemetery Hill.* Chapel Hill: University of North Carolina Press, 1993.

———. *Gettysburg: The Second Day.* Chapel Hill: University of North Carolina Press, 1987.

Piston, William Garrett. *Lee's Tarnished Lieutenant: James Longstreet and His Place in Southern History.* Athens: University of Georgia Press, 1987.

Pois, Robert and Philip Langer. *Command Failure in War: Psychology and Leadership.* Bloomington: Indiana University Press, 2004.

Priest, John M. *Antietam: The Soldiers' Battle*. Shippensburg, PA: White Mane Publishing Co., Inc., 1989.

Quarles, Benjamin. *The Negro in the Civil War*. Boston: Little, Brown and Co., 1953.

Rhea, Gordon C. *The Battle of the Wilderness May 5–6, 1864*. Baton Rouge: Louisiana State University Press, 1994.

———. *The Battles for Spotsylvania Court House and the Road to Yellow Tavern, May 7–12, 1864*. Baton Rouge: Louisiana State University Press, 1997.

———. *Cold Harbor: Grant and Lee May 26–June 3, 1864*. Baton Rouge: Louisiana State University Press, 2002.

———. *To the North Anna River: Lee and Grant May 13–25, 1864*. Baton Rouge: Louisiana State University Press, 2000.

Robertson, James I., Jr. *General A. P. Hill: The Story of a Confederate Warrior*. New York: Random House, 1987.

———. *Stonewall Jackson: The Man, the Soldier, the Legend*. New York: Macmillan Publishing USA, 1997.

Rowland, Thomas J. *George B. McClellan and Civil War History in the Shadow of Grant and Sherman*. Kent: Kent State University Press, 1998.

Royster, Charles. *The Destructive War: William Tecumseh Sherman, Stonewall Jackson, and the Americans*. New York: Vintage Books, 1993.

Scales, John R. *Sherman Invades Georgia*. Annapolis: Naval Institute Press, 2006.

Secrist, Philip L. *The Battle of Resaca: Atlanta Campaign, 1864*. Macon, GA: Mercer University Press, 1998.

Sears, Stephen W. *Controversies & Commanders: Dispatches from the Army of the Potomac*. Boston: Houghton Mifflin Company, 1999.

———. *George B. McClellan: The Young Napoleon*. New York: Tic-knor & Fields, 1988.

———. *Landscape Turned Red: The Battle of Antietam*. New York: Book of the Month Club, 1994.

Shaara, Michael. *The Killer Angels*. New York: Ballantine Books, 1974.

Simpson, Brooks D. *Ulysses S. Grant: Triumph Over Adversity, 1822–1865*. Boston: Houghton Mifflin Company, 2000.

Simpson, Harold B. *Hood's Texas Brigade: Lee's Grenadier Guard*. Fort Worth: Landmark Publishing, Inc., 1970. Vol. 2 of four-volume set of Hood's Texas Brigade.

Smith, Diane. *Command Conflicts in Grant's Overland Campaign: Ambition and Animosity in the Army of the Potomac*. Jefferson, NC: McFarland & Company, 2013.

Smith, Gene. *Lee and Grant: A Dual Biography*. New York: Promontory Press, 1984.

Smith, Jean Edward. *Grant*. New York: Simon & Schuster, 2001.

Smith, John David, ed. *Black Soldiers in Blue: African American Troops in the Civil War Era*. Chapel Hill: University of North Carolina Press, 2002.

Stackpole, Edward J. *They Met at Gettysburg*. New York: Bonanza Books, 1956.

Stern, Philip Van Doren. *Robert E. Lee: The Man and the Soldier*. New York: Bonanza Books, 1963.

Stewart, George R. *Pickett's Charge: A Microhistory of the Final Attack at Gettysburg, July 3, 1863*. Boston: Houghton Mifflin Co., 1959.

Thomas, Emory M. *Robert E. Lee: A Biography*. New York: W. W. Norton & Company, 1995.

Trudeau, Noah Andre. *The Last Citadel: Petersburg, Virginia June 1864–April 1865*. Baton Rouge: Louisiana State University Press, 1991.

Tucker, Phillip Thomas. *Barksdale's Charge: The True High Tide of the Confederacy at Gettysburg, July 2, 1863*. Havertown, PA: Casemate Publishers, 2013.

Waugh, John C. *The Class of 1846: From West Point to Appomattox: Stonewall Jackson, George McClellan and Their Brothers*. New York: Warner Books, Inc., 1994.

Weigley, Russell F. *The American Way of War: A History of United States Military Strategy and Policy*. New York: Macmillan Publishing Co., Inc., 1973.

———. *A Great Civil War: A Military and Political History, 1861–1865*. Bloomington: Indiana University Press, 2000.

Weir, William. *Fatal Victories*. Hamden, Connecticut: Archon Books, 1993.

Werstein, Irving. *Abraham Lincoln Versus Jefferson Davis*. New York: Thomas Y. Crowell Company, 1959.

Wert, Jeffry D. *General James Longstreet: The Confederacy's Most Controversial Soldier—A Biography*. New York: Simon & Schuster, 1993.

———. *The Sword of Lincoln: The Army of the Potomac*. New York: Simon & Schuster, 2005.

Wheeler, Richard. *On Fields of Fury: From the Wilderness to the Crater: An Eyewitness History*. New York: HarperCollins Publishers, 1991.

Wheeler, Tom. *Mr. Lincoln's T-Mails: The Untold Story of How Abraham Lincoln Used the Telegraph to Win the Civil War*. New York: Harper Collins, 2006.

White, Ronald C. *American Ulysses: A Life of Ulysses S. Grant*. New York: Random House, 2016.

Wiley, Bell Irvin. *The Road to Appomattox*. Baton Rouge: Louisiana State University Press, 1994. Reprint of Memphis: Memphis State College Press, 1956.

Williams, Kenneth P. *Grant Rises in the West*. 2 vols. Lincoln: University of Nebraska Press, 1997. Originally vols. 3 and 4 of *Lincoln Finds a General: A Military Study of the Civil War*. New York: Macmillan, 1952.

———. *Lincoln Finds a General: A Military Study of the Civil War*. Vol. 1. Bloomington: Indiana University Press, 1985. Reprint of 1949 edition.

———. *Lincoln Finds a General: A Military Study of the Civil War*. Vols. 2 and 5. New York: The Macmillan Company, 1959. Reprint of 1949 edition.

Williams, T. Harry. *Lincoln and His Generals*. New York: Alfred A. Knopf, Inc., 1952.

———. *McClellan, Sherman and Grant*. New Brunswick: Rutgers University Press, 1962.

Wills, Brian Steel. *George Henry Thomas: As True as Steel*. Lawrence: University Press of Kansas, 2012.

Wilson, David L., and John Y. Simon, eds. *Ulysses S. Grant: Essays and Documents*. Carbondale: University of Illinois Press, 1981.

Woodworth, Steven E., ed. *Civil War Generals in Defeat*. Lawrence: University of Kansas Press, 1999.

———, ed. *Davis and Lee at War*. Lawrence: University of Kansas Press, 1995.

———. *Jefferson Davis and His Generals: The Failure of Confederate Command in the West*. Lawrence: University Press of Kansas, 1990.

———. *Nothing But Victory: The Army of the Tennessee, 1861–1865*. New York: Alfred A. Knopf, 2005.

PERIODICAL ARTICLES

Alexander, Ted, "Antietam: The Bloodiest Day," *North & South*, Vol. 5, No. 7 (Oct. 2002): 76–89.

———. "Antietam Stories of Human Interest and Sites off the Beaten Path," *Blue & Gray Magazine*, XX, No. 1 (Fall 2002): 6–19, 48–62.

———. "Ten Days in July: The Pursuit to the Potomac," *North & South* 2, No. 6 (Aug. 1999): 10–34.

Allen, Stacy D. "Corinth, Mississippi: Crossroads of the Western Confederacy," *Blue & Gray Magazine*, XIX, No. 6 (Summer 2002): 6–25, 36–51.

Bauer, Daniel. "Did a Food Shortage Force Lee To Fight?: An Investigation into Lee's Claim That He had To Attack at Gettysburg Because His Army Lacked Sufficient Rations To Do Anything Else," *Columbiad: A Quarterly Review of the War Between the States*, Vol. I, No. 4 (Winter 1998): 57–74.

Bradley, Michael R. "Tullahoma: The Wrongly Forgotten Campaign," *Blue & Gray Magazine*, XXVII, No. 1 (2010), 6–25, 40–44, 47–50.

Brennan, Patrick J. "Mac's Last Stand: Autumn 1862 in Loudon Valley, Virginia," *Blue & Gray Magazine*, XVII, No. 2 (Dec. 1999): 6–20, 48–57.

Broome, Doyle D., Jr. "Daring Rear-guard Defense," *America's Civil War*, Vol. 6, No. 5 (Nov. 1993): 34–40.

Cheeks, Robert C. "Carnage in a Cornfield," *America's Civil War*, Vol. 5, No. 2 (July 2002): 30–37.

Chiles, Paul. "Artillery Hell! The Guns of Antietam," *Blue & Gray Magazine*, XVI, No. 2 (Dec. 1998): 6–16, 24–25, 41–59.

Clark, John E., Jr. "Reinforcing Rosecrans by Rail: The movement of the Federal Eleventh and Twelfth Corps from Virginia was a wonder of strategy, logistics, and engineering," *Columbiad: A Quarterly*

Review of the War Between the States, III, No. 3 (Fall 1999): 74–95 at 74–87.

"Common Soldier: Dr. John Kennerly Farris, Confederate Surgeon, Army of Tennessee," *Blue & Gray Magazine*, XVII, No. 2 (Dec. 1999): 46–47.

Connelly, Thomas Lawrence. "Robert E. Lee and the Western Confederacy: A Criticism of Lee's Strategic Ability," *Civil War History*, XV, No. 2 (June 1969): 116–32.

Davis, Stephen. "Pat Cleburne's Emancipation Proposal," *Blue & Gray Magazine*, VI, No. 4 (Apr. 1989), 19.

———. "Sherman in North Georgia: The Battle of Resaca," *Blue & Gray Magazine*, XXXI, No. 4 (2015): 6–28, 42–50.

Dolzall, Gary W. "Muddy, Soggy Race to Campbell's Station," *America's Civil War*, Vol. 15, No. 3 (July 2002): 26–32, 80.

Frye, Dennis E. "Burnside Betrayed?: Robert E. Lee's Confederates Were the Official Target at Antietam – But the Union Commander Took Aim at One of His Own," *America's Civil War*, Vol. 28, No. 4 (Sept. 2015): 23–31.

———. "'Through God's Blessing,'" *North & South*, Vol. 5, No. 7 (Oct. 2002): 66–74.

Hattaway, Herman. "The Changing Face of Battle," *North & South*, Vol. 4, No. 6 (August 2001): 34–43.

Jenkins, Robert D., Sr. "Dalton: The Opening of the Georgia Campaign," *Blue & Gray Magazine*, XXXII, No. 1 (2015): 6–30, 41–50.

Krolick, Marshall D., "Gettysburg: The First Day, July 1, 1863," *Blue & Gray Magazine*, V, No. 2 (Nov. 1987): 8–20, 14–15.

Kross, Gary. "Gettysburg Vignettes: Attack from the West," *Blue & Gray Magazine*, XVII, No. 5 (June 2000), 6–22, 44–50.

————. "That One Error Fills Him with Faults: Gen. Alfred Iverson and His Brigade at Gettysburg," *Blue & Gray Magazine*, XII, No. 3 (February 1995): 22, 52–53.

Levin, Kevin M. "Confederate Like Me: Rebels Who Brought Their Slaves to War Assumed a Shared Loyalty to the Confederate Cause —as Do Some History Revisionists Today," *The Civil War Monitor*, Vol. 3, No. 1 (Spring 2013): 60–67, 78–79.

Levine, Bruce. "Black Confederates," *North & South*, Vol. 10, No. 2 (July 2007): 40–45.

Mackowski, Chris and Kristopher D. White. "Second-Guessing Dick Ewell: Why Didn't the Confederate general take Cemetery Hill on July 1, 1863?" *Civil War Times*, Vol. 49, No. 4 (Aug. 2010): 34–41.

Magner, Blake A. "Hancock's Line at Gettysburg, July 3, 1863: 'This Is Going To Be a Hot Place,'" *Blue & Gray Magazine*, XXVI, No. 4 (2009), 6–25, 40–49.

Mallock, Daniel. "Cleburne's Proposal," *North & South*, Vol. 11, No. 2 (Dec. 2008): 64–72, 66–67.

Marvel, William. "More Than Water Under Burnside's Bridge," *America's Civil War*, Vol. 18, No. 6 (Jan. 2006): 46–52.

McMurry, Richard M. "From the West. . .Where the War Was Decided," *North & South*, Vol. 14, No. 1 (May 2012), 12–17.

Newton, Steven H. "Joseph Johnston and Snake Creek Gap," *North & South*, Vol. 4, No. 3 (March 2001): 56–67.

————. "What Talent Might Have Achieved: The Battle of Resaca," *North & South*, Vol. 13, No. 5 (Jan. 2012): 27–36.

———— et al. "The Ten Greatest Blunders of the Civil War," *North & South*, Vol. 8, No. 1 (Jan. 2005): 10–23.

O'Harrow, Robert, Jr. "Victory on His Shoulders: Quartermaster General Montgomery Meigs Set the Stage for Union Success," *America's Civil War*, Vol. 29, No. 6 (Jan. 2017): 26–33.

Person, Gustav J. "Crossing the James River, June 1864: '. . . the real crisis of the war,'" *Engineer* (Sept.–Dec. 2009): 58–64.

Reese, Timothy J. "A typographical shortcut distorts George B. McClellan's reactions to the September 1862 'Lost Order,'" *America's Civil War*, Vol. 17, No. 5 (Nov. 2004), 18–20, 72.

Rhea, Gordon. "Baldy Smith – The Scapegoat of Petersburg," *North & South*, Vol. 14, No. 1 (May 2012): 18–29.

Robertson, William Glenn. "The Chickamauga Campaign: The Battle of Chickamauga: Day 1, September 19, 1863," *Blue & Gray Magazine*, XXIV, No. 6 (Spring 2008), 6–29, 40–52.

———. "The Chickamauga Campaign: The Battle of Chickamauga: Day 2, September 20, 1863," *Blue & Gray Magazine*, XXV, No. 2 (Summer 2008), 6–31, 40–50.

Secrist, Philip L. "Resaca: For Sherman a Moment of Truth," *Atlanta Historical Society Journal* (Spring 1978): 8–41.

Sears, Stephen W. "The Curious Case of the Lost Order," *The Civil War Monitor*, Vol. 6, No. 4 inter 2016): 30-41 and related Note at Ibid., Vol. 7, No. 1 (Spring 2017): 5.

———. "McClellan at Antietam," *Hallowed Ground*, Vol. 6, No. 1 (Spring 2005): 30.

Skoch, George F. "Miracle of the Rails," *Civil War Times Illustrated*, Vol. 31, No. 4 (Oct. 1992): 22–24, 56–59.

Smith, Robert Barr. "Killing Zone at Burnside's Bridge," *Military History*, Vol. 21, No. 2 (June 2004): 34–40.

Stackpole, Edward J. "Showdown at Sharpsburg—Story of the Battle," *Civil War Times Illustrated*, Vol. 1, Issue 5 (August 1962): 4–8, 28–32.

Suhr, Robert Collins, "Old Brains' Barren Triumph," *America's Civil War*, Vol. 14, No. 2 (May 2001): 42–49.

Sword, Wiley. "The Battle Above the Clouds," *Blue & Gray Magazine*, XVIII, No. 2 (Dec. 2000): 6–20, 43–56.

———. "Missionary Ridge," *Blue & Gray Magazine*, XIX, No. 6 (2013), 6–31, 40–50.

Thiele, Gregory A. "McClellan at Antietam: Another View," *North & South*, Vol. 12, No. 4 (Nov. 2010): 31–37.

Welch, Richard F., "Gettysburg Finale," *America's Civil War*, Vol. 6, No. 1 (July 1993): 50–57.

Wert, Jeffry D. "Disaster in the West Woods," *Civil War Times*, Vol. 41, No. 5 (Oct. 2002): 32–39.

Wilson, John. "Miracle at Missionary Ridge," *America's Civil War*, Vol. 12, No. 7 (misprinted as 6) (March 2000): 42–49 at 42–44.

Wittenberg, Eric J. "Sheridan's Second Raid and the Battle of Trevilian Station," *Blue & Gray Magazine*, XIX, No. 3 (Feb. 2002): 8–24, 45–50.

NOTES

PROLOGUE

1.   For a very brief analysis of about thirty major blunders of the Civil War, see Steven H. Newton, Keith Poulter, John Y. Simon, Craig L. Symonds, and Steven Woodworth, "The Ten Greatest Blunders of the Civil War," *North & South*, Vol. 8, No. 1 (Jan. 2005), 10–23, in which five historians each selected ten great blunders (with considerable overlap). For a humorous, informative, and brief look at numerous Civil War mistakes, see Clint Johnson, *Civil War Blunders* (Winston-Salem: John F. Blair, 1997). Neither the cited article nor book explores any blunders in detail.

2.   Lincoln to Henry Halleck, July 6, 1863, in Roy P. Basler, The Collected Works of Abraham Lincoln (New Brunswick: Rutgers University Press, 1953), 8 vols., VI, 318; Lincoln to Halleck, July 7, 1863, Ibid., 319.

3.   Albert Castel with Brooks D. Simpson, *Victors in Blue: How Union Generals Fought the Confederates, Battled Each Other, and Won the Civil War* (Lawrence: University Press of Kansas, 2011), 165.

1

1.   David S. Heidler and Jeanne T. Heidler (eds.), *Encyclopedia of the American Civil War: A Political, Social, and Military History* (New York: W. W. Norton & Company, 2002), 416.

2.   David Christy, *Cotton Is King: or Slavery in the Light of Political Economy* (Cincinnati: Derby & Jackson, 1855), discussed in Frank L. Owsley, *King Cotton Diplomacy: Foreign Relations of the Confederate States of America* (Chicago: University of Chicago Press, 1931, 1959, 1969), 15.

3.   www.teachingamericanhistory.org/library/document/cotton-is-king, quoting *Selections from the Letters and Speeches of the Hon. James H. Hammond, of South Carolina* (New York: John F. Trow & Co., 1866), 311–312 (emphasis added).

4.   Owsley, *King Cotton*, xv–xvi.

5.   Heidler & Heidler, *Encyclopedia*, 418.

6.   This equated to $3.5 billion in 1858 currency (www.historicalstatistics.org/currencyconverter.html), which would be $105 billion in 2015 currency (https://www.measuringworth.com/uscompare/relativevalues.php).

7.   Owsley, *King Cotton*, 3.

8.   Heidler & Heidler, *Encyclopedia*, 180.

9.   Heidler & Heidler, *Encyclopedia*, 418.

10. Owsley, *King Cotton,* 8–9, 14–15.

11. *London Times*, Apr. 29, 1861, quoted in Owsley, *King Cotton*, 11.

12. Williamson Murray and Wayne Wei-Siang Hsieh, *A Savage War* (Princeton: Princeton University Press, 2016), 37.

13. Newton et al., "Ten Greatest Blunders," 14. Four of these five historians identified King Cotton diplomacy as one of the ten biggest blunders of the war.

14. Murray and Hsieh, *Savage War*, 37.

15. Owsley, *King Cotton*, 1.

16. William Howard Russell, *My Diary North and South* (London: T.O.H.P. Burnham, 1863), 51.

17. Owsley, *King Cotton*, 21–22.
18. Allan Nevins, *Ordeal of the Union* (New York: Charles Scribner's Sons, 1947–1950) (8 vols.), V, 97.
19. Nevins, *Ordeal*, V, 18–19.
20. W. H. Chase, *DeBow's Review*, XXX, no. 1 (January 1861), quoted in Nevins, *Ordeal*, V, 18–19. "Major" Chase apparently used a militia or honorary title.
21. R. K. Call to John S. Littell, pamphlet, Feb. 12, 1861, quoted in Nevins, *Ordeal*, V, 97–98.
22. Owsley, *King Cotton*, 23.
23. Confederates imported these often desperately needed items through Mexico or the less-than-airtight blockade.
24. Nevins, *Ordeal*, V, 97.
25. Renata Eley Long, *In the Shadow of the* Alabama: *The British Foreign Office and the American Civil War* (Annapolis: Naval Institute Press, 2015), 24.
26. *Punch*, Mar. 30, 1861, quoted in ibid. at 24–25.
27. Varina Davis, *Jefferson Davis: A Memoir by His Wife* (New York: Belford Company, 1890), 2 vols., II, 160, quoted in Owsley, *King Cotton*, 19.
28. Heidler & Heidler, *Encyclopedia*, 480
29. Heidler & Heidler, *Encyclopedia*, 180, 418.
30. Heidler & Heidler, *Encyclopedia*, 480–81.
31. Owsley, *King Cotton*, 24–27.
32. Nevins, *Ordeal*, V, 100.
33. Bunch to Russell, Aug. 3, 1861, quoted in Owsley, *King Cotton*.
34. Owsley, *King Cotton*, 28-29, quote at 29 (citing Magee to Russell, Aug. 21, 1861).
35. Heidler & Heidler, *Encyclopedia*, 180, 418, 480; Owsley, *King Cotton*, 29–37.
36. Owsley, *King Cotton*, 37.
37. Owsley, *King Cotton*, 39–41.
38. Owsley, *King Cotton*, 41–42.
39. Owsley, *King Cotton*, 41–42, quote at 42.

40. Newton et al, "Ten Greatest Blunders," 14.
41. Murray and Hsieh, *Savage War*, 90.
42. Owsley, *King Cotton*, 42.
43. Newton et al, "Ten Greatest Blunders," 14; Murray and Hsieh, *Savage War*, 76; Owsley, *King Cotton*, 134-35; Christopher Dickey, *Our Man in Charleston: Britain's Secret Agent in the Civil War South* (New York: Crown Publishers, 2015), 218–219.
44. Britain's "dynamic economy" has been credited for its resistance to "crude coercion." Murray and Hsieh, *Savage War*, 37. Although some cotton from the countries listed was of a lower quality than Southern cotton, it was adequate to keep the English mills operating.
45. Murray and Hsieh, *Savage War*, 86; Owsley, *King Cotton*, 141.
46. Owsley, *King Cotton*, 147. For details of the European cotton famine, see Ibid., 134–153.
47. Heidler & Heidler, *Encyclopedia*, 180; Owsley, *King Cotton*, 37.
48. Heidler & Heidler, *Encyclopedia*, 180.
49. Ibid., 481. The blockade became increasingly effective but was never airtight.
50. Murray and Hsieh, *Savage War*, 84–85.
51. Owsley, *King Cotton*, 42.
52. Owsley, *King Cotton*, 193–197, quote at 194.
53. *Economist*, June 3, 1861, quoted in Owsley, *King Cotton*, 194
54. Nevins, *Ordeal*, VI, 243.
55. Heidler & Heidler, *Encyclopedia*, 418.
56. Nevins, *Ordeal*, V, 97.
57. Long, *In the Shadow*, 28.
58. Long, *In the Shadow*, 72.
59. Long, *In the Shadow*, 108-109.
60. Long, *In the Shadow*, 108.
61. Workingmen's views were reflected in a December 1862 letter sent by Manchester workers to Lincoln that thanked him for the "vast progress" he had made toward "erasure of that foul blot on Civilization and Christianity – chattel slavery." Long, *In the Shadow*, 109.

62. Owsley, *King Cotton*, 43–46, 48–49.
63. Confederate Congress, An act to regulate the destruction of property under military necessity, and to provide for the indemnity thereof, March 17, 1862, OR, IV, iii, 1066–67.
64. Owsley, *King Cotton*, 49.
65. Owsley, *King Cotton*, 45–49.
66. Heidler & Heidler, *Encyclopedia*, 180–81, 418–19; quotation at 419. For details of the belated Confederate efforts to make positive use of its cotton resources, see Owsley, *King Cotton*, 360–93.
67. Owsley, *King Cotton*, 392–93.
68. Newton et al., "Ten Greatest Blunders," 17. Long after the war, the Confederacy's President Jefferson Davis and Treasury Secretary Christopher Memminger claimed that the Confederacy would not have been able to ship four million bales of cotton to Europe early in the war. Nevins, *Ordeal*, VII, 3n. If so, why the embargo? Also, the blockade was not a significant *early-war* impediment but worsened each year; one of ten blockade runners was seized in 1861, one of eight in 1862, and one of four in 1863. Owsley, *King Cotton*, 261. "As [British] consuls were reporting, the unreliability of supplies was tied less to the Union blockade in the early years of the war, which was not very effective, than to the continuing embargo on cotton supported by Southern planters and politicians convinced they could squeeze Lancashire until London would bend to their will." Dickey, *Our Man in Charleston*, 307. The ex-Confederate leaders' claims appear to have been a postwar effort to avoid admitting error in their cotton policy and have as much validity as postwar claims that secession had nothing to do with slavery. See Edward H. Bonekemper III, *The Myth of the Lost Cause: Why the South Fought the Civil War and Why the North Won* (Washington: Regnery History, 2015), 31–95.
69. Steven Newton in Newton et al., "Ten Greatest Blunders," 18.

2

1. At Chancellorsville in May 1863, Union Major General Joseph Hooker commanded 130,000 or more troops.

2. General Orders No. 16, April 14, 1862, Department of the Mississippi; Captain Nathaniel H. McLean to Grant, April 14, 1862, John Y. Simon and John F. Marszalek, eds. *The Papers of Ulysses S. Grant* (32 vols.) (Carbondale: Southern Illinois University Press, 1967–2015), V, 48–49.

3. Halleck to Grant, April 14, 1862, *The War of Rebellion: A Compilation of the Official Records of the Union and Confederate Armies*, (Washington: Government Printing Office, 1880–1901) (128 vols.), I, x, part 2, 106.

4. Russell F. Weigley, *The American Way of War: A History of United States Military Strategy and Policy* (New York: Macmillan Publishing Co., 1973), 139; Special Orders No. 35, Department of the Mississippi, April 30, 1862, *Grant Papers*, V, 105.

5. Stacy D. Allen, "Corinth, Mississippi: Crossroads of the Western Confederacy," *Blue & Gray Magazine*, XIX, No. 6 (Summer 2002), 6–25, 36–51.

6. Murray and Hsieh, *Savage War*, 160.

7. Grant, *Memoirs*, I, 377; Peter Cozzens, *The Darkest Days of the War: The Battles of Iuka & Corinth* (Chapel Hill: University of North Carolina Press, 1997), 17; Ronald C. White, *American Ulysses: A Life of Ulysses S. Grant* (New York: Random House, 2016), 229. Grant was unaware that, in the aftermath of Shiloh, Lincoln reputedly had to resist many suggestions that he remove Grant by saying, "I can't spare this man; he fights." T. Harry Williams, *McClellan, Sherman and Grant* (New Brunswick: Rutgers University Press, 1962), 96.

8. Allen, "Crossroads," 12–24, 36 (siege map on 13); Sam R. Watkins, *"Co. Aytch": Maury Grays, First Tennessee Regiment or a Side Show of the Big Show* (Wilmington, N.C.: Broadfoot Publishing Company, 1987) (Reprint of 1882 and 1952 editions), 71.

9.   White, *American Ulysses*, 230.

10.   Grant, *Memoirs*, I, 381–82; Allen, "Crossroads," 24, 36;
      Cozzens, *Darkest Days*, 31–33.

11.   Grant, *Memoirs*, I, 376–81; Robert Collins Suhr, "Old Brains'
      Barren Triumph," *America's Civil War*, Vol. 14, No. 2 (May
      2001), 42–49 at 49.

12.   Grant, *Memoirs*, I, 381–384.

13.   Murray and Hsieh, *Savage War*, 205.

14.   Nevins, *Ordeal*, VI, 152.

15.   Weigley, *American Way of War*, 136.

16.   Williams, *McClellan, Sherman and Grant*, 94.

17.   Murray and Hsieh, *Savage War*, 210–213; Nevins, *Ordeal*, VI,
      169.

18.   William B. Feis, *Grant's Secret Service: The Intelligence War
      from Belmont to Appomattox* (Lincoln: University of Nebraska
      Press, 2002), 114.

3

1.   For a fuller story of McClellan's disastrous Antietam Campaign
      performance, see Bonekemper, McClellan and Failure, 123–140;
      Stephen W. Sears, *George B. McClellan: The Young Napoleon*
      (New York: Ticknor & Fields, 1988), 270–326.

2.   Lincoln called McClellan's undermining of Pope at Second
      Manassas "shocking," "atrocious," and "unpardonable."
      Nevins, *Ordeal*, VI, 185.

3.   Gideon Welles, *Diary of Gideon Welles* (3 vols.) (Boston:
      Houghton Mifflin Company, 1911), I, Sept. 12, 1862, 124.

4.   McClellan to Mary Ellen McClellan, Sept. 5, 1862, 11 a.m.,
      Papers of McClellan, 435.

5.   McClellan to Mary Ellen McClellan, Sept. 7, 1862, 2:30 p.m.,
      Papers of McClellan, 437–438.

6.   Murray and Hsieh, *Savage War*, 221.

7.   Nevins, *Ordeal*, VI, 215–218.

8. McClellan to Halleck, Sept. 8, 1862, 8 p.m., OR, I, xix, part 2, 211.
9. McClellan to Halleck, Sept. 9, 1862, 7:30 p.m., OR, I, xix, part 2, 218-19; McClellan to Halleck, 6 p.m., ibid., 219.
10. McClellan to Mary Ellen McClellan, Sept. 9, 1862, 5 p.m., *Papers of McClellan*, 442.
11. Lincoln to McClellan, Sept. 10, 1862, 10:15 a.m., *Works of Lincoln*, V, 412; McClellan to Lincoln, Sept. 10, 1862, OR, I, xix, part 2, 233.
12. McClellan to Halleck, Sept. 11, 1862, *Papers of McClellan*, 444–45.
13. Welles, *Diary*, I, Sept. 12, 1862, 124.
14. Michael C.C. Adams, *Fighting for Defeat: Union Military Failure in the East, 1861–1865* (Lincoln: University of Nebraska Press, 1978, 1992), 91.
15. McClellan to Halleck, Sept. 11, 1862, OR, I, xix, part 1, 758; Halleck to McClellan, Sept. 11, 1862, ibid. The night before McClellan had written to Pennsylvania's Governor Andrew Curtin that he concurred with an assessment that the Confederates had no less than 120,000 troops at Frederick. Curtin to McClellan, Sept. 10, 1862, 10 a.m., OR, I, xix, part 2, 248; McClellan to Curtin, Sept. 10, 1862, 10:30 p.m., OR, I, xix, part 2, 248–249. The nine thousand Union troops at Harpers Ferry were soon supplemented by about four thousand others who fled there from nearby Martinsburg.
16. Edwin C. Fishel. *The Secret War for the Union: The Untold Story of Military Intelligence in the Civil War* (Boston: Houghton Mifflin, 1996), 217.
17. Gregory A. Thiele, "McClellan at Antietam: Another View," *North & South*, Vol. 12, No. 4 (Nov. 2010): 31–37 at 33 (emphasis added).
18. Lincoln to Orville H. Browning (oral), July 25, 1862, in Theodore Calvin Pease and James G. Randall (eds.), *The Diary of Orville Hickman Browning* (Springfield: Illinois State

Historical Library, 1925-33)(2 vols.), I, 563, cited in Don E. Fehrenbacher and Virginia Fehrenbacher, eds., *Recollected Words of Abraham Lincoln*, (Stanford: Stanford University Press, 1996), 65.

19.   McClellan to Halleck, Sept. 10, 1862, OR, I, xix, part 2, 254–255.

20.   McClellan to Halleck, Sept. 11, 1862, 3:45 p.m., ibid., 253; Lincoln to McClellan, Sept. 11, 1862, 6 p.m., *Works of Lincoln*, V, 15.

21.   Lincoln to McClellan, Sept. 12, 1865, 5:45 p.m., Ibid., 418.

22.   McClellan to Lincoln, Sept. 12, 1862, 9 p.m., Ibid., 418n.

23.   McClellan to Lincoln, Sept. 12, 1862, 9 p.m., OR, I, xix, part 2, 272; McClellan to Halleck, Sept. 12, 1862, 6 p.m., Ibid., 271–272; McClellan to Mary Ellen McClellan, Sept. 12, 1862, 3 p.m., *Papers of McClellan*, 449–450.

24.   McClellan to Lincoln, Sept. 13, 1862, 12 m. [received 2:35 a.m. September 14, 1862], OR, I, xix, part 2, 281. Because of the ambiguous "12 m." dateline, there continues to be a vigorous debate about whether McClellan sent this message at noon on the thirteenth or twelve hours later at midnight. See Timothy J. Reese, "A typographical shortcut distorts George B. McClellan's reactions to the September 1862 'Lost Order'," *America's Civil War*, Vol. 17, No. 5 (Nov. 2004): 18–20, 72; Stephen W. Sears, "The Curious Case of the Lost Order," *The Civil War Monitor*, Vol. 6, No. 4 (Winter 2016), 30-41 at 40; Note, Ibid., Vol. 7, No. 1 (Spring 2017), 5. In either event, McClellan's reaction to the discovery was inexcusably slower than he promised the president.

25.   Sears, "Curious Case," 73.

26.   Murray and Hsieh, *Savage War*, 542.

27.   A. Wilson Greene, "'I Fought the Battle Splendidly': George B. McClellan and the Maryland Campaign" in Gary W. Gallagher, *Antietam: Essays on the 1862 Maryland Campaign* (Kent, OH: Kent State University Press, 1989), 56–83 at 61.

28.   McClellan to Franklin, Sept. 13, 1862, 6:20 p.m., OR, I, xix, part 1, 45-46 at 45; LI, part 1, 826–827.

29.   Sears, *McClellan,* 282; Alan T. Nolan, *The Iron Brigade: A Military History* (Bloomington: Indiana University Press, 1961), 117.

30.   McClellan to Halleck, Sept. 13, 1862, 11 p.m., OR, I, xix, part 2, 281–282.

31.   Heidler & Heidler, *Encyclopedia*, 1831–1832.

32.   Testimony of William B. Franklin, March 30, 1863, U.S. Congress, *Report of the Joint Committee on the Conduct of the War* (House of Representatives, 37th Cong., 3rd Sess.) (3 vols.) (Washington: Government Printing Office, 1863), Part I, 625–628 at 625–626; McClellan to Franklin, Sept. 14, 1862, OR, I, li, part 1, 833 (emphasis added). Franklin's claim that McClellan ordered him to wait for Couch's division flies in the face of his orders from McClellan to move at daylight "[w]ithout waiting for the whole of that division to join." McClellan to Franklin, Sept. 13, 1862, 6:20 p.m., OR, I, xix, part 1, 45–46 at 45.

33.   Murray and Hsieh, *Savage War*, 226–227; Heidler & Heidler, *Encyclopedia*, 513–515, 1831–1832.

34.   Ibid., 514–515.

35.   Nevins, *Ordeal*, VI, 219. Jackson's successful mini-campaign against Harpers Ferry is described in Dennis E. Frye, "'Through God's Blessing'," *North & South*, Vol. 5, No. 7 (Oct. 2002): 66–74. Five hundred African American "contrabands" were captured at Harpers Ferry and returned to slavery. James M. McPherson, *Crossroads of Freedom: Antietam* (Oxford: Oxford University Press, 2002), 114.

36.   Nevins, *Ordeal*, VI, 219.

37.   Murray and Hsieh, *Savage War*, 228–229.

38.   Newton et al, "Ten Greatest Blunders," 17.

39.   Edward Porter Alexander, *The Military Memoirs of a Confederate* (New York: Charles Scribner's Sons, 1907), 245.

40. McClellan to Halleck, Sept. 14, 1862, 9:40 p.m., OR, I, xix, part 2, 289; Sept.15, 1862, 8, 8 (again), and 10 a.m., Ibid., 294–295.

41. Nevins, *Ordeal*, VI, 221.

42. Lincoln to McClellan, September 15, 1862, 2:45 p.m., *Works of Lincoln*, V, 426.

43. Edward Porter Alexander, *Fighting for the Confederacy: The Personal Recollections of General Edward Porter Alexander* (Edited by Gary W. Gallagher) (Chapel Hill: University of North Carolina Press, 1989), 145–146.

44. Murray and Hsieh, *Savage War*, 229.

45. McClellan to Halleck, Sept. 15, 1862, OR, I, xix, part 2, 294–295 at 295.

46. Nevins, *Ordeal*, VI, 223–224.

47. McPherson, *Crossroads*, 114.

48. Thiele, "McClellan at Antietam," 34.

49. Robert C. Cheeks, "Carnage in a Cornfield," *America's Civil War*, Vol. 5, No. 2 (July 2002), 30–37 at 30.

50. Alexander, *Fighting for the Confederacy*, 151.

51. Ibid.

52. For details of the Battle of Antietam, see John M. Priest, *Antietam: The Soldiers' Battle* (Shippensburg, Pennsylvania: White Mane Publishing Co., Inc., 1989); Jay Luvaas and Harold W. Nelson (eds.), *The U.S. Army War College Guide to the Battle of Gettysburg* (Carlisle, Pennsylvania: South Mountain Press, Inc., 1986); and Ted Alexander, "Antietam: The Bloodiest Day," *North & South*, Vol. 5, No. 7 (Oct. 2002), 76–89. McClellan's army suffered about 12,400 casualties, and Lee's army incurred at least 10,300. Heidler & Heidler, *Encyclopedia*, 66; see casualty discussion in McPherson, *Crossroads*, 129 and endnote 56.

53. Alexander, *Fighting for the Confederacy*, 151.

54. Thiele, "McClellan at Antietam," 35.

55. Cheeks, "Carnage," 30–37; Heidler & Heidler, *Encyclopedia*, 60.

56. Jeffry D. Wert, "Disaster in the West Woods," *Civil War Times*, LXI, No. 5 (Oct. 2002): 32-39.

57. Herman Hattaway, "The Changing Face of Battle," *North & South*, Vol. 4, No. 6 (August 2001): 34–43 at 38.

58. Report of Brig. Gen. George Sykes, U.S. Army, commanding Second Division, of the battle of Antietam…, Sept. 30, 1862, OR, I, xix, part 1, 350–52 at 351.

59. Paul Chiles, "Artillery Hell! The Guns of Antietam," *Blue & Gray Magazine*, XVI, No. 2 (Dec. 1998): 6–16, 24–25, 41–59 at 49; McPherson, *Crossroads*, 123–124; Alexander, *Military Memoirs*, 262; Catton, *Mr. Lincoln's Army*, 304.

60. Thiele, "McClellan at Antietam," 35.

61. Alexander, *Fighting for the Confederacy*, 151.

62. Pois and Langer, *Command Failure*, 55.

63. Chiles, "Artillery Hell!" 51–52.

64. Stephen Sears, "McClellan at Antietam," *Hallowed Ground*, Vol. 6, No. 1 (Spring 2005): 30. It is likely that McClellan had downgraded Burnside's role at Sharpsburg because Little Mac's friend Porter had just arrived and disclosed to McClellan that Burnside had forwarded to the War Department copies of telegrams Porter had sent to Burnside. Those messages were highly critical of Pope, detested by McClellan and Porter, and left the accurate impression that Porter and McClellan had deliberately undermined Pope at Second Manassas. After Porter's arrival at Frederick, Burnside was snubbed and criticized by McClellan, formerly Burnside's close friend. Dennis Frye, "Burnside Betrayed?: Robert E. Lee's Confederates Were the Official Target at Antietam—But the Union Commander Took Aim at One of His Own," *America's Civil War*, Vol. 28, No. 4 (Sept. 2015): 23–31.

65. For details on the fighting at Burnside's Bridge, see Robert Barr Smith, "Killing Zone at Burnside's Bridge," *Military History*, Vol. 21, No. 2 (June 2004), 34–40.

66. John C. Waugh, *The Class of 1846: From West Point to Appomattox: Stonewall Jackson, George McClellan and Their Brothers* (New York: Warner Books, Inc., 1994), 385.

67. William Marvel, "More Than Water Under Burnside's Bridge," *America's Civil War*, Vol. 18, No. 6 (January 2006): 46–52.

68. Barr, "Killing Zone," 39.

69. Ibid. Barr wrote, "Although the Young Napoleon had promised to support Burnside, he failed to issue the necessary orders, and just as the regulars were on the verge of punching a hole in the thin Rebel line before them, he recalled them." Ibid.

70. McPherson, *Crossroads*, 128–29.

71. Stephen Sears, *Landscape Turned Red: The Battle of Antietam* (New York: Book of the Month Club, 1994), 256–57.

72. Thiele, "McClellan at Antietam," 36.

73. McClellan to Halleck, Sept. 17, 1862, 1:25 p.m., OR, I, xix, part 2, 312.

74. Waugh, *Class of 1846*, 391.

75. In a famous exchange, Lee asked Hood, "Where is the splendid division you had this morning?" and Hood replied, "They are lying on the field where you sent them...." Nevins, *Ordeal*, VI, 225–226, quotes at 226.

76. Gary W. Gallagher, "'A Great General Is So Rare': Robert E. Lee and the Confederacy" in Gary W. Gallagher and Joseph T. Glatthaar (eds.), *Leaders of the Lost Cause: New Perspectives on the Confederate High Command* (Mechanicsburg, PA: Stackpole Books, 2004), 1–41 at 16.

77. Alexander, *Fighting for the Confederacy*, 146.

78. *Joint Committee Report*, Part I, 41–43; Testimony of Ambrose E. Burnside, Ibid., 637–642 at 642; Testimony of William B. Franklin, March 30, 1863, ibid., 625–628 at 627; Heidler & Heidler, *Encyclopedia*, 66–67; McPherson, *Crossroads*, 129. "At the end of the fighting on the seventeenth, Lee no longer had the strength for anything but defensive action. McClellan did; he had not used his reserve and, according to his own estimate, 15,000

fresh troops had joined him during the battle. They were not used." Adams, *Fighting for Defeat*, 91. Edward J. Stackpole contrasted McClellan's statement that his new fresh divisions were tired and "needed rest and refreshment" with Lee's use of A. P. Hill's exhausted troops the prior afternoon. Edward J. Stackpole, "Showdown at Sharpsburg—Story of the Battle," *Civil War Times Illustrated*, Vol. 1, Issue 5 (August 1962): 4–8, 28–32 at 32.

79. Alexander, *Fighting for the Confederacy*, 153.

80. Murray and Hsieh, *Savage War*, 241.

81. McClellan to Mary Ellen McClellan, Sept. 18, 1862, 8 a.m. (telegram), *Papers of McClellan*, 469; 8 a.m. (letter), Ibid.; Sept. 19, 1862, 8 a.m., ibid.

82. McClellan to Halleck, September 19, 1862, 8:30 a.m., OR, I, xix, part 2, 330; 10:30 a.m., ibid.; 1:30 p.m., OR, I, xix, part 1, 68.

83. George B. McClellan, *Report of Major General George B. McClellan upon the Organization of the Army of the Potomac, and its campaigns in Virginia and Maryland, from July 26, 1861, to November 7, 1862* (House of Representatives, 38th Congress, 1st Session, Ex. Doc. No. 15) (Washington: Government Printing Office, 1864), 211.

84. Alan T. Nolan, *The Iron Brigade: A Military History* (Bloomington: Indiana University Press, 1961, 1994), 144.

85. McPherson, *Crossroads*, 130.

86. Patrick J. Brennan, "Mac's Last Stand: Autumn 1862 in Loudon Valley, Virginia," *Blue & Gray Magazine*, XVII, No. 2 (Dec. 1999): 6–20, 48–57 at 7. Secretary Welles reported on the Key incident: "The President informed us of his interview with Key, one of Halleck's staff, who said it was not the game of the army to capture the rebels at Antietam, for that would give the North advantage and end slavery; it was the policy of the army officers to exhaust both sides and then enforce a compromise which would save slavery." Welles, *Diary*, I, Sept. 29, 1862, 156.

87. Alexander, *Fighting for the Confederacy*, 105–106.

88. Priest, *Antietam*, 290, quoting Porter to Lafayette McLaws, June 16, 1886. Porter, it should be remembered, had recommended that such an order *not* be given by McClellan.

89. Thiele, "McClellan at Antietam," 36, citing Cazenove Lee, quoted in R. E. Lee Jr., *The Recollections & Letters of Robert E. Lee* (reprint: New York: Konecky & Konecky, undated), 416.

90. Thiele, "McClellan at Antietam," 37.

91. Alexander, *Fighting for the Confederacy*, 146.

92. Gary W. Gallagher, "The Maryland Campaign in Perspective," in *Gallagher, Antietam: Essays*, 84–94 at 90.

4

1. Although contending that Confederate failure to use black troops was a major blunder, Keith Poulter added an insightful caveat: "Of course, in order to do so (and not have them desert *en masse* to the enemy) the secessionists would have needed an entirely different outlook on race—in which case there would have been no war." Newton et al., "Ten Greatest Blunders," 17.

2. See Bonekemper, *Myth*. Most of this chapter has been excerpted from that work.

3. DeBow, "Memories of the War," 226–227, quoted in Bruce Levine, *Confederate Emancipation: Southern Plans To Free and Arm Slaves During the Civil War* (Oxford: Oxford University Press, 2006), 9.

4. See Levine, *Confederate Emancipation*, 13 and notes for examples.

5. See Kevin M. Levin, "Confederate Like Me: Rebels Who Brought Their Slaves to War Assumed a Shared Loyalty to the Confederate Cause—as Do Some History Revisionists Today," *The Civil War Monitor*, Vol. 3, No. 1 (Spring 2013): 60–67, 78–79 at 66. The Internet is full of unsupported stories of black Confederate soldiers. Even worse, a 2010 Virginia textbook, *Our Virginia: Past and Present*, asserted that "thousands of

Southern blacks fought in the Confederate ranks, including two battalions under the command of Stonewall Jackson." When challenged, the author claimed she had read this information on the Internet. Ibid., 79.

6. Ibid., 66, citing Kenneth W. Noe, *Reluctant Rebels: The Confederates Who Joined the Army after 1861* (Chapel Hill: University of North Carolina, 2010), 43–44; Andrew Ward, *The Slaves' War: The Civil War in the Words of Former Slaves* (Boston: Mariner Books, 2008), 93.

7. Ibid., 78.

8. Donald C. Pfanz. *Richard S. Ewell: A Soldier's Life* (Chapel Hill: University of North Carolina Press, 1998), 139. Years after the war Davis claimed that the notion of arming slaves was unheard of in 1861 and denied Ewell's version of their conversation. Ewell's story is supported by a July 1862 letter he wrote to his niece stating, "It is astonishing to me that our people do not pass laws to form Regiments of blacks. The Yankees are fighting low foreignors [sic] against the best of our people, whereas were we to fight our negroes they would be a fair offset & we would not be fighting kings against men to use a comparison from chequers." Ibid., "Cleburne's Proposal," *North & South*, Vol. 11, No. 2 (Dec. 2008), 64–72, 66–67; Levine, *Confederate Emancipation*, 18.

9. Ibid.

10. Mallock, "Cleburne's Proposal," 68–69.

11. Cleburne et al to Joseph Johnston et al, Jan. 2, 1864, OR, I, lii, part 2, 586-592 [full text] at 586–587.

12. OR, I, lii, part 2, 588–589.

13. Ibid., 589–591; Don H. Doyle, *The Cause of All Nations: An International History of the American Civil War* (New York: Basic Books, 2015), 270–271.

14. OR, I, lii, part 2, 590 (emphasis added).

15. Ibid., 590–591.

16. Ibid., 592.

17. As early as March 7, 1864, the *New York Times* was lauding the use of black Union troops. Its referral to a "prodigious revolution" reflected growing Northern "acceptance of the Negro as a soldier capable of fighting for the preservation of the Union and for the freedom of the slave." Dudley Taylor Cornish, *The Sable Arm: Black Troops in the Union Army, 1861-1865* (Lawrence: University Press of Kansas, 1956, 1987), xi–xii.

18. Edward E. Baptist, *The Half Has Never Been Told: Slavery and the Making of American Capitalism* (New York: Basic Books, 2014), 245, 246.

19. Benjamin Quarles, *The Negro in the Civil War* (Boston: Little, Brown and Co., 1953), 278.

20. Horton and Horton, *Slavery*, 182–183.

21. Charles Jones Jr., "Negro Slaves During the Civil War: Their Relations to the Confederate Government," *The Magazine of American History with Notes and Queries,* Vol. 16, 175 (1886), quoted in Mallock, "Cleburne's Proposal" at 70.

22. Mallock, "Cleburne's Proposal," 68–69.

23. Mallock, "Cleburne's Proposal," 69 (emphasis added).

24. Walker to Davis, Jan. 12, 1864, OR, I, lii, part 2, 595.

25. Davis to Walker, Ibid., 596.

26. Seddon to Johnston, Jan. 24, 1864, OR, I, lii, part 2, 606–607.

27. Johnston Circular to Division Commanders, Jan. 31, 1864; ibid., 608.

28. Mallock, "Cleburne's Proposal," 71.

29. Under the "Peter Principle" (in this case, the "Double Peter Principle" since he previously had been promoted beyond his abilities), the incompetent Bragg had been elevated to this influential position after he resigned as Army of Tennessee commander following the rout of his army at Chattanooga in November 1863.

30. Mallock, "Cleburne's Proposal," 71.

31. Mallock, "Cleburne's Proposal," 67. Continuing this line of thought was Stephen Davis, who wrote, "Many have thought

since then that had Cleburne taken his staff's advice and not presented his controversial paper at Dalton, he would likely have won promotion to corps commander sometime later. The history of the Georgia campaign, and of the Army of Tennessee, might thus have been dramatically different." Stephen Davis, "Pat Cleburne's Emancipation Proposal," *Blue & Gray*, VI, No. 4 (Apr. 1989), 19.

32. Levine, *Confederate Emancipation*, 38 (emphasis added).

33. Doyle, *The Cause*, 272–273. "But one can hardly help thinking about how [Cleburne's "brilliant but impolitic" proposal's] harsh truths and radical recommendations played on the Confederate president's mind between January…and November 1864 when, facing the failure of impressment policy and an even more desperate manpower situation, he made his own proposal for the radical modification of slavery, as he put it." William A. Blair and Karen Fisher Younger, *Lincoln's Proclamation: Emancipation Reconsidered* (Chapel Hill: University of North Carolina Press, 2009), 141.

34. Seddon to Johnston, Jan. 21, 1864, OR, I, lii, part 2, 606–607 at 606.

35. Lee to Andrew Hunter, Jan. 11, 1865, OR, IV, iii, 1012–1013.

36. Ibid., 1013.

37. Lee to Ethelbert Barksdale, *Richmond Sentinel*, Feb. 23, 1864, quoted in Mallock, "Cleburne's Proposal," 72.

38. *Macon Telegraph and Confederate*, March 30, 1865, quoted in Levine, *Confederate Emancipation*, 55; *Memphis Appeal*, Oct. 31, 1864, quoted in ibid.; *Richmond Examiner,* Feb. 25, 1865, quoted in ibid., 4.

39. *Charleston Mercury*, Nov. 3, 1864, quoted in Levine, *Confederate Emancipation*, 4–5.

40. *Richmond Whig*, Nov. 9, 1864, quoted in Levine, *Confederate Emancipation*, 50.

41. Doyle, *The Cause*, 275; Levine, *Confederate Emancipation*, 4–5.

42. See John David Smith (ed.), *Black Soldiers in Blue: African American Troops in the Civil War Era* (Chapel Hill: University of North Carolina Press, 2002).
43. OR, IV, iii, 1009–1010.
44. Levine, *Confederate Emancipation*, 43–44, 50.
45. Levine, *Confederate Emancipation*, 46.
46. Levin, "Confederate Like Me," 66–67.
47. Levine, *Confederate Emancipation*, 40–59, quote at 59.
48. Blair and Younger, *Lincoln's Proclamation*, 142.
49. Quarles, *Negro in Civil War*, 280–281.
50. Levine, *Confederate Emancipation*, 125.
51. Joseph T. Glatthaar, "Black Glory: the African-American Role in Union Victory" in Gabor S. Boritt (ed.), *Why the Confederacy Lost* (New York: Oxford University Press, 1992), 133–136 at 137, 158.
52. Levine, *Confederate Emancipation*, 157.

5

1. Allen C. Guelzo, however, argued that Lee may have been correct in keeping his army intact because "if Lee had managed to take Washington, the war would have been over in an afternoon." Guelzo also believed the Union did not focus on the real line of operations in the "West," Chattanooga—Atlanta—Savannah—until late 1863. Guelzo to author, April 7, 2015. See Chapter 7 concerning Union delays in attacking Mobile, just south of that line.
2. Lee to James A. Seddon, May 10, 1863, *Papers of Lee*, 482. Chancellorsville was the only significant "late" battle that had been fought by Lee's army since mid-December.
3. Lee to Jefferson Davis, May 11, 1863, *Papers of Lee*, 483–484.
4. James M. McPherson, *Battle Cry of Freedom: The Civil War Era* (New York: Ballantine Books, 1988), 645; Steven E. Woodworth (ed.), *Davis and Lee at War* (Lawrence: University of Kansas Press, 1995), 230.

5.   Lee to John B. Hood, May 21, 1863, *Papers of Lee*, 490.

6.   Harry W. Pfanz, *Gettysburg: The Second Day* (Chapel Hill: The University of North Carolina Press, 1987), 4.

7.   Alexander, *Fighting for the Confederacy*, 222.

8.   McPherson, *Battle Cry of Freedom*, 646–647.

9.   Lee's arguments are reflected in his letters of April and May 1863. Lee to James A. Seddon, April 9, 1863; Lee to Samuel Cooper, April 16, 1863; Lee to Jefferson Davis, April 16, 1863; Lee to James A. Seddon, May 10, 1863; Lee to Jefferson Davis, May 11, 1863; *Papers of Lee*, 430–431, 433–434, 434–435, 482, 483–484. See Thomas Lawrence Connelly and Archer Jones, *The Politics of Command: Factions and Ideas in Confederate Strategy* (Baton Rouge: Louisiana State University Press, 1973), 126–128.

10.   Nevins, *Ordeal*, VII, 84–85, quote at 84.

11.   Lee to Jefferson Davis, June 23, 1863, *Papers of Lee*, 527–528; Herman Hattaway and Archer Jones, *How the North Won: A Military History of the Civil War* (Urbana: University of Illinois Press, 1983, 1991), 401–402, 404. Steven Woodworth noted that, "Calling for Beauregard a month earlier, when the northern invasion itself was still being debated by the cabinet, would have made fatally obvious to the cautious president that what Lee had in mind was an all-out end-the-war gamble." Woodworth, *Davis and Lee*, 238–239.

12.   Hattaway and Jones, *How the North Won*, 414.

13.   Lee to Jefferson Davis, June 25, 1863, *Papers of Lee*, 530, 531.

14.   Lee to Jefferson Davis, June 25, 1863, *Papers of Lee*, 532. George A. Bruce criticized Lee's post-battle rationale that he wanted to draw Hooker away from the Rappahannock and maneuver to gain a battlefield victory: "This discloses a piece of strategy with no definite objective, but one resting on a contingency. There is certainly something quixotic in the idea of moving an army two hundred miles for the purpose of finding a battlefield, leaving his base of supplies one hundred miles or

more at the end of the railroad at Winchester [the railroad actually ended at Staunton, Virginia—one hundred fifty miles from Gettysburg], when able to carry along only ammunition enough for a single battle, as was necessarily the case." George A. Bruce, "Lee and Strategy" in Gary W. Gallagher (ed.), *Lee the Soldier* (Lincoln: University of Nebraska Press, 1996), 117.

15. Alexander, *Fighting for the Confederacy*, 219–220.

16. Jones, "Military Means," in Boritt, *Why the Confederacy Lost*, 67.

17. Thomas Lawrence Connelly, *Autumn of Glory: The Army of Tennessee, 1862–1865* (Baton Rouge: Louisiana State University Press, 1971, 1991), 114.

18. Thomas Lawrence Connelly, "Robert E. Lee and the Western Confederacy: A Criticism of Lee's Strategic Ability," *Civil War History*, XV, No. 2 (June 1969), 116–132 at 124.

19. Ibid. "Lee's Pennsylvania campaign demanded that the Confederacy not use eastern reserves to attempt to lift the Vicksburg siege; Bragg, weakened to aid Johnston [near Vicksburg], was driven from Middle Tennessee by Rosecrans's brilliant Tullahoma campaign; and Johnston's fragment was too small to operate effectively against the heavily reinforced Grant." Hattaway and Jones, *How the North Won*, 415.

20. Richard E. Beringer, Herman Hattaway, Archer Jones, and William N. Still Jr., *Why the South Lost the Civil War* (Athens: University of Georgia Press, 1986), 264, 300; Archer Jones, *Civil War Command & Strategy* (New York: The Free Press, 1992), 168. "If on the other hand [Lee] fought a battle in Pennsylvania, he could choose his position and compel the Union army to fight another battle of Fredericksburg [what Longstreet recommended and Lee did not do]. But again Lee overlooked the political effect of fighting. Even a victorious defensive battle would look like a defeat because of the inevitable retreat of a raiding army forced to concentrate and unable to forage." Jones, "Military Means," in Boritt, *Why The Confederacy Lost*, 68.

21. Alexander, *Fighting for the Confederacy*, 110, 222. Often overlooked is the fact that Meade's nearest supply railhead was inconveniently located about twenty-five miles away at Westminster, Maryland, where most of his quartermaster and subsistence stores remained. Allen C. Guelzo to author, April 7, 2015; Kent Masterson Brown, *Lee, Logistics, and the Pennsylvania Campaign* (Chapel Hill: University of North Carolina Press, 2005), 45–46.

22. "Rather than a menace, Lincoln perceived Lee's raid, like the previous advance to Antietam, as an opportunity to strike the enemy when vulnerable and far from his base, 'the best opportunity' he said, 'we have had since the war began.'" Hattaway and Jones, *How the North Won*, 400.

23. In 1868 Lee allegedly told William Allan that his intentions in moving north were defensive: "First [Lee] did not intend to give general battle in Pa. if he could avoid it—the South was too weak to carry on a *war of invasion*, and his offensive movements against the North were never intended except as parts of a defensive system." William Allan, "Memoranda of Conversations with Gen. R.E. Lee" in Gallagher, *Lee the Soldier*, 7–24 at 13. Lee's actions in 1862 and 1863 seem inconsistent with that description.

24. The two best comprehensive studies of Lee's Gettysburg campaign are Edwin B. Coddington, *The Gettysburg Campaign: A Study in Command* (New York: Charles Scribner's Sons, 1984) and Allen C. Guelzo, *Gettysburg: The Last Invasion* (New York: Alfred A. Knopf, 2013).

25. Weigley, *American Way of War*, 116.

26. William Willis Blackford, *War Years with Jeb Stuart* (Baton Rouge: Louisiana State University Press, 1945, 1993), 211–212.

27. Ibid., 212–213.

28. Lee to his wife, June 9, 1863, *Papers of Lee*, 506, 507.

29. Allen C. Guelzo to author, April 7, 2015.

30. Guelzo, *Gettysburg*, 129, 459. Guelzo's perspective was: "It cannot be repeated too often: Lee did not lack for intelligence— for *strategic* information about the location, strength, and movement of the enemy; what he lacked was screening—*tactical* concealment of his own movements from observation and contact by the enemy." Ibid., 459.

31. In addition, Lee had skilled cavalry with him, including the Sixth, Seventh, Eleventh, and Thirty-fifth Virginia cavalry regiments (heroes of Fleetwood Hill at Brandy Station), that he could have used, but did not, for scouting purposes. Nevertheless, after the war, Lee blamed Stuart for disobeying orders, keeping Lee uninformed and thereby forcing the fighting at Gettysburg. Allan, "Conversations," April 15, 1868, and February 19, 1870, in Gallagher, *Lee the Soldier*, 13–14, 17.

32. Josiah Gorgas, *The Civil War Diary of General Josiah Gorgas*, Frank E. Vandiver and Sarah Woolfolk Wiggins eds. (Birmingham: University of Alabama Press, 1947, 1955), 70.

33. Lee to Jefferson Davis, June 23 and 25, 1863, *Papers of Lee*, 527–528, 530–531, 532–533.

34. Lee to Jefferson Davis, June 25, 1863 (second letter), *Papers of Lee*, 531.

35. For details of Day One, see Guelzo, *Gettysburg*, 137-231; Coddington, *Gettysburg Campaign*, 260–322; Gary Kross, "Gettysburg Vignettes: Attack from the West," *Blue & Gray Magazine*, XVII, No. 5 (June 2000): 6–22, 44–50.

36. Pfanz, *Second Day*, 20.

37. Luvaas and Nelson, *Army War College Guide*, 5; Krolick, Marshall D., "Gettysburg: The First Day, July 1, 1863," *Blue & Gray Magazine*, V, No. 2 (Nov. 1987), 8–20, 14–15. On Buford's critical role on June 30 and July 1 at Gettysburg, see Longacre, Edward, *General John Buford: A Military Biography* (Conshohocken, Pennsylvania: Combined Books, 1995), 179–203; Krolick, "The First Day."

38. Krolick, "The First Day," 15.

39. Coddington, *Gettysburg Campaign*, 281.
40. Gary Kross, "That One Error Fills Him with Faults: Gen. Alfred Iverson and His Brigade at Gettysburg," *Blue & Gray Magazine*, XII, No. 3 (February 1995): 22, 52–53. According to Guelzo, July 1 was the day Lee expected his army to concentrate at Gettysburg-Cashtown. "But he did expect a general engagement thereafter with isolated portions of the AOP [Army of the Potomac]. Lee's ideal scenario would have been for Reynolds' left wing to have rushed pell-mell into the waiting arms of the entire ANV [Army of Northern Virginia] at Gettysburg, and been crushed; Lee could then have waited cheerfully to see if Meade would attack him with the rest of the reduced AOP, or allow him to spend the balance of the summer running rampant through central Pennsylvania." Allen C. Guelzo to author, April 7, 2015.
41. Pfanz, *Second Day*, 22.
42. Ibid., 23.
43. Harry Pfanz concluded, "Obviously [Lee] did not expect a battle that would limit his army's ability to maneuver as early as 1 July or he would not have given hundreds of wagons precedence over much needed infantry." Ibid., 22.
44. Jeffry D. Wert, *General James Longstreet: The Confederacy's Most Controversial Soldier—A Biography* (New York: Simon & Schuster, 1993), 255.
45. Ibid., 72; Coddington, *Gettysburg Campaign*, 315.
46. Allen C. Guelzo presented a contrary view. He said that Lee viewed a general engagement as one involving all three of his corps. "Lee wished to hold off until Longstreet's corps was up; and he had every reason to believe that there was no hurry, and that the attack on Cemetery Hill could wait for the morning. He did not need another Malvern Hill." Allen C. Guelzo to author, April 7, 2015.
47. William Garrett Piston, *Lee's Tarnished Lieutenant: James Longstreet and His Place in Southern History* (Athens: University of Georgia Press, 1987), 49.

48. Douglas Southall Freeman, *Lee's Lieutenants: A Study in Command* (3 vols.)(New York: Charles Scribner's Sons, 1942–1944)(1972 reprint), III, 94–95.

49. Coddington, *Gettysburg Campaign*, 316–317; Guelzo, *Gettysburg*, 213; Gallagher, " 'If the Enemy Is There, We Must Attack Him': R.E. Lee and the Second Day at Gettysburg," 497–521, in Gallagher, *Lee the Soldier*, 508.

50. Coddington, *Gettysburg Campaign*, 320. William Garrett Piston concurred. Piston, *Lee's Tarnished Lieutenant*, 49.

51. Guelzo, *Gettysburg*, 215–216.

52. Chris Mackowski and Kristopher D. White, "Second-Guessing Dick Ewell: Why Didn't the Confederate general take Cemetery Hill on July 1, 1863?" *Civil War Times*, 49, No. 4 (Aug. 2010): 34–41 at 41.

53. Douglas Southall Freeman, *R. E. Lee* (4 vols.)(New York and London: Charles Scribner's Sons, 1934–1935), III, 91; Pfanz, *Second Day*, 111.

54. Hattaway and Jones, *How the North Won*, 406.

55. For details of Day Two (July 2), see Guelzo, *Gettysburg*, 233-370; Coddington, *Gettysburg Campaign*, 359–441.

56. Guelzo, *Gettysburg*, 238–243. "The gentlest conclusion to draw is that Johnston climbed *some other hill*, and thought it was the Round Tops (which, in turn, may account for his surprise at leading [Lafayette] McLaws and [Thomas] Moncure [Longstreet subordinates] along a road and up a rise which, without warning, revealed them to Federal signalmen), and thus completely overlooking the mass of Union troops between Cemetery Hill and the Round Tops that morning." Ibid., 243. Harry Pfanz said there were other early morning probes of the Union left by Colonel Armistead H. Long and, of all people, General Pendleton. Pfanz, *Second Day*, 105–106.

57. Coddington, *Gettysburg Campaign*, 372–374.

58. Ibid.

59. Ibid., 324.

60. Ibid., 361; Pfanz, *Second Day*, 26. Harry Pfanz stated that the exact dialogue will never be known. Pfanz, *Second Day*, 26–27.

61. Lee to Samuel Cooper, Battle Report of Gettysburg Campaign, January 20, 1864, *Papers of Lee*, 376.

62. Alexander, *Fighting for the Confederacy*, 233–234 (emphasis added).

63. Nevins, *Ordeal*, VII, 98.

64. Daniel Bauer, "Did a Food Shortage Force Lee To Fight?: An Investigation into Lee's Claim That He had To Attack at Gettysburg Because His Army Lacked Sufficient Rations To Do Anything Else," in *Columbiad: A Quarterly Review of the War Between the States*, Vol. I, No. 4 (Winter 1998): 57–74. Bauer concluded, "Based on these [food supply] estimates and the political pressures of the period, Meade would most likely have been forced to attack long before food became a problem for Lee. This being the case, the South Mountain strategy [withdrawal to Cashtown] had an excellent chance of succeeding." Ibid., 67.

65. Allen C. Guelzo to author, April 7, 2015.

66. Lee to Samuel Cooper, Battle Report of Gettysburg Campaign, January 20, 1864, *Papers of Lee*, 577.

67. Alexander, *Fighting for the Confederacy*, 236.

68. Piston, *Lee's Tarnished Lieutenant*, 118.

69. Coddington, *Gettysburg Campaign*, 270.

70. Alexander, *Fighting for the Confederacy*, 237.

71. Coddington, *Gettysburg Campaign*, 378; Freeman, *R. E. Lee*, III, 93; Freeman, *Lee's Lieutenants*, III, 115.

72. Alexander, *Fighting for the Confederacy*, 278; Coddington, *Gettysburg Campaign*, 378.

73. Freeman, *R. E. Lee*, III, 150.

74. Coddington, *Gettysburg Campaign*, 378-381; Freeman, *R. E. Lee*, III, 95–97.

75. Piston, *Lee's Tarnished Lieutenant*, 55–58.

76. Coddington, *Gettysburg Campaign*, 382.

77. Ibid., 55–58.

78.   Guelzo, *Gettysburg*, 328–334; Freeman, *R.E. Lee*, III, 100–101. For details and a unique perspective, see Phillip Thomas Tucker, *Barksdale's Charge: The True High Tide of the Confederacy at Gettysburg, July 2, 1863* (Havertown, Pa.: Casemate Publishers, 2013).

79.   Piston, "Cross Purposes" in Gallagher, *Third Day*, 31, 43.

80.   Piston, *Lee's Tarnished Lieutenant*, 58. Lee's uncoordinated attacks at Gettysburg were similar to those of McClellan at Antietam the prior summer.

81.   Bruce pointed to Lee's failure, on both July 2 and 3, to launch properly coordinated attacks: "For two days, Gettysburg presents the spectacle of two desperately fought and bloody battles by less than one third of [Lee's] army on each occasion, the other two thirds looking on, for the conflict was visible from nearly every point on the Confederate lines. Does not all this present another question to solve [than] whether a corps commander was quick or slow? Was the commander-in-chief justified in assigning such a task to such a force?" Bruce, "Lee and Strategy" in Gallagher, *Lee the Soldier*, 122.

82.   Freeman, *R. E. Lee*, III, 101–102; Harry W. Pfanz, *Gettysburg—Culp's Hill & Cemetery Hill* (Chapel Hill: University of North Carolina Press, 1993), 235–283.

83.   Pfanz, *Culp's and Cemetery Hills*, 284–327.

84.   Alexander, *Fighting for the Confederacy*, 234–235. Similarly, Harry Pfanz criticized Lee for leaving Ewell, with one-third of Lee's outnumbered infantry, in an isolated position unsuited to offensive operations. Pfanz, *Second Day*, 426.

85.   Harry Pfanz faulted Lee for his hands-off supervision of Longstreet, whom Lee "… seems not to have hurried…along," and Hill ("He did not rectify Hill's faulty deployment of Anderson's division or his inadequate measures to sustain Anderson's attack…."). Pfanz, *Second Day*, 426–427. For details on Hill's inadequate performance, see Ibid., 99, 114, 386–387.

86. For details of Day Three, see Guelzo, *Gettysburg*, 371–446; Gallagher, *Third Day*, 1–160; Coddington, *Gettysburg Campaign*, 442–534; Blake A. Magner, "Hancock's Line at Gettysburg, July 3, 1863: 'This Is Going To Be a Hot Place'," *Blue & Gray Magazine*, XXVI, No. 4 (2009): 6–25, 40–49.

87. Coddington, *Gettysburg Campaign*, 465–476; Pfanz, *Culp's Hill & Cemetery Hill*, 284–309; Pfanz, *Second Day*, 438.

88. Coddington, *Gettysburg Campaign*, 450.

89. Foote, Shelby, *The Civil War: A Narrative*, 3 vols. (New York: Random House, 1958–1974), II, 525.

90. On this particular Lee-Longstreet dispute, see Piston, "Cross Purposes" in Gallagher, *Third Day*, 31–55.

91. Coddington, *Gettysburg Campaign*, 460. Longstreet later stated that Lee had written to him in the 1863–1864 winter that, "If I only had taken your counsel even on the 3d [July 3], and had moved around the Federal left, how different all might have been." James Longstreet, "Lee's Right Wing at Gettysburg," 339–353, in eds. Robert Underwood Johnson and Clarence Clough Buel, *Battles and Leaders of the Civil War* (4 vols.)(New York: Thomas Yoseloff, Inc., 1956) (Reprint of Secaucus, NJ: Castle, 1887–1888), III, 349.

92. Coddington, *Gettysburg Campaign*, 488.

93. Wert, *Longstreet*, 287.

94. Alexander, *Fighting for the Confederacy*, 254.

95. Alexander, *Great Generals*, 26.

96. Alexander, *Fighting for the Confederacy*, 251.

97. Ibid., 252.

98. Ibid., 258.

99. Ibid., 260; Coddington, *Gettysburg Campaign*, 500.

100. Freeman, *Lee's Lieutenants*, III, 157. Many of the attackers were non-Virginians, especially North Carolinians.

101. Coddington, *Gettysburg Campaign*, 501.

102. Confederate Captain Joseph Graham, of the Charlotte Artillery, wrote in late July 1863 of Pettigrew's infantry "mov[ing] right

through my Battery, and I feared then I could see a want of resolution in our men. And I heard many say, 'that is worse than Malvern Hill,' and 'I don't hardly think that position can be carried,' etc., etc., enough to make me apprehensive about the result...." Gallagher, "Lee's Army" in Gallagher, *Third Day*, 23.

103. Alexander, *Fighting for the Confederacy*, 266; Coddington, *Gettysburg Campaign*, 526; Wert, *Longstreet*, 292.
104. Bruce, "Lee and Strategy" in Gallagher, *Lee the Soldier*, 123–124.
105. Waugh, *Class of 1846*, 487.
106. Piston, *Lee's Tarnished Lieutenant*, 62.
107. Wert, *Longstreet*, 292.
108. Coddington, *Gettysburg Campaign*, 525–526.
109. Freeman, *R. E. Lee*, III, 133–134.
110. Alexander, Fighting for the Confederacy, 278–280.
111. J. F. C. Fuller, *Grant and Lee: A Study in Personality and Generalship* (Bloomington: Indiana University Press, 1957) (Reprint of 1933 edition), 118.
112. Nevins, *Ordeal*, VII, 111.
113. Ernest B. Furgurson, *Chancellorsville 1863: The Souls of the Brave* (New York: Alfred A. Knopf, 1992), 350.
114. Lee to Jefferson Davis, July 29, 1863, *Papers of Lee*, 563.
115. Welch, Richard F., "Gettysburg Finale," *America's Civil War,* Vol. 6, No. 1 (July 1993), 50–57.
116. Alexander, *Fighting for the Confederacy*, 271. But Lincoln and much of the Union army were greatly disappointed about the lack of an attack ensuring Lee's escape. For details of the post-Gettysburg chase, see Ted Alexander, "Ten Days in July: The Pursuit to the Potomac," *North & South,*" 2, No. 6 (Aug. 1999): 10–34.
117. Coddington, *Gettysburg Campaign*, 535–574.
118. Gorgas, *Diary*, 75.
119. Longstreet, however, was in many ways his own worst enemy. He lashed out at critics with his own inaccurate and impolitic

version of events, especially in James Longstreet, *From Manassas to Appomattox: Memoirs of the Civil War in America* (New York: Smithmark Publishers, Inc., 1994) (reprint of 1896 edition).

120. Michael R. Bradley, "Tullahoma: The Wrongly Forgotten Campaign," *Blue & Gray Magazine*, XXVII, No. 1 (2010): 6–25, 40–44, 47–50.

121. Michael Fellman, *The Making of Robert E. Lee* (Baltimore: Johns Hopkins University Press, 2000), 149–150.

122. Ibid., 92.

123. William C. Davis, *Crucible of Command: Ulysses S. Grant and Robert E. Lee—The War They Fought, the Peace They Forged* (New York: Da Capo, 2015), 327–328.

124. Ibid., 330.

125. Lee to Samuel Cooper, Battle Report of Gettysburg Campaign, January 20, 1864, *Papers of Lee*, 576.

126. Lee's attacks at Gettysburg "were an unhappy caricature of the most unfortunate aspects of his tactics." Woodworth, *Davis and Lee*, 245. On the plentitude of food available for Lee's army, see Bauer, "Food Supplies?"

127. Ed. Robert Hunt Rhodes, *All for the Union: The Civil War Diary and Letters of Elisha Hunt Rhodes* (New York: Orion Books, 1991) (reprint of Andrew Mowbray Inc., 1985), 117.

128. Jones, "Military Means," in Boritt, *Why the Confederacy Lost*, 68.

129. Thomas L. Livermore, *Numbers & Losses in the Civil War in America: 1861–1865* (Millwood, N.Y.: Kraus Reprint Co., 1977) (Reprint of Bloomington: Indiana University Press, 1957), 102–103.

130. Lee to Jefferson Davis, July 31, 1863, *Papers of Lee*, 565.

131. Because of the misleadingly positive newspaper reports, Lee had cautioned his wife that "You will have learned before this reaches you that our success at Gettysburg was not as great as reported." Gary W. Gallagher, "Lee's Army Has Not Lost Any of Its

Prestige: The Impact of Gettysburg on the Army of Northern Virginia and the Confederate Home Front," 1–30, in Gallagher, *Third Day*, 18. Lee to his wife, July 12, 1863, *Papers of Lee*, 547.

132. Lee to Jefferson Davis, July 31, 1863, *Papers of Lee*, 565.

133. Bell Irvin Wiley, *The Road to Appomattox* (Baton Rouge: Louisiana State University Press, 1994) (Reprint of Memphis: Memphis State College Press, 1956), 64–65.

134. Winston Groom, *Shrouds of Glory: From Atlanta to Nashville: The Last Great Campaign of the Civil War* (New York: The Atlantic Monthly Press, 1995), 42.

135. "Principally, [Gettysburg] cost the Confederacy an immense number of killed and wounded, far greater in proportion to Lee's resources than the battle losses suffered by the Union. As President Davis later wrote, stressing the casualties: 'Theirs could be repaired, ours could not.'" Hattaway and Jones, *How the North Won*, 415.

136. Guelzo, *Gettysburg*, 461.

6

1. For details on the Battle of Chickamauga, see William Glenn Robertson, "The Chickamauga Campaign: The Battle of Chickamauga: Day 1, September 19, 1863," *Blue & Gray Magazine*, XXIV, No. 6 (Spring 2008): 6–29, 40–52 and "The Chickamauga Campaign: The Battle of Chickamauga: Day 2, September. 20, 1863," *Blue & Gray Magazine*, XXV, No. 2 (Summer 2008): 6–31, 40–50. Historians have generally treated that battle as a two-day battle (September 19–20, 1863), but there was considerable crucial fighting on the day before (September 18).

2. Freeman, *Lee's Lieutenants*, III, 221–222.

3. Connelly and Jones, *Politics of Command*, 134–135.

4. Ibid., 135; Steven E. Woodworth, *Davis and Lee at War* (Lawrence: University of Kansas Press, 1995), 255; Lee to James Longstreet, Aug. 31, 1863, *Papers of Lee*, 594.

5. Connelly, *Autumn of Glory*, 150–153; Hattaway and Jones, *How the North Won*, 444. Hattaway and Jones compared Lee's ultimate acquiescence with his position in May 1863 (when he insisted on keeping Longstreet for his Gettysburg Campaign): "Lee ran less risk, had less emotional investment, and hence less dissonance in September than he had had in the spring. He felt less need to keep all of his forces in Virginia; the need in the West appeared more pressing after the defeats in Mississippi and Tennessee. [Thus] he could easily accede to Davis's desire to apply the conventional strategy and reinforce the west with troops sent by rail from Virginia." Ibid., 374.

6. Connelly, *Autumn of Glory*, 152, 191. Because of Longstreet's delayed arrival, Connelly concluded, "The [Confederate] concentration at Chickamauga, often eulogized by historians, is more myth than genuine fact." Ibid., 152.

7. Peter Cozzens, *The Shipwreck of Their Hopes: The Battles for Chattanooga* (Urbana: University of Illinois Press, 1994), 390.

8. McDonough, *Chattanooga*, 226.

9. A long-standing dispute between Bragg and his generals was exacerbated by this latest failure.

10. John Wilson, "Miracle at Missionary Ridge," *America's Civil War*, Vol. 12, No. 7 (misprinted as 6) (March 2000): 42–49 at 42–44.

11. Grant, *Memoirs*, I, 583–584: II, 17–19; James Lee McDonough, *Chattanooga: A Death Grip on the Confederacy* (Knoxville: The University of Tennessee Press, 1984), 49.

12. McDonough, *Chattanooga*, 45; Feis, *Grant's Secret Service*, 177. Grant's descriptions of the Chattanooga Campaign are in Ulysses S. Grant, "Chattanooga," in Johnson and Buel, *Battles and Leaders*, III, 679–711 and Grant, *Memoirs*, II, 17–88.

13. John E. Clark, Jr., "Reinforcing Rosecrans by Rail: The movement of the Federal Eleventh and Twelfth Corps from Virginia was a wonder of strategy, logistics, and engineering," *Columbiad: A Quarterly Review of the War Between the States*,

III, No. 3 (Fall 1999): 74–95 at 74–87; George F. Skoch, "Miracle of the Rails," *Civil War Times Illustrated*, XXXI, No. 4 (Oct. 1992): 22–24, 56–59; John E. Clark, Jr., *Railroads in the Civil War: The Impact of Management on Victory and Defeat* (Baton Rouge: Louisiana State University, 2001), 146–209; Thomas Weber, *The Northern Railroads in the Civil War, 1861–1865* (Bloomington: Indiana University Press, 1952, 1999), 181–186; Robert O'Harrow, Jr., "Victory on His Shoulders: Quartermaster General Montgomery Meigs Set the Stage for Union Success," *America's Civil War*, Vol. 29, No. 6 (Jan. 2017): 26–33.

14. Grant, *Memoirs*, II, 27–30; McDonough, *Chattanooga*, 53–54.

15. Grant, *Memoirs*, II, 29–39; McDonough, *Chattanooga*, 54–58, 76–85; Cozzens, *Shipwreck*, 48–65; Wiley Sword, "The Battle Above the Clouds," *Blue & Gray* Magazine, XVIII, No. 2 (Dec. 2000): 6–20, 43–56 at 13–14.

16. Cozzens, *Shipwreck*, 107–108.

17. Bruce Catton, *Grant Takes Command* (Boston: Little, Brown and Company, 1968, 1969), 55–56.

18. Grant, *Memoirs*, II, 38–39.

19. Grant, *Memoirs*, II, 40–41; McDonough, *Chattanooga*, 88-94; Cozzens, *Shipwreck*, 74–100; Sword, "Battle Above Clouds," 16–19. Grant apparently got a laugh when the quartermaster in charge of the stampeding mules requested that they receive promotion to the rank of horse. B. A. Botkin (ed.), *A Civil War Treasury of Tales, Legends and Folklore* (New York: Promontory Press, 1960), 332–333.

20. McDonough, *Chattanooga*, 226–227.

21. Grant, *Memoirs*, II, 41–42.

22. Lee to Davis, Sept. 11, 1863, *Papers of Lee*, 599.

23. Lee to Davis, Sept. 14, 1863, Ibid., 600–601 (emphasis added).

24. Lee to Davis, Sept. 23, 1863, Ibid., 602–603 (emphasis added).

25. Cozzens, *Shipwreck*, 103.

26. Ibid.

27. McDonough, *Chattanooga*, 226.
28. Longstreet may have taken as many as seventeen thousand to twenty thousand troops away from Chattanooga. Richard N. Current (ed.), *Encyclopedia of the Confederacy* (4 vols.) (New York: Simon & Schuster, 1993), Vol. 2, 895, 897.
29. Cozzens, *Shipwreck*, 103–105; Wilson, "Miracle," 44–45; Edward H. Bonekemper, III, *How Robert E. Lee Lost the Civil War* (Fredericksburg: Sergeant Kirkland's Press, 1998), 142–143; Connelly, "Lee and Western Confederacy," 129; Wert, *Longstreet*, 320–21.
30. Cozzens, *Shipwreck*, 105.
31. Grant, *Memoirs*, II, 48–52; Sword, "Battle Above Clouds," 43; Cozzens, *Shipwreck*, 125.
32. Grant, *Memoirs*, II, 62–64; McDonough, *Chattanooga*, 106–120, 129–140; Cozzens, *Shipwreck*, 159–178; Wilson, "Miracle," 45; Sword, "Battle Above Clouds," 44–56.
33. Marszalek, *Sherman*, 283.
34. Grant, *Memoirs*, II, 75–78; McDonough, *Chattanooga*, 143–160; Cozzens, *Shipwreck*, 199–244.
35. Wilson, "Miracle," 46.
36. McDonough, *Chattanooga*, 228.
37. McDonough, *Chattanooga*, 161–180; Wilson, "Miracle," 46–48. See Wiley Sword, "Missionary Ridge," *Blue & Gray Magazine*, XIX, No. 6 (2013): 6–31, 40–50.
38. McDonough, *Chattanooga*, 181-89; Roy Morris, Jr., *Sheridan: The Life and Wars of General Phil Sheridan* (New York: Crown Publishers, Inc., 1992), 144–145; Wilson, "Miracle," 48; Catton, *Grant Takes Command*, 81–82.
39. Wilson, "Miracle," 48; Morris, *Sheridan*, 145; McDonough, *Chattanooga*, 167.
40. Cozzens, *Shipwreck*, 390.
41. McDonough, *Chattanooga*, 182–185.
42. Wilson, "Miracle," 49; Morris, *Sheridan*, 146; Cozzens, *Shipwreck*, 289-99.

43. McDonough, *Chattanooga*, 230.

44. Grant, *Memoirs*, II, 81–83; Wilson, "Miracle," 49; Smith, *Grant*, 280; Morris, *Sheridan*, 148; McDonough, *Chattanooga*, 214–225; Doyle D. Broome Jr., "Daring Rear-guard Defense," *America's Civil War*, Vol. 6, No. 5 (Nov. 1993): 34–40; Watkins, *"Co. Aytch"*, 125.

45. William Farrar Smith, "Comments on General Grant's 'Chattanooga'" in Johnson and Buel, *Battles and Leaders*, III, 714–777 at 717. Years later, when Grant was asked if Bragg had thought his position was impregnable, Grant responded with a smile, "Well, it *was* impregnable." Foote, *Civil War*, II, 859.

46. Gary W. Dolzall, "Muddy, Soggy Race to Campbell's Station," *America's Civil War*, Vol. 15, No. 3 (July 2002): 26–32, 80.

47. Jacob Dolson Cox, *Military Reminiscences of the Civil War* (New York: Charles Scribner's Sons, 1900) (2 vols.), II, 20–41.

48. Lincoln to Grant, Nov. 25, 1863, *Works of Lincoln*, VII, 30; Grant, *Memoirs*, II, 98; Lincoln to Grant, Dec. 8, 1863, *Works of Lincoln*, VII, 53; Simpson, *Hood's Texas Brigade*, 359-81. On activity at Knoxville, see Johnson and Buel, *Battles and Leaders*, III, 731–752.

49. Wilson, "Miracle," 49.

50. Foote, *Civil War*, II, 859.

51. John Kennerly Farris to Mary Farris, December 26, 1863, quoted in "Common Soldier: Dr. John Kennerly Farris, Confederate Surgeon, Army of Tennessee," *Blue & Gray Magazine*, XVII, No. 2 (Dec. 1999): 46–47 at 47, from "Letters to Mary: The Civil War Diary of Dr. John Kennerly Farris," *Franklin County Historical Review*, Vol. XXV, Winchester, Tennessee (1964).

52. Davis, *Jefferson Davis*, 527–31.

53. McDonough, *Chattanooga*, 219.

54. Nevins, *Ordeal*, VII, 211.

55. Bruce Catton, *This Hallowed Ground: The Story of the Union Side of the Civil War* (Garden City, NY: Doubleday & Company, Inc., 1956, 1962), 371.

56.   Cozzens, *Shipwreck*, 391.

7

1.   Galveston, a less significant Gulf port, remained open until the end of the war.

2.   Wheelan, *Libby Prison Breakout*, 11. Allan Nevins asserted that as early as the spring of 1862 Admiral Farragut's fleet should have been sent against then weakly fortified Mobile. Nevins, *Ordeal*, VI, 113.

3.   Sherman to Grant, July 12, 1863, noon, OR, I, xxiv, Part 3, 522–523.

4.   Banks to Grant, July 18, 1863, OR, I, xxiv, part 3, 527–528 [errors in original].

5.   Grant to Halleck, July 18, 1863, *Grant Papers*, IX, 70; OR, I, xxiv, part 3, 529–530.

6.   Halleck to Grant, July 22, 1863, *Grant Papers*, IX, 71n; OR, I, xxiv, part 3, 542.

7.   Grant, *Memoirs*, I, 579.

8.   Grant to Halleck, July 24, 1863, *Grant Papers*, IX, 108-111 at 109; OR, I, xxiv, part 3, 497–498.

9.   Grant to Halleck, August 1, 1863, *Grant Papers*, IX, 137–138; OR, I, xxiv, part 3, 569.

10.   *Grant Papers*, IX, 138n.

11.   Halleck to Banks, July 24, 1863, OR, I, xxxviii, 652–653.

12.   Halleck to Grant, July 30, 1863, *Grant Papers*, IX, 159n; OR, I, xxiv, part 3, 562 and Halleck to Grant, Aug. 6, 1863, *Grant Papers*, IX, 159n; OR, I, xxiv, part 3, 578. As late as August 10, Banks was still opining to Grant that "I still think it of the utmost moment that that port [Mobile] should be in our hands." Banks to Grant, August 10, 1863, OR, I, xxvi, part 1, 673–674 at 674.

13.   Halleck to Grant, Aug. 3, 1863, OR, I, xxiv, part 3, 571.

14.   Grant to Dana, Aug. 5, 1863, *Grant Papers*, IX, 145–147 at 146.

15. Lincoln to Banks, Aug. 5, 1863, *Works of Lincoln*, VI, 364–366 at 364.

16. Lincoln to Grant, Aug. 9, 1863, *Works of Lincoln*, VI, 374–375 at 374; *Grant Papers*, IX, 197n; OR, I, xxiv, part 3, 584.

17. Ibid.

18. Edward H. Bonekemper, III, *Lincoln and Grant: The Westerners Who Won the Civil War* (Washington: Regnery Publishing, 2015), 270–271; Smith, *Grant*, 261–262; Grant, *Memoirs*, I, 578.

19. Grant to Lincoln, Aug. 23, 1863, *Grant Papers*, IX, 195–197 at 196.

20. Grant, *Memoirs*, I, 578-79. Grant's attitude toward Halleck turned sour after Grant learned that Halleck had tried to derail his career after his early 1862 victories at Forts Henry and Donelson and had not, as Halleck claimed, saved Grant from Washington-originated criticisms (which actually had been Halleck's complaints to Washington).

21. Murray and Hsieh, *Savage War*, 352–353, 510–511.

22. Edward T. Cotham Jr., *Sabine Pass: The Confederacy's Thermopylae* (Austin: University of Texas Press, 2004); Current, *Encyclopedia*, Vol. 3, 1357; Vol. 4, 1584.

23. Current, *Encyclopedia*, Vol. 1, 233; Vol. 4, 1584.

24. See Chapter 6 for details of the Chickamauga Campaign.

25. Rawlins to Sherman, Sept. 22, 1863, *Grant Papers*, IX, 229–230; OR, I, xxx, part 1, 161–162.

26. Grant to Halleck, Sept. 22, 1863, *Grant Papers*, IX, 229: OR, I, xxx, part 1, 161–162.

27. Sherman to Rawlins Sept. 22, 1863, *Grant Papers*, IX, 230n; OR, I, xxx, part 3, 773.

28. Grant to Col. John C. Kelton, Sept. 25, 1863, *Grant Papers*, IX, 237-38; OR, I, xxx, part 3, 841.

29. Grant to Halleck, Sept. 30, 1863, *Grant Papers*, IX, 251-53 at 253; OR, I, xxx, part 3, 944.

30. Grant to Halleck, Oct. 5, 1863, *Grant Papers*, IX, 263; OR, I, xxx, part 4, 97; Hurlbut to Halleck, Oct. 1, 1863, OR, IX, part 4, 4, enclosing L. Trager's undated spy report, Ibid., 4–8.

31. Halleck to Grant, Oct. 11, 1863, *Grant Papers*, IX, 253n; OR, I, xxx, part 4, 274.

32. See Chapter 6 for details of the Chattanooga Campaign.

33. Murray and Hsieh, *Savage War*, 357, 359.

34. Catton, *Grant Takes Command*, 93.

35. Dana to Stanton, Nov. 29, 1863, OR, I, xxxi, part 2, 71-72, quote at 72.

36. Grant to McPherson, Dec. 1, 1863, *Papers of Grant*, 9, 480–81 at 481.

37. Grant to Halleck, Dec. 7, 1863, *Grant Papers*, IX, 500–501; OR, I, xxxi, part 3, 349–350.

38. Halleck to Grant, Dec. 17, 1863, *Grant Papers*, IX, 501n; OR, I, xxxi, part 3, 454.

39. Halleck to Grant, Dec. 21, 1863, *Grant Papers*, IX, 501-502n; OR, I, xxxi, part 3, 458.

40. Dana to Grant, Dec. 21, 1863, *Grant Papers*, IX, 502n; OR, I, xxxi, part 3, 457–458.

41. Grant to Halleck, Dec. 23, 1863, *Grant Papers*, IX, 551-52 at 551; OR, I, xxxi, part 3, 473.

42. Halleck to Grant, Jan. 8, 1864, *Grant Papers*, IX, 17-18, quote at 17; OR, I, xxxii, part 2, 40–42. On January 10 Dana sent Grant a telegram with a different message. It stated that Dana was authorized to say that Grant could undertake a Mobile campaign as soon as he deemed everything safe in east Tennessee. It then discussed the situation there. Dana to Grant, Jan. 10, 1864, *Grant Papers*, X, 18n; OR, I, xxxii, part 2, 58. Halleck and Dana clearly were not on the same page. But it is unclear if or when Grant received Dana's wire. *Grant Papers*, X, 18n.

43. Grant to Halleck, Jan.15, 1864, *Grant Papers*, X, 14-17; OR, I, xxxii, part 2, 99–101.

44. Over the 1863-64 winter, Jefferson Davis and his new military advisor Braxton Bragg, along with Lee, were unrealistically urging that Joseph Johnston, new commander of the Confederate Army of Tennessee, launch an offensive into Tennessee. Johnston appropriately rejected that recommendation because of his inadequate resources and the logistical difficulties of such an operation into an area where living off the mountainous and barren land was impossible.

45. Halleck to Grant, Jan. 18, 1864, OR, I, xxxii, part 2, 126–127, quote at 127.

46. Grant to Thomas, Jan. 19, 1864, *Grant Papers*, X, 45-46; OR, I, xxxii, part 2, 142–143.

47. Grant, *Memoirs*, II, 119–120.

48. Sherman to Banks, March 4, 1864, OR, I, xxxiv, part 2, 494.

49. Grant to Banks, March 15, 1864, *Grant Papers*, X, 200–201, quotes at 201; OR, I, xxxiv, part 2, 610–611.

50. Grant to Halleck, March 25, 1864, *Grant Papers*, X, 223-24, quote on 223; OR, I, xxxiii, 729. Grant wrote similarly to Sherman, who responded, "If Banks can…carry Mobile and open up the Mobile River he will in a measure solve the most difficult part of my problem, *Provisions*." Grant to Sherman, April 4, 1864, *Grant Papers*, X, 251–253; Sherman to Grant, April 9, 1864, *Grant Papers*, X, 253–254n.

51. Halleck to Grant, March 25, 1864, *Grant Papers*, X, 224n; OR, I, xxxiii, 729.

52. Grant to Halleck, March 28, 1864, *Grant Papers*, X, 231-32; OR, I, xxxiii, 752–3.

53. Grant to Banks, March 31, 1864, *Grant Papers*, X, 242-43; OR, I, xxxiv, part 1, 11.

54. Grant, *Memoirs*, II, 119–120.

55. Newton et al., "Ten Greatest Blunders," 17. The campaign also had a seamy side as the navy superseded the army in private profits, for its officers reaped from seizures of cotton and other commodities. Nevins commented, "On the Red River in the

spring of 1864, the carnival of trade and speculation reached its height for a single campaign." Nevins, *Ordeal*, VII, 359.

56.   Grant to Banks, April 17, 1864, *Grant Papers*, X, 298.

57.   Hunter to Grant, April 28, 1864, *Grant Papers*, X, 308n.

58.   Hunter to Grant, May 2, 1864, *Grant Papers*, X, 308n.

59.   Grant to Halleck, May 3, 1864, *Grant Papers*, X, 395.

60.   Newton et al., "Ten Greatest Blunders," 14.

61.   Murray and Hsieh, *Savage War*, 425, 428.

62.   Newton et al., "Ten Greatest Blunders," 18.

8

1.   For details of Sherman's Atlanta Campaign and the missed opportunity at Resaca, see Richard M. McMurry, *Atlanta 1864: Last Chance for the Confederacy* (Lincoln: University of Nebraska Press, 2000); Albert E. Castel, *Decision in the West: The Atlanta Campaign of 1864* (Lawrence: University Press of Kansas, 1992); Stephen Davis, *Atlanta Will Fall: Sherman, Joe Johnston, and the Yankee Heavy Battalions* (Wilmington: Scholarly Resources, Inc., 2001); Robert D. Jenkins, Sr., "Dalton: The Opening of the Georgia Campaign," *Blue & Gray Magazine*, XXXII, No. 1 (2015): 6–30, 41–50.

2.   Benson Bobrick, *Master of War: The Life of General George H. Thomas* (New York: Simon & Schuster, 2009), 220.

3.   Brian Steel Wills, *George Henry Thomas: As True as Steel* (Lawrence: University Press of Kansas, 2012), 253; Bobrick, *Master of War*, 220–221.

4.   Joint Committee, *Supplemental Report*, Vol. 1, 198, quoted in Bobrick, *Master of War*, 220–221.

5.   David Evans, *Sherman's Horsemen: Union Cavalry Operations in the Atlanta Campaign* (Bloomington: University of Indiana Press, 1996), xxix.

6.   Don Piatt and Henry V. Boynton, *George H. Thomas: A Critical Biography*, 525, quoted in Bobrick, *Master of War*, 230.

7. John R. Scales, *Sherman Invades Georgia* (Annapolis: Naval Institute Press, 2006), 186.
8. James Lee McDonough, *William Tecumseh Sherman: In the Service of My Country: A Life* (New York: W. W. Norton and Company, 2016), 475.
9. Wills, *Thomas*, 253.
10. Bobrick, *Master of* War, 230–231; Jenkins, "Dalton," 7–8; Steven H. Newton, "What Talent Might Have Achieved: The Battle of Resaca," *North & South*, Vol. 13, No. 5 (Jan. 2012): 27–36 at 28.
11. Confederate strength would later increase to as much as 75,000.
12. Sherman to Grant, April 10, 1864, OR, I, xxxii, part 3, 312-14; *Grant Papers*, Vol. 10, 253–254n.
13. McMurry, *Atlanta 1864*, 60.
14. Sherman to Thomas, May 5, 1864, OR, I, xxxviii, part 4, 39–40.
15. Jenkins, "Dalton," 9, 19; quote at 19. Others claim that Wheeler disobeyed his orders because he was skirmishing with Union cavalry. Murray and Hsieh, *Savage War*, 429.
16. McMurry, *Atlanta 1864*, 61. For an informative discussion of Johnston's role in enabling a Snake Creek Gap flanking movement, see Steven H. Newton, "Joseph Johnston and Snake Creek Gap," *North & South*, Vol. 4, No. 3 (March 2001): 56–67.
17. Hooker to Whipple, May 7, 1864, 3:30 p.m., OR, I, xxxviii, part 4, 58.
18. Whipple to Hooker, May 7, 1864, ibid.
19. McMurry, *Atlanta 1864*, 63.
20. Kilpatrick to Hooker, May 7, 1864, OR, I, xxxviii, part 4, 61.
21. Hooker to Whipple, May 8, 1864, 9:30 a.m., Ibid., 76.
22. Jenkins, "Dalton," 26–27; Castel, *Decision in the* West, 135. On the evening of May 8, Brigadier General John Corse, Sherman's inspector general, reported the arrival of cavalry at Davis' Cross-Roads on the Chickamauga and Second Cavalry Division

commander Garrard's hesitancy due to fear of a large enemy force, a mere three days' rations, absence of forage, and inadequate grazing grass. A likely frustrated Sherman wrote an endorsement on Corse's message telling him to write Garrard to "keep up with infantry" and "hurry to McPherson." Corse to Sherman, May 8, 1864 and Sherman's endorsement, OR, I, xxxviii, part 4, 85. But it was way too late.

23. McMurry, *Atlanta 1864*, 63–64.
24. Jenkins, "Dalton," 27.
25. McMurry, *Atlanta 1864*, 64; Jenkins, "Dalton," 27.
26. Ibid.
27. McPherson to Sherman, May 9, 1864, 12:30 p.m., OR, I, xxxviii, part 4, 105.
28. Jenkins, "Dalton," 27.
29. William Tecumseh Sherman, *Memoirs of General W. T. Sherman*, 2 vols. (New York: Literary Classics of the United States, Inc., 1990) (reprint of 1885 second edition), II, 33. Sherman's memoirs are not known for their accuracy—especially in taking responsibility himself or casting blame on others.
30. Jenkins, "Dalton," 27.
31. McMurry, *Atlanta 1864*, 65; Jenkins, "Dalton," 27.
32. Newton, "What Talent Might Have Achieved," 29.
33. McPherson to Sherman, May 9, 1864, 10:30 p.m., OR, I, xxxviii, part 4, 106.
34. Whipple to Hooker, May 9, 1864, OR, I, xxxviii, part 4, 92.
35. Whipple to Hooker, May 9, 1864, OR, I, xxxviii, part 4, 93.
36. Whipple to Kilpatrick (care of Hooker), May 9, 1864, OR, I, xxxviii, part 4, 96.
37. Kilpatrick to Brigadier General Washington Elliott, Thomas's chief of cavalry, May 9, 1864, 8:30 p.m., OR, I, xxxviii, part 4, 96–97.
38. Sherman to Halleck, May 10, 1864, 7 a.m., OR, I, xxxviii, part 4, 111.
39. Sherman to Halleck, 7:30 p.m., May 10, 1864, ibid.

40. Castel, *Decision in the West*, 144.
41. Report of Major General Patrick R. Cleburne, C.S. Army, commanding division, of operations May 7-27 [1864], Aug. 16, 1864, OR, I, xxxviii, part 3, 720–726 at 721.
42. Jenkins, "Dalton," 27.
43. Scales, *Sherman Invades*, 162.
44. Jenkins, "Dalton," 27.
45. Davis, *Atlanta Will Fall*, 43–44.
46. Davis, *Atlanta Will Fall*, 42.
47. McMurry, *Atlanta 1864*, 65–66, quote at 66.
48. OR, I, xxxviii, part 3, 721.
49. Sherman, *Memoirs*, II, 32, 34.
50. Vincent J. Esposito (ed.), *The West Point Atlas of American Wars*, 2 vols. (New York: Frederick A. Praeger, 1959, 1964), I, Map 145 narrative.
51. James C. Bradford (ed.), *Oxford Atlas of American Military History* (New York: Oxford University Press, 2003), 90.
52. Frances H. Kennedy (ed.), *The Civil War Battlefield Guide* (Boston: Houghton Mifflin Company, 1990), 173.
53. Warner, *Generals in Blue*, 307.
54. Terry L. Jones, *Historical Dictionary of the Civil War*, 2 vols., Second edition (Lanham, Md., Scarecrow Press, 2011), II, 1355.
55. See discussion below of Scales's criticism of both McPherson and Sherman.
56. Scales, *Sherman Invades*, 168.
57. McDonough, *Sherman*, 477, 479.
58. Heidler and Heidler, *Encyclopedia*, 1294. There is some confusion about the dates, but the article's meaning is clear.
59. Stephen Davis, "Sherman in North Georgia: The Battle of Resaca," *Blue & Gray Magazine*, XXXI, No. 4 (2015): 6–28, 42–50 at 17.
60. Philip L. Secrist, *The Battle of Resaca: Atlanta Campaign, 1864* (Macon, Ga.: Mercer University Press, 1998), 64.
61. Wills, *Thomas*, 255.

62. Sherman, *Memoirs*, II, 32; Bobrick, *Master of War*, 231–232.

63. Sherman to Halleck, May 10, 1864, quoted in Bobrick, *Master of War*, 232.

64. Sherman to Grant, June 24, 1864, in *Grant Papers*, Vol. 11, 263 (complete with grammatical and spelling errors). An edited quote appears in Bobrick, *Master of War*, 235.

65. William Warner to Mrs. General William T. Sherman, Feb. 22, 1876, in Sherman, *Memoirs*, II, Appendix, 507–516 at 508–509, as selectively quoted in Bobrick, *Master of War*, 232–233.

66. Ibid., 509, as selectively quoted in Bobrick, *Master of War*, 233.

67. Warner to Mrs. Sherman, Feb. 22, 1876, in Sherman, *Memoirs*, II, Appendix, 509 (emphasis added).

68. McDonough, *Sherman*, 477–478.

69. McMurry, *Atlanta 1864*, 55–58, 64–65; quote at 64.

70. McMurry, *Atlanta 1864*, 65.

71. Scales, *Sherman Invades*, 162–163.

72. Ibid., 186.

73. Evans, *Sherman's Horsemen*, xxxii.

9

1. Smith, *Grant*, 368.

2. Three of the four railroads supplying Lee's army ran though Petersburg.

3. Gustav J. Person, "Crossing the James River, June 1864: '…the real crisis of the war,'" *Engineer* (Sept.–Dec. 2009): 58–64, quotation at 60.

4. Grant to Halleck, June 5, 1864, Simon et al., *Grant Papers*, XI, 19–20 at 19. As to the morale of his army, Grant dubiously asserted to Chief of Staff Halleck, "The feeling of the two Armies now seems to be that the rebels can protect themselves only by strong intrenchments, whilst our Army is not only confidant [*sic*] of protecting itself, without intrenchments, but that it can beat and drive the enemy whenever and wherever he can be found without this protection." Ibid., 20.

5.   Ibid.
6.   Esposito, *West Point Atlas*, I, Map 137 narrative.
7.   "Lee and Grant, 1864," 56–57; Eric J. Wittenberg, "Sheridan's Second Raid and the Battle of Trevilian Station," *Blue & Gray Magazine*, XIX, No. 3 (Feb. 2002): 8–24, 45–50.
8.   Person, "Crossing the James," 60; Ronald C. White, *American Ulysses: A Life of Ulysses S. Grant* (New York: Random House, 2017), 363 (one-day variation in dates between sources).
9.   "Lee and Grant, 1864," 57.
10.   Person, "Crossing the James," 60–61.
11.   Esposito, *West Point Atlas*, I, Map 137 narrative.
12.   https://www.nps.gov/parkhistory/onlinebooks/civil_war-series/11/sec16.htm.
13.   Alexander, *Fighting for the Confederacy*, 420.
14.   Smith, *Grant*, 370.
15.   Person, "Crossing the James," 63. Grant may have elected to use slower but immediately available ferry transportation to quickly start his crossing and avoid the risks of (1) a tenuous beachhead and (2) possible conflict between bridge construction and the arrival of the Eighteenth Corps flotilla coming up the James.
16.   Person, "Crossing the James," 63. The 2,170-foot bridge consisted of 101 pontoon boats, had an eleven-foot-wide roadway between guardrails, and contained a floatable hundred-foot draw that could be moved to allow for passage of vessels. Ibid.
17.   Lee to James Seddon, June 13, 1864, 10 p.m., *Papers of Lee*, 776–777; Lee to Davis, June 14, 1864, 12:10 p.m., Ibid., 777–778.
18.   Lyman, Theodore, "MHSM [Military Historical Society of Massachusetts] Papers V5: Operations of the Army of the Potomac, June 5-15, 1864," http://www.beyondthecrater.com/resources/mhsm-papers/mhsm.
19.   Hattaway and Jones, *How the North Won*, 589.
20.   Lee to Beauregard, June 17, 1864, OR, I, vol. 40, ii, 664–665.
21.   Fuller, *Grant and Lee*, 223.

22. Lee to Bragg, June 15, 1864, 12:20 p.m., *Papers of Lee*, 781; Lee to Davis, June 15, 1864, 12:45 p.m., Ibid., 780.

23. Lee to Beauregard, June 16, 1864, 10:30 a.m., OR, I, vol. 40, ii, 659; 40 *Papers of Lee*, 784; Thomas, *Lee*, 337; Alexander, *Fighting for the Confederacy*, 429.

24. Lee to Beauregard, June 16, 1864, 4 p.m., OR, I, vol. 40, ii, 659; *Papers of Lee*, 785; Alexander, *Fighting for the Confederacy*, 429.

25. Lee to Beauregard, June 17, 1864, 6 a.m., OR, I, vol. 40, ii, 664; Thomas, *Lee*, 337.

26. Lee to Beauregard, June 17, 1864, noon, OR, I, vol. 40, ii, 664; Lowry, *Fate of the Country*, 53; Freeman, *R. E. Lee*, III, 417; Alexander, *Fighting for the Confederacy*, 430.

27. Lee to Beauregard, June 17, 1864, 4:30 p.m., OR, I, vol. 40, ii, 665; *Papers of Lee*, 789; Alexander, *Fighting for the Confederacy*, 430.

28. Foote, *Civil War*, III, 438; Lowry, *Fate of the Country*, 56; Freeman, *Lee's Lieutenants*, III, 534; Freeman, *R. E. Lee*, III, 421; Trudeau, *The Last Citadel*, 51; Alexander, *Fighting for the Confederacy*, 430.

29. Alexander, *Fighting for the Confederacy*, 430–431.

30. Lee to E.H. Gill, June 18, 1864, 3:30 a.m., *Papers of Lee*, 791; Alexander, *Fighting for the Confederacy*, 431.

31. Noah Andre Trudeau, *The Last Citadel: Petersburg, Virginia June 1864–April 1865* (Baton Rouge: Louisiana State University Press, 1991), 22–25.

32. David Alan Johnson, *Battle of Wills: Ulysses S. Grant, Robert E. Lee, and the Last Year of the Civil War* (Amherst, N.Y.: Prometheus Books, 2016), 207–208; White, *American Ulysses*, 364.

33. Grant to Halleck, June 14, 1864, *Grant Papers*, XI, 45.

34. Robert Hunt Rhodes (ed.), *All for the Union: The Civil War Diary and Letters of Elisha Hunt Rhodes* (New York: Orion Books, 1991) (originally Andrew Mowbray Incorporated, 1985), 161–163, quotation at 161–162.

35. Details of the June 15–18 failed Union attacks can be found in Thomas J. Howe, *The Petersburg Campaign: Wasted Valor, June 15–18, 1864* (Lynchburg: H. E. Howard, Inc., 1988).

36. Trudeau, *Last Citadel*, 35; Gordon Rhea, "Baldy Smith: The Scapegoat of Petersburg," *North & South*, Vol. 14, No. 1 (May 2012): 18–29 at 19.

37. Trudeau, *Last Citadel*, 35–36.

38. White, *American Ulysses*, 366.

39. Howe, *Petersburg*, 21–22, quotation at 22.

40. Rhea, "Baldy Smith," 21–23.

41. Ibid., 23–25; Hattaway and Jones, *How the North Won*, 589–590.

42. Alexander, *Fighting for the Confederacy*, 422.

43. See Chapter 2.

44. Murray and Hsieh, *Savage War*, 397.

45. Rhea, "Baldy Smith," 25.

46. Esposito, *West Point Atlas*, Map 138 narrative; Howe, *Petersburg*, 34–35.

47. P. G. T. Beauregard, "Four Days of Battle at Petersburg," in Johnson and Buel, *Battles and Leaders*, 4:541.

48. Howe, *Petersburg*, 35.

49. Rhea, "Baldy Smith," 25–28.

50. Diane Smith, *Command Conflicts in Grant's Overland Campaign: Ambition and Animosity in the Army of the Potomac* (Jefferson, N.C.: McFarland & Company, 2013), 195.

51. Howe, *Petersburg*, 29. On the morning of the fifteenth, Meade gave Hancock on-again, off-again orders about whether to await sixty thousand rations. That process delayed Hancock for at least three hours, and his troops nevertheless marched without the rations—not knowing their assignment. Ibid., 29–30.

52. Rhea, "Baldy Smith," 19, 20, 23; Smith, *Command Conflicts*, 196.

53. Ibid., 24, 26.

54. Trudeau, *Last Citadel*, 36, 39–40.

55. Johnson, *Battle of Wills*, 208; Grant, *Memoirs*, II, 294–295, quotation at 295.
56. Smith, *Command Conflicts*, 196.
57. Trudeau, *Last Citadel*, 43.
58. Howe, *Petersburg*, 35–37.
59. Grant, *Memoirs*, II, 296.
60. Howe, *Petersburg*, 42–43.
61. Ibid., 47–51; Trudeau, *Last Citadel*, 44–46.
62. Howe, *Petersburg*, 51-52; Trudeau, *Last Citadel*, 47–48.
63. Howe, *Petersburg*, 56–58.
64. Ibid., 59–60.
65. Johnson, *Battle of Wills*, 209.
66. White, *American Ulysses*, 369; Howe, *Petersburg*, 62–105; Trudeau, *Last Citadel*, 48–50.
67. Howe, *Petersburg*, 104–105.
68. White, *American Ulysses*, 369. In the June 18 attack, Colonel Joshua Chamberlain of the Twentieth Maine, a hero at Gettysburg, was seriously injured and Grant promoted him to brigadier general.
69. Meade to John H. Martindale, June 18, 1863, OR, I, xl, part 2, 205.
70. Johnson, *Battle of Wills*, 210; Howe, *Petersburg*, 106–135; Bonekemper, *How Lee Lost*, 163; Trudeau, *Last Citadel*, 53–54; William F. Fox, *Regimental Losses in the American Civil War, 1861–1865: A Treatise on the Extent and Nature of the Mortuary Losses in the Union Regiments, with Full and Exhaustive Statistics Compiled from the Official Records on File in the State Military Bureaus and at Washington* (Dayton: Morningside House, 1985) (Reprint of Albany: Brandow Printing Company, 1898), 36.
71. Heidler and Heidler, *Encyclopedia*, 1497.
72. Grant refused Hancock's suggestion for a full investigation of the Petersburg failure. He did not need that unproductive distraction or possible embarrassment. Johnson, *Battle of Wills*, 211.

73. Grant, *Memoirs*, II, 298.

74. Rhea, "Baldy Smith," 27.

75. Porter, *Campaigning with Grant*, 210–211.

76. Johnson, *Battle of Wills*, 211.

10

1. Grant to Sherman, April 4, 1864, *Papers of Grant*, Vol. 10, 251–253 at 252.

2. Sherman to Grant, April 10, 1864, OR, I, xxxii, part 3, 312–314; *Papers of Grant*, Vol. 10, 253–254n.

3. Some historians blame Johnston more than Hood for Atlanta's fall. "Arguably Johnston's retreat guaranteed the fall of Atlanta. Many think it would have been lost earlier if J[ohnston] had remained." Richard McMurry to author, March 11, 2017.

4. James Donnell, *Atlanta 1864: Sherman Marches South* (New York: Osprey Publishing, 2016), 88; Murray and Hsieh, *Savage War*, 443; Castel, *Decision in the West*, 523–524.

5. McDonough, *Sherman*, 544–545.

6. Sherman *Memoirs*, II, 581.

7. See Chapter 8.

8. Castel, *Decision in the West*, 530.

9. Ibid., 540–541.

10. Donnell, *Atlanta 1864*, 89.

11. Murray and Hsieh, *Savage War*, 444.

12. Esposito, *West Point Atlas*, I, Map 148 narrative.

13. T. Harry Williams, *Lincoln and His Generals* (New York: Alfred A. Knopf, Inc., 1952), 338.

14. Nevins, *Ordeal*, VIII, 153–154.

15. John Marszalek, *Sherman: A Soldier's Passion for Order* (New York: The Free Press, 1993), 283. "Kennesaw" was the battle of Kennesaw Mountain on June 27, 1864, in which Sherman, against Thomas's pleas, had attacked an impregnable position and suffered about three thousand casualties. On Sherman's behalf, Marszalek adds: "Sherman's decision to avoid a bloody

clash [at Atlanta] ensured the tremendous success of his campaign.... Atlanta was one of the most important Union victories of the war. Not only was it the capture of a major railroad and manufacturing center, but it gave Abraham Lincoln the impetus to hold on to the presidency in the November election." Ibid., 283–284.

16.   Castel, *Decision in the West*, 539.

17.   Ibid., 540. Castel compares this situation with Snake Creek Gap (see Chapter 8): " Twice, first at the beginning of the campaign and then at the end of it, Thomas presented Sherman with plans that offered a splendid chance of making it impossible for the South to continue the war in the West and, as a result, in the East as well. On the first occasion, Sherman implemented the plan in an inadequate fashion; on the second, he did not implement it at all." Ibid.

18.   Ibid., 542.

19.   Grant, *Memoirs*, II, 649–650.

20.   Sherman to Grant, December 16, 1864, in William T. Sherman, *Memoirs of General William T. Sherman*, second edition, 2 vols. (New York: D. Appleton and Company, 1889), II, 207–210 at 209 (emphasis added).

21.   Sherman's marches through Georgia and the Carolinas are examples of "hard war," not "total war." The latter is characterized by massive rapes and killings of innocent civilians. See "Did the North Win by 'Total War'?" in Bonekemper, *Myth*, 247–253.

22.   Sherman to Lincoln, December 22, 1864, *Works of Lincoln*, VIII, 182n. Lincoln telegraphed his thanks on December 26. Lincoln to Sherman, December 26, 1864, ibid., 181–182.

23.   Sherman to Hardee, Dec. 17, 1864, in Sherman, *Memoirs*, II, 210–211 at 211.

24.   Hardee to Sherman, Dec. 17, 1864, in Sherman, *Memoirs*, II, 211–212 at 211.

25. Sherman to Grant, Dec. 18, 1864, in Sherman, *Memoirs*, II, 212–13 at 213.
26. McDonough, *Sherman*, 578.
27. Sherman, *Memoirs*, II, 216.
28. Sherman, *Memoirs*, II, 216–217.
29. McDonough, *Sherman*, 578–579.
30. Sherman's Report, OR, I, xliv, 7–14.
31. Marszalek, *Sherman*, 308.
32. Castel, *Decision in the West*, 558, 565.
33. Sherman biographer Marszalek succinctly explains that "Sherman wanted to avoid pitched battle of maim and killing. Sherman tried to fight a war of destruction not killing because he had always promised his friends in the South that once they gave up he would become their best friend." Marszalek to author, April 1, 2017.
34. The Georgia militia had gone home.

INDEX

Nevins, Allan, 4, 6, 22, 40, 76, 104, 128

New Orleans, LA, 7, 9, 14, 130–31, 135, 138–39, 144

O

Official Records, 65, 190

Orchard Knob, 121–23

Overland Campaign, the, 66, 146, 173–74, 185, 190–91

Owsley, Frank L., 2, 4–5, 8–9, 11, 13–14

Oxford Atlas of American Military History, 163

P

Pascagoula Bay, 138

Peach Orchard, 94–95

Pemberton, John, 75, 81, 106

Petersburg, VA, 70, 173–75, 178–91

Pettigrew, J. Johnston, 101, 104–5

Pickett, George E., 103–6

Pickett's Charge, 77, 99–101, 104

Pinkerton, Allan, 33

Polk, Leonidas, 146, 157, 161, 170

Pope, John, 19, 29, 33, 55

Porter, David D., 145

Porter, Fitz John, 33, 46, 54

Posey, Carney, 96

Potomac River, 29, 31–32, 34, 36, 39–41, 46, 51–52, 55–56, 76, 91, 105–6, 109, 194

Punch, 6

R

Rappahannock River, 75, 79

Red River Campaign, the, 144–46, 169

Resaca, GA, 149–51, 153–54, 156–67, 169–71, 199

Rhea, Gordon, 191

Rhett Jr., Robert Barnwell, 67

Rhodes, Elisha Hunt, 109, 181–82

Richmond, VA, 33, 56, 64, 66, 70, 74–76, 80, 106, 109, 112–13, 119, 125, 127, 130, 173–76 178–81, 186, 188–89, 191

Richmond Examiner, 67, 69

Richmond Whig, 67–68

Rocky Face Ridge, 150–51, 160, 164

Rome, GA, 152–54, 158, 162

Rosecrans, William, 24, 106, 111–15, 119, 134–36, 138

Russell, John, 7–8

Russell, William Howard, 4

S

Savannah, GA, xiv, 8–9, 193–94, 199–204

Schofield, John, 150–51, 153, 158, 163, 166–67, 169

Sears, Stephen, 35, 49

Second Manassas, 29, 55, 95

Seddon, James, 65–66, 68, 74–75, 112

Seminary Ridge, 86, 91–92, 96, 101, 103

Sharpsburg, MD, 28, 38–41, 43, 45–46, 48, 51, 54

Shenandoah Valley, the, 175

Sheridan, Philip, 23, 54, 122–23, 125, 174–75

Sherman, William T., xiii–xiv, 22–23, 25, 54, 66, 111–12, 116,